TEARS OF GLORY

MICHAEL PEARSON

TEARS of GLORY

THE HEROES OF VERCORS, 1944

MAPS BY RAFAEL PALACIOS

Doubleday & Company, Inc., Garden City, New York
1979

Library of Congress Cataloging in Publication Data

Pearson, Michael.
   Tears of glory.

   Bibliography.
   Includes index.
      1. World War, 1939-1945—France—Vercors.
   2. Vercors, France—History. I. Title.
   D762.V4P42   940.53′44′98   78-216
   ISBN 0-385-11446-X

For Robert

List of Maps

The Massif

The Vercors massif, with its sheer walls thousands of feet tall, dominates the plain of the Rhône and Isère rivers like some vast monolithic cathedral. From every direction, those immense gaunt ramparts form a high, often endless skyline. For long stretches they are white, sometimes furrowed into semi-pillars, sometimes darkened by scrub or trees thrust out from the rock face, sometimes enfolded for a few miles within rugged mountain peaks. Mostly, however, they are stark and monotonous, forming a great natural acropolis that stands isolated, its foothills washed by four rivers—near, but not linked, to the great Alpine mass that spreads east to Switzerland and Italy.

The Vercors is shaped like a gigantic arrowhead, thirty miles long by twenty miles wide—a geological phenomenon, fashioned by erosion. It is made of limestone—not of granite, like the higher Alps—and bitter weather has combed it into gorges, gouged from it deep grottoes, and formed within it a huge plateau that, enclosed within soaring cliffs, is remote indeed. It can be reached from the surrounding plain only by a few steep, narrow roads that have been hewn and tunneled from the mountain, that span deep ravines by way of slender bridges.

This enormous natural citadel was designed for drama, yet strangely it was ignored by history until 1944. In that critical summer, when the Allied armies invaded Europe, the massif became the setting of the most famous saga of the French Resistance or even of the Resistance throughout Europe. Since then, partly because of controversy that often creates myths from war, the story of the Free Republic of the Vercors has become a legend.

It is the truth behind this legend—the bravery, the sadness, the humor, the charm, the defiance, the brutality, the hopes, the betrayal—that this book aspires to relate.

Principal Characters

On the Vercors Plateau

BEAUME (Vincent)
Chief of the Second Bureau of the Vercors Military Commander, responsible for security, police, prison, courts, and intelligence.

BEAUREGARD (Captain Costa de)
Military commander of the Vercors northern sector.

CAMMAERTS (Francis)
Chief of the Jockey Circuit of secret agents operated by F Section of the British SOE (Special Operations Executive).

CHABAL (Sergeant Major, later Lieutenant, Abel)
Commander of a unit from the Grenoble regiment of the BCA (Bataillon des Chasseurs Alpins).

CHAVANT (Eugène)
The "Patron," or civil administrator, of the Vercors.

DESCOUR (Colonel Marcel)
Commander of Region 1, the Rhône-Alps district of the Secret Army, later called the FFI (Forces Françaises de l'Intérieur).

FARGE (Yves)

Civil administrator of southeastern France, appointed from Algiers.

GEYER (Captain Narcisse)

Military commander of the Vercors from December 1943 to June 1944, after which date he was commander of the southern sector.

HOPPERS (Lieutenant Vernon)

Leader of an American OSS (Office of Strategic Services) unit, parachuted into the Vercors.

HUET (Major, later Colonel, François)

Military commander of the Vercors from June 1944.

LONGE (Major Desmond)

Leader of a liaison team from RF Section of the British SOE, parachuted into the Vercors.

MYERS (Lieutenant Chester)

Second in command of the OSS team, parachuted into the Vercors.

PRÉVOST (Jean)

Celebrated French writer, who took part in devising the idea of turning the Vercors into a mountain fortress, and became one of its five regional commanders.

ZELLER (Colonel, later General, Henri)

The Secret Army (later FFI) Commander of southeastern France.

In Algiers

BÉTHOUART (General Marie Édouard)

Chairman of the National Defense Committee, effectively General de Gaulle's chief of staff.

CAFFEY (General Benjamin)

Commander of the Second Bureau and Special Operations on the staff of Allied Forces Headquarters, Mediterranean Theater.

COCHET (General Gabriel)

DMS (Military Delegate for the Southern Sector of France)—effectively commander in chief of French forces within southern France, responsible to General Koenig in London.

CONSTANS (Colonel Jean)

Head of the Action Department of the Direction Générale des Services Spéciaux and French delegate in the Special Projects Operations Center—effectively the senior officer on the receiving end of radio messages from the Resistance.

DE GAULLE (General Charles)

President of the provisional French government in Algiers.

GRENIER (Fernand)

Minister for Air in the provisional French government.

ROOKS (Major General Lowell)

Deputy Chief of Staff, Allied Forces Headquarters, Mediterranean Theater.

SOUSTELLE (Jacques)

Director of the Direction Générale des Services Spéciaux and holder of other posts concerned with both the government and the French forces in the interior—effectively a very important lieutenant of De Gaulle.

WILSON (General Sir Henry Maitland)

Commander in Chief, Allied Forces, Mediterranean Theater.

In London

KOENIG (General Pierre)
> Commander in Chief, FFI, but with tactical direction of the Northern Sector of France (Cochet commanding the Southern Sector).

CHAPTER 1

At about a quarter to ten on June 13, 1944, Major François Huet, military commander of the Vercors plateau, rode his Peugeot 75 fast through the main street of St.-Nizier, blaring his horn. The sun was above the high peaks of the Chartreuse range to the northeast and the morning air in the little mountain town was already warm.

On that beautiful cloudless day, the ugly noise of the speeding motorcycle seemed obscene, but the people the officer passed knew well enough the reason for his haste.

He had made good time from the hotel in St.-Martin that was serving as his headquarters. It was less than half an hour since the phone call had warned him that a German column was approaching up the little road at the foot of the massif below St.-Nizier.

Huet always looked stiff and awkward, no matter what he was doing, but on the motorcycle he seemed especially inflexible. His arms, as he gripped the handlebars, were rigid. His head, which he always held high, appeared to have no independent movement, as though it were fixed by an unseen clamp to his neck and body.

Outside the town the road steepened sharply down toward the pass, and Huet checked his speed. The temporary command post of Captain Costa de Beauregard, who was in charge of the Vercors northern sector, was a roadside villa, and as the major approached from St.-Nizier he was standing on the balcony, binoculars to his eyes, looking down the mountain.

Huet pulled up before the villa, pushed his way hurriedly through the group of men gathered waiting for orders around the front door, and walked briskly—Huet never ran—up the stairs of the villa to the balcony with its spectacular view of Grenoble and the wide, flat valley of the Isère.

"How many are there?" he asked.

"About four hundred," answered Beauregard, "maybe a few less." The lookouts had not stopped to count, so eager were they to shout the alert. "They're still quite a way off."

Huet took the glasses the captain handed him and studied the mountainside beneath him. The St.-Nizier pass on the northeast of the massif was the easiest of the eight approaches into the Vercors, but even this was steep—a cliff standing more than three thousand feet above the banks of the river, broken occasionally by terraces. Below them the road wound upward in elongated loops, passing through several little hamlets, from the town of Seyssins near the foot.

The long gray column of troops was still on the lower levels of the mountain road, looking at that distance like an enormous slow-moving centipede. Through the glasses, Huet could just make out the young officer at the head of the column—blond, his hat jaunty. Huet moved his glasses sideways, pan-ning like a camera along the line of marching men, searching for any sign of mountain guns.

"No artillery?" he queried with relief.

"Heavy machine guns that they're manhandling," answered Beauregard. "They've left their transport at La Tour-Sans-Venin—that's a hamlet about three kilometers above Seyssins." Huet did not need to be told where La Tour was. He had lived all his life at Coublevie, only ten miles to the north. He knew the Vercors well.

This was the first attack by the Germans since he had assumed command of the plateau a week ago. Indeed, it was the first *attack* there had ever been, for the passes had never seriously been defended before. During the two years that the rugged mountains and thick forest of the Vercors massif had provided cover for camps of Maquis guerrillas, several enemy columns had swept across the plateau on punitive raids, burning houses and arresting villagers, but no real attempt had been made to stop them. The basic tenet of guerrilla warfare was: never, never try to hold a position. Do as much damage as possible, then disappear.

D Day, a week before, had changed all that. The Allied armies had invaded Normandy. The French underground had been summoned, in coded messages broadcast by the BBC, to rise against the Germans. The Vercors was outlaw country no longer. It was a base of the French Resistance under the orders of General de Gaulle and the Allied commanders in Algiers. It was an area of Free France. The nearest liberating troops were more than five hundred miles away, but the sheer cliffs of gnarled gray rock that formed a wall to the Vercors interior imparted a sense of protection, a feeling of remoteness from the surrounding country below that was controlled by the Germans. In fact, for days the Tricolor, banned since the Occupation, had been fluttering defiantly, in full view of the barracks in Grenoble, from Les Trois Pucelles (the Three Virgins), the

strange three-fingered obelisk that stuck upward like an arm
from the higher slopes of Le Moucherotte—until Huet had ordered the flag to be struck because it was needlessly provocative. He, too, had felt this false sensation of safety provided by
the Vercors cliffs but knew he must resist it.

Responding to his orders, Huet had mobilized the Vercors,
summoning the Resistance men impatiently awaiting his call in
the towns and villages of the plain around the massif to join
the resident Maquisards* from the camps on the plateau. Now,
as he studied the advancing German column through binoculars, nearly three thousand men were at their posts within the
Vercors. Some four hundred of them were ranged on either
side of the St.-Nizier pass—on a deep shelf that, like a giant
roller-coaster, followed the concave, curving shape of the mountain, dipping to the little road in the middle from high levels at
each end.

Huet's men were courageous but he knew they were inexperienced, unschooled, and certainly unprepared for exposure to
enemy fire.

Their arms were minimal: Sten submachine guns, no-
toriously inaccurate, that had been dropped by parachute;
sporting weapons; a few First World War machine guns that
constantly jammed; and "Gammon" grenades—small canvas
bags, packed with explosive, that made a lot of noise but did
little damage.

This was the material that Huet had with which to fight the
trained, fully equipped troops of the Wehrmacht. Only two
weeks before, Eugène Chavant, the civilian "Patron" of the
Vercors, had been promised at French headquarters in Algiers
that four thousand paratroopers and proper weapons—mortars

---

* The word "Maquis" was borrowed by the French Resistance from rebels
in Corsica who chose it because it was the name of tough undergrowth
that proliferated in the mountains. Its tenacious qualities, they felt, reflected their own determination.

and mountain artillery—would be sent onto the plateau, but these had not arrived yet. Huet hoped fervently that they would come soon, for although the few hundred enemy marching up the road toward them could only be a preliminary move to test his defenses or perhaps to gain control of the easiest pass, this action was certain to be followed very soon by a major assault. By then the invasion by the Allies of the South of France would have been launched, but even that coast was 150 miles away on the far side of very rugged country. Who knew how long it would take them to reach Grenoble—or Valence, on the other side of the massif?

For a few moments, Huet surveyed the immense valley three thousand feet below—through which Napoleon had passed with his army on the surprise march on Paris after his escape from Elba. The city of Grenoble lay exposed, seeming strangely compact, bordered as it was by two rivers—the Isère, flowing north around the foot of the Vercors cliffs toward the Rhône; and the Drac, running from the south along the whole east side of the massif—and set against a background of the immense mountain ranges of the Chartreuse and the Belledonne.

That morning there was a light haze over the city but some landmarks were clearly visible—the cathedral with its great dome; the university complex at St.-Martin-d'Hères in the far distance; and nearer, in the angle formed by the two rivers, the barracks of the 6th BCA, the Bataillon des Chasseurs Alpins, Grenoble's own regiment of mountain infantry. Now it was a base for enemy troops and the headquarters of General Karl Pflaum, commander of the Wehrmacht's 157th Reserve Division. Through the glasses, Huet could see the black Swastika flying from the mast on the parade ground.

The German column approached a hamlet called Pariset and the troops broke off the road into the nearby fields to the north. "They're aiming for Charvet Hill," said Beauregard, "or possibly the railroad track—both maybe."

Huet studied the terrain to the left of his line, carefully examining the little mountain railroad that connected Grenoble to St.-Nizier. In peacetime winters, it brought skiers to the plateau; in summer, walkers and campers. It was set on a small embankment that provided a smooth surface for the track as it crossed the rugged indentations of the side of the massif. It could provide good cover for advancing troops.

He switched his attention to the Charvet farm, high on the hill—at the left extremity of the switchback shelf that his defenders were manning. It was the usual cluster of farm buildings: a farmhouse, a barn, some sheds.

The German plan was fairly clear—the classic outflanking move of an attacking army. If the Germans reached the Charvet farm and set up a heavy machine gun on its elevated position, they would be able to fire down on Beauregard's line. His men, who would have no effective cover against shooting from this direction, would be forced to fall back. At the same time, a thrust would no doubt be made from the cover of the railroad track. It was vital that the Germans should be prevented from taking Charvet Hill.

Clearly, reinforcements were badly needed, but before Huet ordered any men to be transferred from other parts of the plateau he had to find out if the Germans were approaching any of the other passes. The only way he could discover this or issue any instructions was by phone to his headquarters from the café in St.-Nizier. For, although the internal telephone system in the Vercors was very good, there were no mobile means of communication, no walkie-talkies or short-range radio.

As Huet rode back to the town on his motorcycle, the problems he faced must have seemed insuperable. Certainly, on this warm June morning, the command of the Vercors appeared very different from the appointment that had been assigned to him four weeks before in Lyon.

CHAPTER 2

Light rain had been falling in Lyon on that afternoon in early May when Huet had followed his orders and joined Colonel Marcel Descour as he strolled "along the left sidewalk of the Rue du Plat going in the direction of the Perrache district," as Descour recalls.

Descour was the Secret Army Commander of Region 1 of the twenty districts into which France was divided. He was accompanied by his chief of staff, a tall grim man named Dom Guétet who had temporarily abandoned his habit as a Benedictine monk to help direct the Resistance forces in the Rhône Valley and much of the Alps to the east of it.

All three were wearing brimmed felt hats and the same shabby shapeless suits worn by most men who worked in offices in Lyon. They looked like clerks—anonymous, ordinary people of the city.

Nowadays Descour—whose own commander had recently

been arrested—always conducted his discussions and issued his orders in the open air, preferably in busy streets. He had learned by experience that secret meetings held indoors were vulnerable to discovery by the Gestapo, and the very fact that everyone present was alert for the dreaded hammering on the door created tension and overreaction.

It was because of this kind of extra-taut setting, so Descour believed, that Alain le Ray, a previous military commander of the Vercors, had angrily offered his resignation when faced with criticism—and indeed why Descour had accepted it, which he now knew was an "absurd and unfortunate" mistake. In fact, it was because of the chaotic personal conflict that had resulted in the Vercors from Le Ray's replacement that Descour was now in the process yet again of appointing a military commander.

This time, the colonel was sure he had the ideal officer for this vital post—a post, at least, that would become vital as soon as the Allies invaded Europe. For he knew thirty-nine-year-old François Huet very well. Both of them came from the same kind of strongly Catholic army families. They had worked together before the war when Descour, who was five years older than the major, had been aide-de-camp to General Maurice Gamelin. More recently, the colonel had called on Huet in the Lyon suburb of Crépieux-la-Pape, where, under cover of an ex-officers' association, the major had operated an intelligence network called "Les Druides." They had talked about the Vercors, which, as Descour knew, was a familiar area to Huet since he lived so close to the massif. The old rapport that had existed between them had become renewed. They were much the same sort of man, both marked by a degree of personal reserve. Huet, with his awkward movements and his cold blue eyes, was by nature a little formal. Descour, with thin pointed features, a pencil mustache, and black hair brushed tight to his head, was also something of an introvert. His talent lay in skillful organizing rather than dashing leadership, which, of course, made him well suited to the direction of a clandestine force.

As the three men strolled along the street, a German patrol passed them, marching in the direction of the station ahead. Troops were a common sight in Lyon, since it was the headquarters of the German Army in the South, but it was still unnerving to hear the tramp of feet approaching from behind and then, after the patrol had passed, to watch the shoulders of the soldiers moving under the gray uniforms as they swung on up the street ahead of them.

"The time has come, François," said Descour. "I want you to take command in the Vercors."

Since their first meeting at Crépieux-la-Pape the two men had talked much about "Operation Montagnards," the plan to transform the Vercors on the day that Europe was invaded into a vast fortress base in the heart of German-occupied territory—and about Huet's assuming command to direct it. For this remote plateau, enclosed in its tight ring of mountains and sheer cliffs, dominated the main routes north from the south coast of France—the great valley of the Rhône, the traditional road for armies advancing from the Mediterranean, and the Route Napoléon that curled through the mountains from Nice via Digne. Railroad lines, roads, and rivers all converged near this gigantic massif, shaped like an arrow pointing north.

The Vercors plan—conceived two years before by Pierre Dalloz, an expert mountaineer who lived on the plateau, and his friend Jean Prévost, the writer—was brilliantly simple: when the Allied troops landed on the south coast of France, an operation that was scheduled to coincide with the big invasion across the Channel, the few hundred Maquisards in the Vercors camps would be joined by Resistance men from the plain. The passes would be closed so that thousands of paratroopers could safely be dropped onto the plateau and reinforced by other contingents of the French Secret Army. From within the massif the Germans could then be attacked from the rear as they tried to fight off the invading force in the south. Their supply lines could be devastated.

As a plan its scope was enormous, but if the timing of the operation was not executed with precision, it could end in disaster on a big scale. For the threat that this fortified natural citadel with its tiny access roads, most of them tunneled through rock, would pose to the Germans would be immense. Once the paratroopers were flown in with artillery and mortars, the Vercors would be so formidable that an assault could be successful only at an enormous cost in German lives. The danger for the French would lie in the period before they arrived, when the passes would be held only by Resistance men. If the enemy could mount a major attack fast enough, the Maquisards would not be able to hold out for long—and if they failed, they could expect ruthless punitive reprisals.

From the moment of its first proposal, Operation Montagnards had been warmly received by the French Resistance leaders. Funds had been allocated to develop it and General de Gaulle had personally approved it in London—and indeed this had been signaled to the Vercors on the French service of the BBC in a coded message, *"Les Montagnards doivent continuer à gravir les cimes"* ("The mountaineers must continue to climb the heights").

By the May afternoon that Colonel Descour summoned François Huet to the meeting in the Rue du Plat in Lyon, he had received no firm instructions about the operation. But plans for the Secret Army to launch a complex nationwide program of sabotage at the time of the invasion—to disrupt communications and hinder troop movements—were well advanced. Descour was certain, correctly it was to turn out, that orders would be sent to him to mobilize the Vercors, and he wanted to be ready for them when they came. There were,

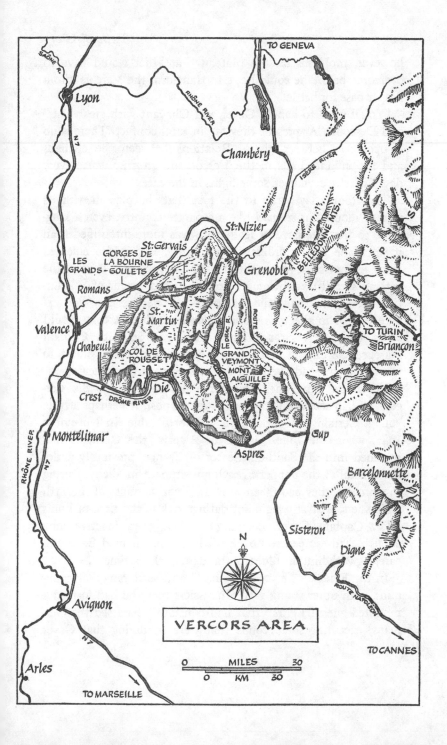

TO GENEVA

SAÔNE R.

Lyon

RHÔNE RIVER

N 7

Chambéry

ISÈRE RIVER

BELLEDONNE MTS.

St:Nizier

St:Gervais

GORGES DE
LA BOURNE

LES
GRANDS-GOULETS

Grenoble

Romans

ISÈRE R.

St:-
Martin

ROUTE NAPOLÉON

LE DRAC R.

TO TURIN

Briançon

Valence

Chabeuil

COL DE
ROUSSET

LE
GRAND
VEYMONT

MONT
AIGUILLE

Crest

DRÔME RIVER

Die

RHÔNE RIVER

Montélimar

N 7

Gap

Aspres

Barcelonnette

N

Sisteron

Digne

ROUTE NAPOLÉON

Avignon

N 7

VERCORS AREA

Arles

0   MILES   30

0   KM   30

TO CANNES

TO MARSEILLE

however, problems on the plateau that Huet would have to overcome before he could hope to transform the Vercors into a proper base for battle.

"You'll need to handle Geyer and Chavant with great tact," said Descour. "At present they are in total conflict. There is no co-operation between them. Relations between the civilians and the military units in the Vercors are growing worse every day. There've even been some fights in the cafés."

The trouble lay partly in the fact that the plateau with its ring of mountains *seemed* like a separate country, even a kingdom, so that the issue of leadership was more intensified than it would be in any ordinary community. But it also emerged from an inevitable personality clash. For Eugène Chavant, the veteran socialist politician, the one-time red mayor of St.-Martin-d'Hères, the man who was acknowledged as the "Patron" by everyone in the towns and villages of the Vercors, would never under any circumstances have got on with Captain Narcisse Geyer, the brash, audacious young cavalry officer to whom Descour had given military command of the plateau.

Yet at the time when Descour had sent Geyer to the Vercors, he had seemed highly suited to the post, if perhaps a trifle young. Certainly his reputation was formidable. In November 1942, when the Allies landed in Algeria, the Germans had marched into the Southern Sector of France, previously under the control of the puppet French government in Vichy. During this process, they had taken over the Lyon barracks of the 11th Cuirassiers, a cavalry regiment dating back to the time of Louis XIV. Captain Geyer, deciding he had been inactive long enough, had escaped south on a white horse named Bouccaro, carrying with him the blue silk standard of the regiment.

In the Forêt de Thivollet in the Grand-Serre range of mountains, with other young 11th Cuirassiers men, he had formed a mounted guerrilla group that had constantly harassed the Germans, executing some coups that were so daring that Geyer soon became something of a legend—which was why Descour thought he might be ideal for the wild country of the Vercors.

Geyer did not, in fact, come from the mold that the colonel would truly have liked. He did not, for example, attend the officers' training school at St.-Cyr, the French equivalent of West Point or Sandhurst. He went to Saumur, which was open to talented young men whose parents could not afford the high St.-Cyr fees. But he had an outstanding war record. Seconded to a tank regiment under the command of De Gaulle, then a colonel, he had won the Croix de Guerre and earned special citations for gallantry. He was clever, courageous, and a bold leader, highly respected by his men. He was also erratic and had a dangerous sense of humor. Descour, who had also served with the 11th Cuirassiers, knew well enough the story of the day Geyer had let loose the regiment's white stallions—which was typical of Geyer at his irresponsible worst.

Although the regiment was now a tank unit, the 11th Cuirassiers on ceremonial occasions rode specially bred white Arab stallions that were stabled in their Lyon base. At an early moment in the German take-over of the barracks, a number of horse-drawn wagons were sent to collect urgent items of military equipment needed by the Wehrmacht.

As Geyer wandered past the line of wagons on the parade ground, he noticed that some of the animals were mares in heat—a condition that mares experience more often than most big animals—and it gave him an idea. Unobtrusively, he strolled to the stables and released the regiment's stallions from their stalls. The horses were quick to appreciate their opportunity. The result, witnessed by Geyer, who wandered innocently back onto the parade ground, smiling happily, was glorious chaos as the stallions tried to mount the mares. The wagons overturned. The animals paired with the mares in the traces took fright. Horses were rearing, kicking, trying to break away from the carts, dragging them on their sides.

For the regiment in its humiliation it was a moment of superb revenge, but it could have resulted in horrific repercussions. Geyer, so Descour believed, needed to be controlled. Also, conditions in the Vercors were fraught with difficulties. The Resistance was manned mainly by civilians, but even the soldiers who were there were supplied with food by people who lived in the villages. There was no scope for much in the way of military bravura. The situation, therefore, in December 1943, when Geyer had ridden his horse into the square of St.-Martin and looked around him with the somewhat superior air that characterizes some cavalry officers, had demanded diplomacy. And Geyer, for all his other qualities, was no diplomat.

"The matter is highly delicate," Descour counseled Major Huet. "The conflict has got to be stopped, but we can't afford to lose Captain Geyer." As they both knew, there were plenty of untrained civilians available, but professional, combat-hardened officers, especially those who had demonstrated courage and initiative, were scarce. "Perhaps," Descour mused, "it might be wise to point out that you're not actually superseding him but have been appointed to a kind of broader role, above him."

Huet understood what he meant. The Vercors in its mobilized state, manned by thousands of fighting men, would be a very different command from its present situation as a Maquis base. "I'll do my best," he said, "to handle the matter as tactfully as possible."

CHAPTER 3

Early in the morning of May 17, a few days after Colonel Descour had talked with Huet in Lyon, Eugène Chavant—the Patron they had discussed—sat at his usual table in the café-bar of the Hôtel Breyton in St.-Martin-en-Vercors.

St.-Martin, which had become the headquarters village of the Vercors because of its site in the center of the plateau, was set on the side of a hill separated by a lush green valley from the towering heights of the Roche Rousse, one of the craggy mountain ridges that were a feature of the interior of the massif. There was a small main square, bordered on one side by an old church, with massive wooden doors, and on another by the Mairie, a miniature town hall of faded stone. One corner was dominated by a voluminous three-hundred-year-old lime tree, which had been planted on the orders of the Duc de Sully, the man who put Henry IV of Navarre on the throne of France.

Facing the church and the tree from across the road that

passed along one side of the square was the Hôtel Breyton, an old building of peeling white stucco between great timber beams. Its claim to be a hotel was somewhat specious, considering it had only three bedrooms, but if the Vercors could be likened to a kingdom, this was its palace.

For Chavant, the crowded café was a working office. It was here that he held his meetings, talked with the people who were always waiting to see him, and gave his orders.

He was a dour, quiet-speaking man with gray hair, a deeply lined face, and a short thick mustache. On this May morning his brown eyes were alight with unusual excitement, for a message had arrived from one of the Allied intelligence networks. At last, after an abortive start three weeks before, he was going to Algiers—to the Allied Forces Mediterranean Headquarters, to the seat of General de Gaulle's provisional French government, to discuss the fortress role that the Vercors would play after the invasion of Europe. Also, he planned to demand the replacement of Captain Geyer, who, from the moment Chavant had first encountered him six months before at a secret meeting in a sawmill near the village of St.-Julien-en-Vercors, had inspired in him a violent, obsessive antipathy. And Chavant was not the kind of man to disguise his feelings. It emerged in a kind of smoldering hostility. His nickname, "the Boar," used with affection by friends and with derision by others, was well enough chosen.

Chavant had been a founder of the Vercors in its present form as a Resistance base. He had been one of five men who in the summer of 1941, three years before, had sat around a table in the Café de la Rotonde near Grenoble Station and conceived the idea of setting up camps in the Vercors for refugees from the political police—first for Jews, then for others who were seen as politically undesirable, and finally, and most important, for young men who wanted to avoid being drafted into

the STO (Service du Travail Obligatoire), the Nazi forced-
labor corps.

From the earliest days, it had been Chavant's role in Grenoble to interrogate the people who sought the safety of the Vercors before sending them up in the Huillier autobus to Villard-
de-Lans, the Vercors' largest town, where the Huillier office
would be alerted by telephone to expect a "package."

What Chavant saw as a refuge the military men of the Resistance—men and officers of the French Army—saw as an ulti-
mate base for offensive operations. They, too, began to set up
camps on the plateau. The partnership was not easy. Together
with most of his colleagues, Chavant was a left-wing socialist
and a veteran combatant of the class war. He had first learned
about battle as a private soldier in the trenches in the First
World War, emerging at the end of the hostilities as a sergeant
—young, but already gnarled. He had immersed himself in
labor politics, often leading strikes during the thirties, until
eventually, running under a Socialist ticket, he had become
mayor of St.-Martin-d'Hères on the fringe of Grenoble.

By contrast, most of the military officers interested in the
Vercors were right-wing, usually from gilded backgrounds and
the elite training of St.-Cyr.

A degree of co-operation between the two had, however,
been forced on them by the fact that they faced a common
enemy and shared the same problems. The camps needed food
and money to pay for it. The trucks of Victor Huillier's transport company, which took milk and butter from the Vercors
farms to the plain, brought back meat, flour, and vegetables for
both kinds of Maquisards.

Cash was channeled to both organizations from Allied
sources through a false account in the name of a beekeeper
called François Tirard in the Banque Populaire in Villard-de-
Lans. The ledger was kept on toilet paper so that it could easily

be flushed away if there was fear of detection. Shopkeepers were paid in vouchers that were later exchanged for money.

Raids by troops or police were a constant danger to both military and civilian camps, and they shared the alert system. Lookouts were posted on a twenty-four-hour rota at key points around the massif. Sightings of approaching police cars or troop columns were phoned to the Vercors electricity station. The warning signal was the flashing three times of all the lights in the plateau. Immediately the camps would be evacuated, the Maquisards scattering through the forests, but the residents of the villages would just check that anything compromising was properly hidden and carry on with their life as normal.

At first Eugène Chavant had merely been one of several leaders of the Vercors administration. Then came the trauma of the spring of 1943. The Italians—who at that time policed southeastern France for the Germans—set out to purge the illegal Vercors camps. In March, when the snow still lay in the passes, they raided the plateau and arrested fourteen men, several of them couriers who were close to the leadership, and the OVRA, Mussolini's equivalent of the Gestapo, interrogated them. During the weeks that followed, the police returned to the plateau several times. On two occasions they headed straight for Maquis enclaves—one civilian and one military—in remote parts of the plateau. Each time they were too late to find anyone, since the Maquisards had responded to the warning signal, but it indicated that the Grenoble authorities were becoming extremely well informed.

In subsequent raids they searched houses and made more arrests. Finally, to the shock of everyone in the Vercors, they came for Dr. Léon Martin, who with Chavant had been one of the founders of the Vercors in its illegal form.

In May the campaign rose to crisis. News reached the Vercors that there was a tank truck filled with gasoline in a garage at Mens on the plain. It had broken down, but the repairs were complete. Gasoline in the Vercors—indeed, in France as a whole—was in desperately short supply and Victor Huillier's trucks that serviced the Maquis camps were facing a very serious shortage. A commando *corps franc* of thirteen men was dispatched to hijack the tank truck and bring it to the plateau.

The raid was a disaster. There was an unexpected sentry on duty who caused a delay. The tank truck was blocked by another vehicle, also in for repairs and immobile, and it turned out to have a diesel engine, not a gasoline motor, as the team had been informed, with no oil in the tank.

The team had to accept failure and withdraw, but valuable time had been lost and it was already dawn as they headed back to the Vercors in their truck. At Le Pont-de-Claix on the ring road that encircled the massif they were stopped at a temporary road block manned by troops, and arrested. The Vercors license plate was enough to make the OVRA question the thirteen men vigorously, and disparities in their stories quickly emerged.

The interrogations yielded big results. That day the police raided the Vercors town of Lans-en-Vercors and found six tons of dynamite. It was the start of a new aggressive phase in the purge. Arrest followed arrest, including those of two more leaders—one of whom was later charged with collaborating with the enemy—and the Vercors administration collapsed. Those who had not been taken by the police made for cover. Chavant himself went into hiding in the little mountain town of Chamrousse in the Belledonne range to the east of the Vercors.

When at last, several weeks later, he cautiously emerged from hiding he was the unchallenged leader of the Vercors, acknowledged by everyone as Patron—even if there was a price on his head and he was known only by his cover name of Clément.

At the beginning, when he had helped set up the early

camps, the Vercors had for Chavant been a convenience, a suitable place for his purpose. But he had now worked closely with the men and women of the plateau for more than two years, had shared with them risks, sorrows, and even achievements, and the massif had become deeply personal to him. Although he had been born on the plain and lived all his life in the Grenoble area, he saw the Vercors as *his* territory, the villagers as *his* people, and this sense of possession, of belonging, was mutual.

Until then he had never heard of Operation Montagnards, which the military men had been working on so assiduously, but the concept of the mountain fortress had enormous appeal to him, partly because it was a way to fight the enemy, but also because it would give his plateau a role of great stature in the war. It would ensure for it a name in history. Also he had much respect for Captain Alain le Ray, the first military commander to be appointed to the Vercors within the hierarchy of what was to become the Secret Army. Le Ray was a brilliant skier and mountaineer and was, in fact, one of the few men who had escaped from the German cliff-top prison of Colditz.

So, with a certain jealous and suspicious caution, Chavant began to work with the army officers whose background and aspirations and viewpoints were so different from his own. The situation was highly delicate. The natural conflict between civilians and soldiers was heightened by the utterly different philosophies of the guerrillas, who saw themselves more as patriotic bandits than as troops, and of the career officers, brought up to regard discipline and training and even drill as of supreme importance.

Considering the difficulties, Chavant and the officers established a relationship that, though fragile, was surprisingly good. He still insisted on retaining personal control of the camps of civilians—which was most of the camps—but he accepted that they must ultimately be directed by military experts and play their vital part in preparing the strategic plan to turn the Vercors into an offensive citadel. For their part, the army men acknowledged Chavant's role as Patron, and when a five-man "Military Committee" of the Vercors, consisting of both soldiers and civilians, was set up to run the plateau and ease the frictions, there was no question about his status as its president.

The Military Committee helped to patch up many of the problems between the two groups, but it did not solve them all. The French, who had experienced so many revolutions, had a traditional built-in distrust of the Army. During an Allied parachute drop of weapons some of Chavant's civilians, who had not yet accepted the new discipline, made off in the darkness with some of the munitions—a fact which London learned of with displeasure and which lay at the roots of Le Ray's angry resignation scene with Colonel Descour.

By December 1943, however, the new situation, with Chavant as the accepted outlaw chief of outlaw country, was working well; then it was transformed dramatically by two new factors. First, the Italians signed an Armistice with the Allies. They were replaced in southeastern France by German troops and the Gestapo—a far more ruthless enemy. Second, Captain Narcisse Geyer arrived in the plateau to take over the military command from Le Ray.

At their first strained meeting in the sawmill at St.-Julien, when Geyer came over for a preliminary visit, Chavant's first impressions of the new military commander filled him with foreboding. The fair-haired captain was very short and slight— almost small enough to be a jockey. Like many men of his build, he was aggressive in a breezy kind of way, with a rather facile cocky grin which he probably overused at this first confrontation in an effort to thaw his icy reception. If he did, then it certainly failed. Chavant treated him with what Geyer recalls as a "suspicious hostility" that hardly paved the way for a suc-

cessful partnership. It is doubtful, too, if Geyer paid the Patron
the respect that he had come to expect on his plateau, for the
young officer was not that kind of man. Certainly Chavant was
appalled by the meeting with Geyer, and it is tempting to wonder if the Patron, for all his socialism, had not been a little
impressed by Le Ray's background. For he came from impecca-
ble social and literary circles and had indeed married the
daughter of the great François Mauriac.

By contrast, Geyer, whose father had been killed as a young
lieutenant of very slender means in the last days of the First
World War, came from a very different setting. He had clambered to his present status without influence, by ambition and
merit—and a brilliance in the saddle at the military riding
school at Fontainebleau that always tended to impress French
generals with their atavistic worship of cavalry. His newest
post, "Chef Départemental du Vercors," was his first command
and he believed its title meant what it said: namely, "Chief."
He had been appointed to it formally within the hierarchy of
the Secret Army that was directed from London and Algiers.
And who, for that matter, had appointed Eugène Chavant?

So the two men looked at each other across the floor of the
sawmill, in competition for the role of leader: the mature,
skilled politician, the fervent socialist, the peasant cobbler's son
with an intelligence and a revolutionary faith that had enabled
him to clamber above the origins of which he was proud; and
the wiry, rather arrogant young cavalry officer whose courage
and dash had helped *him* overcome the disadvantages of his
own background.

Chavant presented obstacles from the start. Stubbornly he
refused to permit Geyer to have any dealings with the civilian
camps or even to give training to the Maquisards in the weapons that were parachuted onto the plateau. Months later, an
American OSS team was to report with amused surprise that
some men of the Vercors Maquis did not even know properly

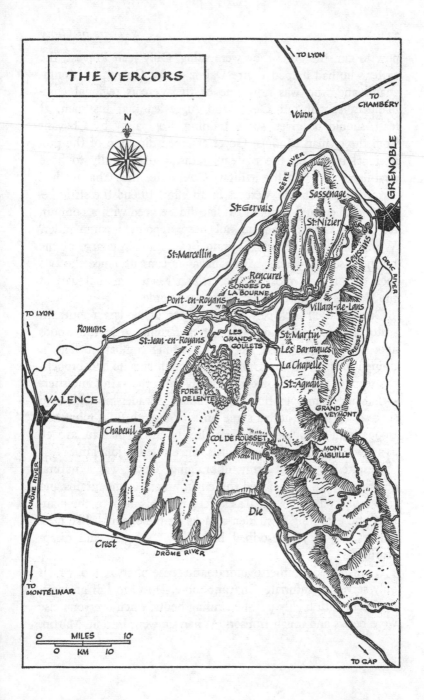

how to aim the guns they were using. Only Jean Prévost, the
writer who had helped Pierre Dalloz design Operation Montagnards and who was now one of the Vercors regional commanders, sought out Geyer and suggested that his men, at
least, should be given some training. Kept away by Chavant
from the civilian Maquis, Geyer assumed direction of the professional troops on the plateau, refusing disdainfully to have
anything to do with the Military Committee that Chavant had
formed to govern the Vercors in an effort to end the strife between soldiers and civilians. What did he need with a committee, asked Geyer? Had he not been appointed commander?
Wisely, however, he left Captain Beauregard in charge of the
northern sector, where, with Chavant's consent, since the two
men got on well, most of the civilian Maquis in that part of
the Vercors were also under Beauregard's orders.

Geyer himself took personal command of the larger southern
sector and set up headquarters in a farmhouse in the woods
above St.-Martin. There he built a strong combat nucleus of
trained men. From the Grand-Serre mountains he had brought
the team of mounted officers—mostly from the 11th Cuirassiers
—that had been operating there under his leadership with such
success. To this he added some units of the 6th BCA mountain
troops from Grenoble that were already on the plateau, as well
as a few tough civilian Maquisards who elected to join him.

Despite his formal army upbringing, Geyer was a natural
guerrilla leader. He enjoyed the environment of mountains and
forests and was exhilarated, as indeed were his men, by the planning and executing of sudden attacks on the enemy—"like mos-
quitoes," as Geyer described his policy, "stinging and disappearing."

He displayed a rather overdramatic sense of style, too, which
only served to infuriate Chavant more. He wore full uniform,
complete with highly polished riding boots, when everyone else
wore berets and rough trousers. When he went into St.-Martin,

or anywhere else, he would normally go by horse, accompanied by an escort of mounted officers.

In his room in the farmhouse that was his headquarters, the blue silk standard of the 11th Cuirassiers—with its motif of the royal arms of the fleurs-de-lis and the golden sun of Louis XIV—was pinned across one wall. He also wore a small badge of fleurs-de-lis on the breast of his jacket, which Chavant believed to be a deliberate provocation to him—the flaunting of monarchist politics before a known and ardent socialist.

Horses were Geyer's passion—and they were yet another reason for his worsening relations with Chavant. The captain believed that they were an ideal method of fast and flexible transport in the rugged terrain of the Vercors where there were only a few roads suited to motor vehicles. So he encouraged his men to acquire them during their *coups de mains*. One of the most daring escapades was carried out by a young 11th Cuirassiers officer named Yves Beesau, heir to a large estate in Normandy and the descendant of a long line of celebrated generals. Beesau discovered that the German commandant in Romans, on the ring road to the west of the Vercors, owned a beautiful chestnut mare. On a mission to the town on other business, Beesau slipped into the stables, forced the grooms at gunpoint to saddle the animal, and rode away at full gallop down Romans' main street. Surprisingly, he got away quite easily and a few hours later rode into Geyer's camp with a broad grin on his face. Bowing with elaborate ceremony, he offered the mare as a gift to his commander.

Chavant was furious when he heard of it because he regarded the coup as stupidly provocative. And indeed, this involved a policy issue on which Geyer and Chavant were in complete opposition, as they were on most things. The Patron wanted the Vercors to retain a low profile, for with good reason he feared the retaliation that the Germans might inflict on the people in the villages. But Geyer was fighting a war. He had not escaped from the enemy at the regiment's Lyon barracks in order to stay inactive on a remote plateau.

Within days of his arrival on the massif, his men had been dispatched on a series of raids against the enemy on the plain. Apart from the big barracks at Grenoble, there were small enemy garrisons in several local towns. These were key targets for sudden strikes by *corps francs* from the Vercors—such as an attack on January 4 that garnered 3,000 kilograms of dynamite, a Citroën truck, a couple of horses, and a supply of telephone cable that was badly needed for the internal communications system of the plateau.

Geyer's men shot Germans in roadside ambushes, hijacked their transport, and executed a raid on a gasoline depot that, like the fiasco at Mens, proved abortive. The police, who had clearly been forewarned, opened fire, using people in the streets as shields so that the Maquisards could not shoot back. The unit only just succeeded in withdrawing without loss.

Geyer was not the only leader to insist on an aggressive policy. Several militant Resistance units—*groupes francs*, as they were known—soon began to make the Vercors their base. From the plateau they would swoop on targets in the towns on the plain, machine guns firing and tires screaming. Naturally Chavant did not approve of these operations either, but the militant teams did not regard him as their chief, since they took their orders direct from Algiers. Also, these attacks were part of a growing campaign of sabotage that was being executed by the Resistance throughout France, but this did not impress Chavant. The Vercors was different. It was compact. Its surrounding mountains formed a clear, definable border that other places did not have. If it was used as a base for offensive operations, there could be no arguing that the sabotage squads were just passing through, as the people in towns on the plain could plead. The Vercors villages, therefore—and especially the farms —were exceptionally vulnerable to reprisals.

By January of 1944 the sympathies of the people of the plateau had become polarized, centering on one or other of the
two leaders. Chavant, of course, had the faithful support of the
residents of the Vercors—and, in particular, of the men who
administered it—and most of the Maquis civilians. Geyer at-
tracted the men who sought action, which included most of the
soldiers. Certainly he commanded a motley collection. There
was a Russian deserter, one of many prisoners of war from the
Eastern Front whom the Germans had conscripted into the
Wehrmacht. There was a sauce chef from Maxim's restaurant in
Paris. There was "Le Barbu" ("the Bearded"), who was
brought at gunpoint to Geyer one day by one of the sentries.

Le Barbu was a huge muscular priest who had been sent to
investigate the Vercors by his bishop—and had become fascinated by what he saw. After his first visit he returned to the
plateau in direct defiance of his bishop's orders and offered his
services to Geyer. The captain's face broke into a twisted grin—
twisted because a cigarette always drooped from his mouth
when he was not on horseback—and pondered aloud the
fighting value of a man of God. Le Barbu responded with a big
laugh that shook his great shoulders.

"I can kill the Germans with my cross," he roared, "and
then read the funeral mass over them." He had come to the
plateau to fight—and indeed Geyer put him in command of
one of the key entrances into the plateau at Les Barraques—but
he also conducted services. Always, though, even when he wore
his cassock, he carried on his belt a revolver and several grenades. Le Barbu was constantly prepared for surprise attacks.

Then there was young Sergeant Abel Chabal of the 6th
BCA, Grenoble's Alpine Regiment, who was building up a
commando unit of tough, highly trained troops, who could
shoot, move fast across mountain country even in deep snow,
and respond with instant obedience to orders.

Geyer's camp was always full of brave, high-spirited, competitive young men who laughed a lot and took too many risks. There was mocking conflict between the 6th BCA, the Alpine troops who had grown up in the mountains, and the 11th Cuirassiers, who were expert riders but not very adept on skis. The value of the horses was limited in heavy snow, and in those early weeks of 1944 the "cowboys," as they were nicknamed by their Alpine comrades, just did their clumsy best, muttering about the spring when their animals would prove their worth.

Very soon after Geyer assumed his post, however, Chavant's fears of retaliation seemed to be justified. On January 19 two senior officers of the Feldgendarmerie (German military police) from Valence, accompanied by a Dutch journalist, very unwisely drove without an escort up the steep, winding, snow-covered road from Die in the south with a black Swastika flag fluttering from the hood of their car. They entered the plateau by way of the narrow tunnel at the pass of the Col de Rousset, and an overkeen group of Maquisards on guard arrested them as hostages.

Geyer did not approve of the action—though he happily displayed the black Swastika flag on his wall beside the regimental standard of the 11th Cuirassiers—because he did not consider the three hostages worth the provocation. To release them, however, posed problems. They had seen far too much. They had recognized men whose families lived in the plain. They were yearning for revenge for their mutilated dignity.

Predictably, two days later a Feldgendarmerie detachment came up the same road to look for them. They were met by heavy fire as they emerged from the tunnel at the Col de Rousset—and retreated fast, with casualties. This was too much for the German authorities. A convoy of thirty trucks, with heavy arms, was signaled from Pont-en-Royans at the foot of the massif on the west. As the column approached up the twisting tunneled road that bordered the deep gorge called Les Grands-

Goulets, the waiting Maquisards attacked it; but the combat was uneven and after a two-hour battle the Germans broke through. The French were not truly trying to stop them. They were just operating the classic technique of doing as much damage as possible—which was easy on those mountain roads— and then withdrawing. They killed a lot of the enemy and suffered only one French casualty; but the Germans responded by burning all the houses in the little hamlet of Les Barraques.

Later, Geyer insisted that his orders to withdraw at an earlier stage had been carried out only by his 11th Cuirassiers, being ignored by some of the other units, and claimed that if they had been followed, the reprisals would have been less severe. The incident emphasized the problems of command in this type of mountain environment—especially when there was conflict between the leaders. For there was no real discipline, no courts-martial for disobedience of orders.

If there were gaps in the Vercors administration, they were revealed only too starkly a week later by tragedy. A unit of veteran Alpine troops from the Grenoble Regiment, the 6th BCA, had deliberately opted for independence from the main Vercors command and installed themselves in the little village of Malleval in the northwestern foothills of the massif.

Malleval was outside the Vercors' protective ring of mountains but it was in high, wild country, approachable only by a narrow road from below, and there was an easy upward escape route to the Pas du Follet, which overlooked it at 3,500 feet. Because the village was not within the compass of the plateau warning system, a member of the unit was always on duty at the foot of the approach road, where there was a telephone to give warning of danger.

At dawn on January 29, the Germans attacked Malleval. They surprised the duty sentry, cut the telephone line, and advanced up the road. Already a detachment had been sent above the village to cover the escape route to the Pas du Follet.

The fact that the telephone was dead was discovered very fast in Malleval. Immediately the 6th BCA commander, Lieutenant Gustave Eysseric, ordered a withdrawal to the pass, but he and his men did not get far. Most of them, including Eysseric himself, died in the first bursts of machine gun fire from the enemy troops who were waiting above them.

The Germans planned to make an example of Malleval, and this time there could be no arguments about subtle tactics of "mosquito stings." They killed thirty BCA men, finishing off the wounded with revolvers. Only five survived, by gaining cover in the confusion of the battle or by pretending to be dead. Then the Germans set the whole village on fire, locking eight of the inhabitants—including a Jewish doctor and his wife—in their homes so that they were burned alive.

The tragedy of Malleval was traumatic for the Vercors. It became one of those disasters which people employ to indicate a date. "Before Malleval . . ." they would say. It was an indication that the battle was growing fiercer—not only in and near the Vercors but through the whole area. Throughout the early months of 1944 the French Resistance was gaining confidence as it became more unified, as the direction from London and Algiers became stronger, as the expectation grew of the Allied invasion. And the Germans were responding to this new mood, executing punitive attacks wherever it seemed to be most prevalent. News came into the plateau of assaults in other areas, including one awful massacre at Glières to the north of the massif. For these at least, Chavant could not hold Geyer responsible, but he could argue with some justification that relations between the French and the occupying authorities had grown more sensitive, so that less was needed to incite retaliation.

In March the fallibility of the Vercors warning system was savagely revealed. Suddenly, in the early light of dawn, the men posted on the approach to the Gorges de la Bourne—the deep

crevice in the massif that divided the north and south sectors—
saw a German column of forty-five trucks approaching along
the road from Villard. This was deep inside the plateau. The
alert should have been given at least an hour before. The Maquisards opened fire, but it was only a gesture. The Germans
were intent on specific targets about which they had been fully
informed. They made straight for Colonel Descour's district
command post in a house near St.-Julien and blew it up, gun-
ning down the men who tried to escape from the blazing
building.

Geyer, in his camp above St.-Martin, some two miles away,
heard the explosions and ordered his men to drop back at once
into the hills with the horses—just in time. For his farmhouse
headquarters, too, was on the Germans' list, and even though it
was empty when they arrived, they set it on fire as a matter of
principle. To fan Chavant's fears, they burned nine farms before returning to the plain.

Clearly the raid did not satisfy them, for in April a large
force of Milice, in their dark blue uniforms, came up onto the
plateau with supporting German troops. They set up temporary
headquarters in the towns of Vassieux and La Chapelle-en-Ver-
cors, not far from St.-Martin. The Milice were political police,
directed by the French puppet government at Vichy. They
worked closely with the Gestapo, employing the same brutal
methods, but since they were acting against their own coun-
trymen they were hated even more.

This was a punitive expedition, designed to clean up the Vercors from within as a base of "terrorists," as the Germans called
the men of the Resistance. And the concern with which the authorities viewed the plateau was indicated by the size of the operation. For the total force amounted to nearly a thousand
men.

For eight days, from April 16 to 24, the Milice conducted a
campaign of terror. They arrested suspects, took hostages, and

interrogated villagers about the positions of Maquis camps and arms dumps. Torture was regularly employed. When one woman who lived near Rousset insisted that she did not know the position of any local Maquis camps, the police beat her, set her home alight, then dragged her along the road behind a car with her feet tied to the rear fender.

Within hours of the arrival of the Milice on the plateau, they announced their intention of shooting twelve men who had been arrested at random—and their lives were saved only by the passionate intervention of Father Gagnol, the curé of Vassieux, who insisted that they were all innocent.

The district Milice chief, the most loathed man in the area, stayed in La Chapelle's Hôtel Bellier in order to supervise the operation—and brought with him his mistress. Nicknamed "Colonel Maude," she acted as prosecutor at the tribunals held in hotels in Vassieux and La Chapelle to try suspected "terrorists," and personally controlled the torture that was a frequent feature of them. Often she had her victims stripped naked in front of her. During one investigation, Henri Bellier, the owner of the hotel, was forced to sit in a red-hot frying pan. André Giroud, a Vassieux farmer, was beaten so badly he was unable to walk after the interrogation. Some of the victims, such as a Pole named Schwartz, failed to survive the handling by the Milice and died later in the hospital.

Physically, Colonel Maude was an attractive woman, but she had an appetite for cruelty, not limited to adults. Holding up the screaming eight-year-old child of François Bonthoux, she snarled, "Smile or I'll kill you!"

Well informed as the authorities always were, the Milice knew the identity of the Resistance leaders and made a big effort to find them. Colonel Maude had in fact visited the Vercors anonymously before the Milice operation on a surveillance trip. In the Hôtel Bellier she had asked to see the military commander on the pretext that she was searching for her brother who was in the Maquis. Geyer had already heard that she had been asking suspicious questions in the bus on her way to La Chapelle, but he wanted to take a look at her. When she raised the question of her brother, he had insisted, "You're mistaken. There's no Maquis in the Vercors."

By the time Colonel Maude returned with the Milice force, even Geyer was not contesting that it was time for a low profile, with no provocative raids, no stealing of beautiful horses. After the big German raid in March, he had moved his camp to the thick cover of the Forêt de Lente, France's largest virgin forest, which covered much of the high country on the west of the plateau. Chavant himself went underground during the purge, protected by the people of the Vercors and especially by Mme Breyton in St.-Martin.

One evening when the smoke-filled café of the Hôtel Breyton was full of villagers, Chavant was eating dinner in the kitchen that adjoined the café since it was too dangerous for him to dine in public. Suddenly the noise of conversation faded. Everyone was looking at the door to the square. A Milice officer was standing there in the hated blue uniform, looking carefully around the room. He walked slowly into the silent café, his footsteps seeming loud, and approached Mme Breyton, who was standing in front of the door that led to the kitchen. About forty, she was a dark-haired, ample woman who had spent all her life in the country and had two sons in the Resistance. She had a strong, formidable personality—as her customers knew well enough.

"Madame," said the *milicien*, "I'm looking for Monsieur Chavant."

"He's not here, monsieur," she said. "I haven't seen him for days." Her stance in the doorway was firm, but everyone in the café knew that she was all that stood between the Patron and arrest. They expected the officer to push her aside or at least call in his men to institute a search of the hotel. But to everyone's astonishment, he suddenly appeared unequal to the challenge. He turned on his heel and walked out of the café. Very slowly and hesitantly, since it was hard to believe he had accepted Mme Breyton's somewhat overdogmatic assurance about the absence of Chavant, conversation started again.

By the time the Milice had been on the plateau for a week, one man had been shot resisting arrest, a number of people had been interrogated under torture, some had been transported to police headquarters in the plain, but no one had been ritually executed within the Vercors—an event which, it soon became evident, was regarded by the authorities as a vital deterrent against "terrorism."

On Sunday, April 23, a tribunal, in which Colonel Maude played a prominent role, sat in trial of three men in the Hôtel Allard in Vassieux. All were stripped naked. One was tortured. They were condemned to death and sentence was ordered to be carried out that day.

Once again Father Gagnol, the curé of the town, intervened to try to save their lives. This time he was met by curt refusal and consent was given only with reluctance to his request to hear their confessions. Afterward each man was given a cigarette and a glass of wine, provided by Mme Allard. During his last minutes alive, André Doucin, an ex-artillery officer who ran a chemist's shop, asked the hotel proprietress to help console his three children and his wife, who was pregnant with a fourth.

Then the condemned men were stood against a wall opposite the Hôtel Allard under the eyes of a horrified crowd of townspeople. They were ordered to prepare themselves and, without blindfolds, they faced the raised rifles of the Milice execution squad. The noise of the shots, not quite simultaneous, was heightened by the confines of the buildings of the town. And the three Frenchmen died—at the orders of a French tribunal, at the hands of the French police, as a warning to French "terrorists." The same tribunal had that morning sentenced six other men to transportation to a German concentration camp named Dachau.

It was the most terrible Sunday that the Vercors had ever known, though it served to bind the people of the plateau even closer in hatred than they had been before—and it was soon to be avenged.

The next day the sadistic Colonel Maude and her lover departed with his political police and the threads of normal life were picked up once again on the plateau. Once more Chavant was seen openly in the café of the Hôtel Breyton and Geyer rode back into town with his usual escort of young officers. He began preparations to set up a new headquarters, about two miles away from St.-Martin, in a farm backed by woods on a hill—with plenty of wild country behind him for fast withdrawal and a good field of vision so that approaching danger could be spotted in good time. The farm was part of a hamlet called La Rivière because it overlooked the valley of the little Vernaison; this valley provided a route south through St.-Agnan toward the Col de Rousset.

Chavant began to worry about Operation Montagnards. It was early spring and already the snow that always clung late to the Vercors meadows was almost gone. The big brown and white cattle were already cropping the young grass. If the invasion was to come this year, as it must, the date could not be far away. And until now, although missions from the three Allied services that controlled secret agents in France had visited the Vercors, there had been no definite orders.

The Patron decided that it was vital for him to go to Algiers to clarify the situation, and suddenly he was given the opportunity. An intelligence network controlled by the American OSS obtained a copy of a chart showing in precise detail the German defense positions along the entire south coast of France. A document of such value could be taken only by personal emissary to Allied headquarters where the invasion from the Mediterranean was being prepared, and Chavant was selected as the courier.

By that morning of May 17, therefore, when Chavant sat in the café of the Hôtel Breyton handling last-minute matters that needed his attention, everything had been settled for his departure with a comrade named Jean Veyrat. The Renault that was to take them on the first lap of the journey to the coast was driven into the square of St.-Martin, and Chavant bade good-by to his little cabinet in the café.

The two men drove through the charred ruins of Les Barraques and down the steep, narrow road that reached to the plain through tight bends and tunnels on the edge of the cliffs of Les Grands-Goulets, with the fabulous view that still made the tough veteran strike leader catch his breath. It was a beautiful day and the sky was a fine blue above the giant, soaring heights on the far side of the gorge.

Five days later, at 2 A.M. on the morning of May 22, they waited in the darkness on the beach at Cape Camarat, near St.-Tropez, flashing a torchlight on a prearranged signal. They were picked up in a rubber boat and transported out to sea where a flotilla of four U. S. Navy motor launches was waiting. A few hours later they arrived in the harbor of Bastia in Corsica and were flown on to Algiers. For Chavant, as the plane circled over the Aéroport de Maison-Blanche, it was a fine moment. They had arrived. Soon he would know the plans for his plateau.

CHAPTER 4

The old pirate port of Algiers was a strange place indeed during the last week of May 1944. In offices installed in Arab palaces on the hill beneath the ancient Bey fortress of the Kasbah worked the Allied officers who were directing the war in the Mediterranean and also the men who were planning to rule France once the Germans were driven north. It was a city of faction and jealousy and dispute although enormous efforts were being made by reorganization to reduce the quarreling in the common cause.

At the head of the military machine was the British General Sir Henry Maitland Wilson, who was responsible to General Eisenhower in London for the operations of Allied forces in the Mediterranean Theater. Most of these troops were in action in Italy, where, during the past few months, the war had not been progressing well. The Germans had succeeded in stopping the Allied advance, and an ambitious attempt to break the months-old stalemate by landing a force behind the enemy lines at Anzio had almost proved disastrous. At last, however, an Allied offensive had broken through the German defense, and Wilson's armies were once more moving toward Rome. Meanwhile, an assault on the South of France, intended originally to coincide with the invasion of Western Europe from Britain, had been planned since January—although the check in Italy, with its demands on resources, had caused serious delays.

The relations between the Allied High Command and the French were ambivalent. First, there was a lingering element of distrust by the Americans and the British of French security, in which they believed there had been leaks—and their suspicions were not eased by the knowledge, as the people of the Vercors could so unhappily endorse, that many Frenchmen were actively supporting the Germans.

Then, no one in Washington or Whitehall had been much in favor of Charles de Gaulle, who was seen as a waspish, arrogant, and very junior general who had appointed himself leader-in-exile of the Free French. But by May 1944 De Gaulle had defeated Henri Giraud, his U.S.-backed rival, and was the unchallenged head of the provisional French government, sitting temporarily on French colonial soil in Algiers. Also, he had built up an immense following among the people of France, to whom he had been broadcasting regularly with great eloquence. The communists, too, who were strong in the French underground, had made an uneasy deal with him, agreeing to sink their differences until the Germans were defeated, in return for representation in his provisional Cabinet in Algiers.

De Gaulle, therefore, with this unity of support, had a lot to sell the Allies, who, no matter how lukewarm or even hostile they might be, believed that the disruption of German communications within France was vital to the prospects for success of the invasion.

In May, as a result of De Gaulle's new leverage, the direction of the Resistance was being handed over to the French—under the over-all control of the Allied commander in chief. The underground in northern France was under the orders of the FFI (Forces Françaises de l'Intérieur, as the Secret Army was now called) in London, and the Southern Sector of the country was run from Algiers.

As part of this change, all the organizations concerned with the Resistance—the American OSS, the British SOE, and the French BCRA—were being merged in Algiers into a single unit called SPOC (Special Projects Operations Center). When Eugène Chavant arrived in the city, this transformation was not quite complete, but for all practical purposes three SPOC colonels—American, British, and French—acted in liaison to service the French underground in preparation for "Operation Anvil," the Allied invasion of the South of France.

The Frenchman was Colonel Jean Constans, who was also a senior executive officer in the Direction Générale des Services Spéciaux (DGSS), which played a big role in directing the Secret Army. Constans, in short, was in both camps: the French, through the DGSS, which De Gaulle controlled, and the Allied military command, through SPOC.

In practice, Constans was the senior officer at the headquarters end of the radio communications from the Maquis bases within the Southern Sector of France—the man who, when they signaled for arms or supplies, had to arrange delivery through his Allied colleagues. He was, therefore, to play a most significant role in the story of the Vercors, which would depend so heavily on headquarters.

It was to this colonel that Chavant was brought within hours of his arrival in Algiers. Constans was a career officer with the same kind of traditional military background as Colonel Descour and Major Huet. In his forties, bald, with bushy eyebrows, he was a man of great enthusiasm, and his excitement about the Vercors grew as Chavant explained why he had come. The Patron spoke in glowing terms of the strategic potential of the great massif and insisted that the doubts about the operation arising from the lack of firm orders must be completely removed so that the people of the plateau could know what was expected of them. "On this point," Constans recalls, "Chavant wanted a precise answer—yes or no—and wanted this answer from the highest authority, which in this case meant General de Gaulle."

Constans listened to the Patron with great interest and arranged for him to meet other members of the military staff. Over the next few days, Chavant went from meeting to meeting of senior officers. Hunched over large-scale maps of the Vercors, he explained the rugged nature of the plateau, its high cliffs, its narrow twisting passes that could be held so easily, its hills, its forests. He answered question after question about his capacity to provision paratroopers, about the strength of the Maquisards in the camps, about the men awaiting their summons in the plain, about parachute landing grounds, about suitable sites for the construction of air strips.

At each conference he encountered enormous enthusiasm for the plan, which was known to all his interrogators in theory but which he now brought to life for them in practice. Constans himself spoke eagerly of flying personally into the Vercors.

The Patron, made cautious by experience, was not an impressionable man, but as the days passed, his mood of optimism grew. These generals and colonels and air commodores treated him as a man of stature and their informed questions made a deep impact on him. "I was facing senior Allied officers," he told writer Paul Dreyfus.* "They knew what they were talking about."

During one meeting, he was asked, "How many paratroopers could you accommodate in the Vercors?"

This was a difficult question. He did not want to suggest too many in case the operation suddenly seemed impractical to them. He knew that there were many other Maquis groups who would be competing for the available resources. Carefully, he proposed, "Two thousand five hundred."

"Two thousand five hundred?" came the response. "We're planning to send you four thousand. Could you cope with this many—feed them, support them?"

Chavant smiled firmly. "Of course," he said. "The Vercors is very big. The pasture is rich. We also have food resources in the plain."

Although Chavant's main purpose was to obtain clarification about the Vercors operation, he did not lose the opportunity to complain about Captain Geyer. (By now, of course, Colonel Descour had already done what was necessary and Huet was at that moment on his way to take command of the plateau.)

Chavant, however, was determined to get his "precise answer —yes or no" about Operation Montagnards from the highest authority—and he got it. Although there is no doubt about the validity of the answer, which is unchallenged by anyone, it has caused great controversy.

General de Gaulle controlled his government and the various French organizations through a complex network of committees, but a key figure on most of them was a thirty-two-year-old ex-anthropologist named Jacques Soustelle.

Soustelle was a rare character. His career had been brilliant. By the age of twenty-five, as a doctor of philosophy, he had been appointed assistant director of the prestigious Musée de

* *Vercors: Citadelle de la Liberté.*

l'Homme in Paris. He had conducted field studies, which won academic acclaim, of ancient Indian tribes in Mexico, which is where he was when France fell in 1940. Soustelle hurried to London to offer his services to De Gaulle, to whom a friend was aide-de-camp. It was the beginning of a close and trusting relationship between the General and the anthropologist. Soustelle soon became a minister in De Gaulle's Cabinet. By May of 1944, when De Gaulle had at last brought the provisional French government under his control, Soustelle had become a man of great power, often acting as a channel for the General's instructions and wishes.

Soustelle does not recall meeting Chavant that May, but he does not question the written order he signed for the Patron to take back to France to Colonel Descour. Issued under the heading of the Comité Français de Libération Nationale (effectively the French government in Algiers) and dated May 30, 1944, it declared: "The directives issued in February 1943 by General Vidal for the organization of the Vercors continue to be valid. Their execution will be pursued by the regional and departmental staff under the control of DMR 1 [Colonel Descour] in liaison partly with the Maquis mission sent from London and partly with headquarters in Algiers."

Soustelle signed the order "for General de Gaulle," and today he insists that he would never have done this without a direct instruction from the General himself. So there is no question that De Gaulle personally approved Operation Montagnards under its other title of the Plan Vidal, so called because this was the cover name of General Charles Delestraint, who had originally been in charge of planning the operation.

The Maquis mission from London to which Soustelle referred was headed by a young English major named Desmond Longe, and consisted of Americans, British, and Frenchmen. It was primarily a liaison mission to keep London and Algiers closely informed about events in the Vercors. To enable it to do this it had four radio operators, equipped with the most sophisticated and high-powered equipment available.

Longe and most of his mission had not yet left England for the Vercors—although one or two of his team were already waiting for him in Algiers—because all air traffic between Britain and North Africa had been stopped for security reasons. The invasion of Europe was scheduled for five days' time, but Soustelle of course did not know this, for so far the facts had been kept even from General de Gaulle himself.

Once Chavant had been given the Soustelle order, the purpose of his visit to Algiers had been achieved. With his friend Jean Veyrat, he was flown back into France by a small Lysander aircraft, which landed on a remote meadow in the Ain Département, to the north of Lyon.

In addition to the order from Soustelle, Chavant brought with him some 2,500,000 francs in 500-franc notes and a new set of signal codes. But his first priority was to meet Colonel Descour, who, after being informed through underground contacts that Chavant wished to see him, arranged one of his secret open-air meetings at a crossroads in the Lyon suburb of Villeurbanne on June 5. Chavant was conducted to the meeting place and, strolling with Descour, handed him two sealed gray packages, in one of which was the Soustelle order, and told him of the plans he had discussed in Algiers to turn the Vercors into a citadel.

Descour smiled as Chavant told him of his experiences. "Well, Patron," he said, "it seems that Operation Montagnards is going to happen after all."

CHAPTER 5

On June 4, as Chavant was traveling from Ain to Lyon for his meeting with Colonel Descour, two important visitors arrived at French headquarters in Duke Street in London to see General Pierre Koenig. They were General Sir Colin Gubbins, head of the SOE, and Colonel David Bruce, chief of the OSS.

Koenig had taken up his appointment as commander in chief of the FFI (Forces Françaises de l'Intérieur) only four days before, and even now he still awaited official confirmation. He was, therefore, as he was to describe it in testimony, still somewhat "in the blue" at this early stage.

His appointment had been welcomed by everyone in the French forces because he was a national hero. In May 1942 Koenig, in command of an outpost of ten thousand men in the North African desert at Bir Hacheim, had held off two divisions of Rommel's Afrika Corps for three weeks of day-and-night attack. Finally, in darkness, with only twenty-two shells

left for his guns, he had led his battered force in a breakout
through the German lines and rejoined the British Army. It
was a brilliant action and, as Robert Aron, the French historian, put it: "From then on Koenig became a symbol of victory. . . ."

Koenig's two callers on June 4 came to the point of their
visit very quickly. In a few hours' time the invasion of Europe
would be launched. The plans had long been made for a
French uprising to coincide with this. A series of specific attacks on rail, road, and telephone communications as well as on
troop concentrations would be unleashed by the Resistance
forces.

However, as has been seen, the original plan was to mount
two assaults: a major operation on the Channel coast of France
and a secondary attack in the South. Now, since plans for the
second had been delayed, everyone in French headquarters had
assumed that only the Resistance in the Northern Sector of
France would be summoned into action. It was this assumption
that Koenig's two visitors had come to dispel.

"The Supreme Commander," explained Gubbins, "wishes us
to call out the South as well. It's vital to the success of the operation that the enemy should not know until the last possible
moment exactly what assaults he is facing and from which directions."

Koenig understood the thinking behind the request. If the
Germans believed that there might be an attack from Algiers
or Italy, they would be forced to keep major forces in the Mediterranean region. But the general also understood the enormous risk. Once they were called to action, the Resistance men
in the South would assume that an invasion of the Mediterranean coast of France was imminent. For everyone recognized
that without the support of an invading army the rising was
sure to fail—with results that would be disastrous.

Koenig, therefore, was being asked to co-operate in the deception of the men under his command that would lead to the sacrifice of many of their lives.

There was, however, a compelling additional risk factor. From the start of the planning, good weather had been regarded as an essential element of the operation. Now, even though it was high summer, there was a gale blowing up in the English Channel, which would mean that the invading force would have to go ashore through heavy surf with all the extra dangers and delay that this would bring.

"This makes it even more essential," Gubbins insisted, "that the enemy should be kept ignorant of the points of assault until our troops in these unfavorable conditions have established a firm bridgehead on French soil—even more vital that we should do everything possible to disrupt the Germans' communications and prevent them moving reinforcements to the attack area."

For Koenig, as for all the other commanders, the overriding factor was the successful liberation of France. It was the kind of terrible decision that generals often had to make, and Koenig really had little choice but to agree.

"I hope," he said, "that at the earliest possible moment I may be permitted to issue an order to the southern Maquis to withdraw from combat." This at least would allow many Resistance men to escape into the mountains.

"Of course," his visitors agreed. All they needed was a few vital days.

It was a decision that was to provoke a storm of criticism of the victor of Bir Hacheim, especially from the communists. It was a decision, too, that was to have enormous repercussions on the Vercors plateau.

That night, after the 11:30 news on the BBC radio service to France from London, the announcer read out seventy coded messages that ordered the Resistance into action. To the uninitiated, they sounded like gibberish. "Giraffe, why do you have so long a neck?" was one. "The cats mate in the front garden," "The mare is chestnut," "In the green forest is a big tree," were others.

Some of them were the lines of poems of which the previous lines had been broadcast a few days before, thus giving the "Act now" signal as a follow-up to the earlier "Prepare for action" order.

All were instructions to Resistance forces to start operations against specific targets to which they had been allocated. Most conformed to four different color plans, the color being a theme of the message—"green," for example, relating to sabotage to railroad tracks—but there were also special individual signals to certain units. One message that some people waiting in the Vercors believed to have been broadcast that night was *"Le chamois des alpes bondit"* ("The chamois leaps from the mountains") which was supposed to be the signal to activate Operation Montagnards. However, the list of transmitted messages in the BBC archives does not include it.

In any event, the summons turned out to be premature. On the advice of his meteorologists, General Eisenhower postponed the invasion for twenty-four hours in the hope of an easing of the gale that was churning the waters of the English Channel.

The next day, in the afternoon of June 5, around about the time that Chavant was giving Colonel Descour his new order from Jacques Soustelle about Operation Montagnards, François Huet arrived in the Vercors to assume his command. He traveled by autobus up the massif from Grenoble, by way of the twisting mountain road that passed through Sassenage village— and on through the Engins tunnel that had been bored through the rock wall known as the Grandes Côtes at a point where there was a bend in the course of the narrow Furon River.

The bus rattled on up the cleft in the Furon valley with its sheer, high rock sides—and then suddenly the vehicle was inside the Vercors in flat, open country marked by some young wheat, but mostly by rich green pasture.

For Huet the ride was familiar. He had been making trips onto the plateau ever since he could remember—for picnics in the summer with the family in the woods, for skiing in the winter from the high ground that he now had to consider with a commander's eye. The swaths that had been cut through the hillside timber to make the pistes for the ski runs would now form fields of fire.

The word *plateau* suggests a broad flat plain, but although the Vercors has a good deal of open country within its surrounding mountains, the interior also is broken by deep gorges and a series of long, high ridges. Some of these, like the Roche Rousse opposite St.-Martin, are bare rock, chipped and furrowed by erosion, often into strange shapes. Others are thick with woods. Mostly the valleys are roughly parallel to each other, cutting the massif from north to south, but the conformation is not always so regular.

The road that reaches southwest from the Engins tunnel through the broad fields of Lans to Villard lies through one of these wide valleys, with long, high, timbered mountains on either side. To Huet's right, through the windows of the bus, was the great Côte du Mas, with its long crest clothed by the close, tall firs of the Forêt de Guinney. The pass through it, which Huet knew well, even though he could not see it from the road, was the Col de la Croix-Perrin, the most important strategic position in that part of the Vercors.

After passing through the steep streets of Villard, between timber Alpine houses with roofs staked to hold the snow in winter, the bus turned and headed north within another valley. Like the open country of Lans, this, too, lay between high ridges of mountains and was, in fact, on the other side of the Col de la Croix-Perrin from the road from the Engins tunnel. They passed through Méaudre and traveled on to Autrans, the bus terminal and most northern town on the plateau. In peacetime, both Autrans and Méaudre were skiing resorts, as indeed, of course, was Villard.

At Autrans, Huet clambered down from the bus, shouldered his pack, and then for some two hours walked up the tiny track that wound up the slopes of the Montagne de la Molière until he came to Plénouze, where he knew Beauregard was camped. It was remote enough. The captain and his men lived in an old shepherds' barn, hidden in trees.

The arrival of Huet, panting from the long climb, as one of Beauregard's men later noted unkindly, took them a little by surprise. Hastily, Beauregard, who felt that some sort of gesture was needed to welcome his new commander, ordered his men to form up in ranks.

These were not soldiers. They were Chavant's civilians—the type of men who had given the word *Maquis* so emotive a meaning to the French under the Occupation. They did not believe in drill and had little time for the military concept of discipline. However, they respected Beauregard, who had succeeded in keeping a foot in both camps during the plateau conflict, and, with a certain obvious reluctance, they stood before Huet in three ragged lines. They were a pathetic bunch—without uniforms, unshaven, their clothes in tatters, wearing shoes with broken uppers or homemade moccasins roughly sewn with twine.

Only seven could present arms in response to Beauregard's order, since the others had no weapons, and even the armed ones carried nothing more lethal than sporting shotguns. "We do have a machine gun as well," Beauregard murmured as he saw the look of stark disbelief in Huet's eyes.

It was a moment of farce, but Huet, who had been an in-

structing officer at St.-Cyr, who had daily watched cadets
drilled to a precision that had seemed barely human, appreciated the captain's gesture. Solemnly he inspected the men as
carefully as if they had been on parade with buttons sparkling
and shoes polished to a high shine. He asked questions of one
or two of them. Then, according to a witness, he stood rigidly
to attention and saluted. In fact, for all its absurdity, the moment was rather moving.

It was a fine evening and, from the high position of
Plénouze, the view of the interior of the Vercors was
magnificent. Huet stood with Beauregard and surveyed the
huge area of his command, the valleys scooped from the mountains, emerging from areas of open country like fingers on a
hand. In the distance, across the Gorges de la Bourne, was the
southern sector of the plateau, and on its far edges in the
southeast the high peaks of Le Grand Veymont and Mont
Aiguille, the Vercors' highest mountains.

Huet spent the night in the old barn at Plénouze with
Beauregard, whom he knew quite well. The captain was a good-
looking young man with thick black hair and a boyish face that
made him look younger than his thirty years. His eminent family came from Savoy and had provided the French cavalry with
officers for generations. "Now," Eugène Chavant told Francis
Cammaerts, an SOE leader, as he took him to meet Beauregard
for the first time, "you're going to meet a real aristocrat." In
fact Beauregard had broken with family tradition and had
opted for the infantry, joining Grenoble's Alpine BCA Regiment when he left St.-Cyr.

He had been one of the first of the military men to be involved with the Vercors, had helped in the planning of Operation Montagnards, and had been a member of the Military
Committee of the Vercors. But, like Chavant, he did not get
on with Narcisse Geyer, regarding him as too brash and reck-
less. Beauregard, too, favored the low profile. In fact, he would

not even permit his men to go into the Vercors towns carrying
a gun in case they were compromised in a search.

Early next morning, Beauregard was awakened by a messenger
from Autrans. He brought momentous news: the Allied armies
were landing on the beaches of Normandy! For a few moments
the sleepy captain could hardly comprehend the full meaning
of what he had just heard, even though the Resistance had
been alerted and he had known it was imminent. For months,
like the other Maquisards in the Vercors, he had been living
underground, had even been hunted by the Germans and the
Milice. He had known the humiliation of defeat and occupation, had witnessed the burning of the Vercors farms, had seen
the arrest of comrades, had shared the trauma of the April executions in Vassieux. Throughout this time, the one event of
which they had all dreamed—the event that would start the liberation, that would signal the Resistance onto the offensive—
was the invasion. At last on that crisp morning it was a reality.
At last, after all the planning, all the talk, and all the conflicts,
the Vercors would shortly become a mountain fortress.

Deeply affected by his emotion, Beauregard roused Huet and
together they hurried on foot down the mountain to the road,
then drove to St.-Martin.

The Vercors towns, like those of most of France, were in
delirium. The BBC French service had just carried the news
that "this morning an immense armada of upwards of four
thousand ships with several thousand smaller craft crossed the
Channel. Eleven thousand first-line aircraft are supporting the
assault." Autrans and Méaudre were filled with cheering people
as Beauregard, waving happily to the many he knew, inched
the car through the crowded streets. But St.-Martin, the headquarters town to which many people had hurried as soon as
they heard the news, presented an almost incredible sight. People flung their arms around one another and kissed. Others
danced, shouting with excitement. Some were crying. Men with

joyous faces hammered the car as the captain drove it slowly to the square and parked it near the old lime tree.

As the two men made their way across the square, Beauregard was repeatedly hugged—by old women, Maquisards, children. Grinning broadly, he made hurried introductions of Huet as "our new military commander" and led the way into the crowded café of the hotel where the expansive Mme Breyton, her eyes shining, shook hands with the major and offered him a celebratory cognac.

In the towns of the plain around the Vercors much the same scene was being enacted, though in some places the presence of the Milice and the Germans acted as a curb on demonstrations of delight that were too uninhibited. "In Grenoble, Romans, Bourg-de-Péage, Valence," wrote Paul Dreyfus, "on this day of June 6, the excitement was at a peak. From these towns the Vercors was seen as a fantastic citadel encircled, above the dark wall of pines, by the white ring of limestone cliffs. The young people had made a thousand visits there, walking and climbing. The older ones had hunted hares and grouse. One way or another they all knew the footpaths of this grim powerful massif. In those intoxicating hours, it seemed impregnable."

In the Hôtel Breyton, the Vercors administrators held an impromptu meeting. Chavant, of course, had not yet returned, but most of the others were present—Dr. Samuel, the most important civilian after the Patron; Malossane, who was in charge of the southern sector; Tessier, who administered the north; Huillier, released from prison after the Italian armistice, who provided most of the transport; Honnard, who was a kind of quartermaster responsible for basic supplies.

There was much news from the plain, where already the Maquis had been in action, blowing up railroads and ammunition dumps, harassing German troops. The enemy had struck back, too. A tank column was at that moment fighting a battle near Crest on the ring road against Resistance men stationed in the Vercors southern foothills.

There was talk, too, of the radio message *"Le chamois des alpes bondit,"* which many people believed to have been transmitted but only one man, Marcel Chapuis, in charge of the plateau's signal contacts, appeared to have actually heard—or thought he had. For he must have been mistaken in his eagerness for the message that would mobilize the Vercors. As has been noted, the official BBC records indicate that it was never transmitted.

Everyone at that heady meeting was eager for action. Even if there was a glimmer of doubt about the *"chamois"* message— and there was very little—there was no question that the last lines of a poem by Verlaine (". . . *Blessent mon coeur d'une langueur monotone"*) had ordered the entire Resistance into a nationwide rising, nor that the words "In the green forest is a big tree" had specifically signaled the Maquis of the Drôme Département to launch a campaign of sabotage. For many people had heard these two messages. The big southern sector of the Vercors, including the town of St.-Martin, where they were at that moment, was in the Drôme Département. So surely, as one man insisted, the Vercors Resistance also should be in combat.

Huet shook his head. "I've had no orders to mobilize the plateau and you know as well as I do that if this is done too soon it could end in disaster. We must be sure that the paratroops are ready to leave Algiers."

The men in the café knew this. They were fully aware that the mobilization of the Vercors, the blocking of the passes, the calling up of the men waiting in the towns on the plain, was a very different decision to the execution of swooping attacks on railroad yards. There could be no disappearing from the massif. Once it was mobilized, it would be there, defiant, immobile, a great fortress inviting German counterattack and reprisals. But after years of brutal oppression they craved action.

The meeting had not been in progress long when there was a clatter of hoofs outside the hotel and Captain Geyer rode into the crowded square with several young officers. He leaped from his horse and strode into the café, grinning broadly. "Bravo!" he declared from the entrance. "*C'est le grand boum!* Now we're going to have some sport!"

Seeing Huet, whom he had met, he bowed with just a touch of irony, sat down, and lit the inevitable cigarette. Huet acknowledged him coolly and continued what he had been saying before the entrance of the exuberant captain had interrupted him. He urged everyone to stay as calm as possible and certainly to avoid any action that might prematurely provoke the Germans.

His words were greeted with silence. When a radio message from General Koenig in London was brought to him, he read it out, hoping that it would give them encouragement, make them feel involved even if they could not yet attack the Germans. Addressed to the Resistance throughout the nation, both South and North, Koenig's stirring call declared that "the battle for the liberation has been launched" and appealed to all to put aside their political differences and "realize the need for total co-operation in the aim of driving the enemy from France." When Huet had finished reading out the words of the hero of Bir Hacheim, everyone in the café applauded, but it only served to increase their sense of anticlimax. No group of men could have been more eager to drive the enemy from France, as their commanding general urged, but Huet's orders to do nothing were frustrating.

Certainly Koenig had seemed to have overcome his hesitation when Gubbins and Bruce had sought his help in Duke Street on June 4. Having undertaken to help fool the Germans about the dangers of attack from the Mediterranean, he had thrown himself wholeheartedly into the deception.

At last, since there was nothing in fact to be decided, the meeting in the Hôtel Breyton began to break up. Huet sat down with Geyer to discuss the issues raised by his arrival. As Descour had suggested, he tried to make his appointment as Geyer's superior officer as palatable as possible. "My purpose," he said, "is to supervise the military liaison of the Drôme and Isère départements." These were the two counties that the massif straddled, part of the plateau being in each.

Geyer looked at him quizzically. "Major," he said, as he recalls, "you're doing what I had to do when I took over from Le Ray. You're telling me you're replacing me as commander of the Vercors."

Huet knew he was treading on delicate ground and his task was not made easier by the fact that, with Descour, he did not like Geyer. This was not just a matter of a personal antipathy. He did not favor the type of officer Geyer represented.

Huet had grown up in the traditional mold of the French Army. He had served with colonial troops in Africa. He was a big regiment man, accustomed to working with armies in relatively conventional warfare. It was only with a great effort of will that he could adjust his mind to the concept of mountain conflict, and even now he viewed the Vercors as an enormous stronghold, a gigantic version of the French forts in the deserts, and planned his tactics accordingly.

By contrast, Geyer at thirty was ten important years younger. Virtually all his battle experience had been gained since 1939 when warfare had depended on a high speed of movement. He was, in fact, a strange mixture as a character. His passion for the regimental standard, his belief in the use of horses in battle, his dash were all pure eighteenth-century in nature. He would have been welcomed in the ranks of Lafayette. Yet at the same time his understanding of small-group tactics was utterly up to date.

In the anger of his meeting with Huet, he recalls, it crossed his mind to leave the Vercors, to retire to the plain with his 11th Cuirassiers and some of his BCA troops, but it was only a momentary reaction. He knew that truly he had to stay—and it was just as well he did. For Geyer controlled the only trained troops on the plateau, the only men who were now used to working as fighting teams. Some of these were civilians, but they had been schooled and drilled during the past months in company with the regular troops. Furthermore, Geyer directed the only military organization on the plateau, limited though it was. His men were on duty at the passes and were based strategically through the Vercors, so that they could be moved fast to potential trouble spots. Huet had to live with him, despite his disapproval, despite the fact that they had very different ideas on how things should be done, and the technique he adopted to handle this delicate situation was, so far as he could, to ignore the captain.

Huet established his headquarters in the Hôtel Breyton, occupying one floor while the civil administration took over the one above, and began to build a team of staff officers—until this grew too large and all the military men had to move to bigger premises up the road. Technically, in the new hierarchy, Geyer was in command of the southern sector, but he was not consulted by his senior officer. They worked in their own headquarters, Huet at St.-Martin and Geyer in his new command post in the farm at La Rivière. It was a remote arrangement for so small a command as the Vercors plateau and hardly ideal for the immense changes that would be involved when thousands of men were called up from the plain.

Meanwhile, on the evening of that joyous day of June 6, General de Gaulle broadcast to the French nation. In the towns and villages of the Vercors, people listened to that rich dramatic voice declaring that "the supreme battle is being fought. . . . For the sons of France, wherever they are, whoever they are, the simple and sacred duty is to fight the enemy by every means at their disposal."

This additional call, with all its underlying emotion, did nothing to ease the impatience of the Vercors Maquisards. But in fact they would not have to wait much longer.

CHAPTER 6

The next day, June 7, Chavant returned to the Vercors in triumph. He clambered down from the little bus that had brought him up from Pont-en-Royans to St.-Martin to be welcomed by his friends, who streamed out of the Hôtel Breyton to greet him.

Sitting with them around a table in the café, he reported on his visit to headquarters. He told them that there was no longer any doubt about the role of the Vercors, that they must prepare to receive four thousand paratroopers, that he had returned with a formal order to Colonel Descour from De Gaulle himself. "The General will almost certainly be establishing his headquarters here in the Vercors," he said. "We must find him a suitable house." Everyone was impressed by this last piece of information, but not surprised because there had been talk of it when the General had first given his approval to Operation Montagnards in 1943.

That night the Patron met Huet. Since there had been so much friction between Chavant and Geyer—and even, for all their mutual respect, a degree of conflict with his predecessor, Le Ray—Colonel Descour had taken steps this time to ensure that the relationship between the Vercors civil chief and the new military commander did at least start off under the best possible conditions. He had asked Father Johannes Vincent, the curé of the Vercors village of Corrençon, to supervise the introduction of the two men. The priest was a convivial man who had played a leading part in establishing the Vercors as a refuge and had long been on the Germans' list of wanted men.

Despite Descour's precautions, there were a few tense moments when Chavant and Huet confronted each other on the neutral ground of a house in St.-Agnan village. For Chavant's lifelong distrust of military officers made him cautious, and the success of his mission to Algiers had given new strength to his confidence in his role in the Vercors. To Father Vincent's anxiety, the Patron made no concessions, failing even to extend his hand for the routine courtesy. He planted his knuckles firmly on his hips, his eyes hostile as he studied Huet. "Good morning, monsieur," he growled. "We have to work together, but I must warn you now that I'm a socialist, I'm against the Church, and I'm against the Army."

Huet stared back at him coldly. "And I, monsieur," he answered, "must inform you that I am a professional soldier, I have nothing to do with politics, and I'm a practicing Catholic."

There was a brief moment of silence as the two men regarded each other. Then suddenly Chavant let out a great laugh and extended both hands to Huet. "I like people who have convictions," he said warmly. "I'm sure we'll get on very well."

And that night he took him to a meeting of the chiefs of the civilian camps, which was held in the school of Rencurel in the northern sector. Chavant had always accepted that, once Operation Montagnards was activated, he would have to relinquish his control of his camps to the military. "Major Huet," he declared, "is your new commanding officer."

Operation Montagnards had not by then been activated, of course, but the next evening, on June 8, Colonel Descour arrived in the Vercors with Dom Guétet. Some of his staff had gone on ahead of him to set up a new headquarters in a remote forest house, named Rang-des-Pourrets, about five miles south of St.-Martin. Among them were his radio operators, who had established a transmission station in a nearby barn. Descour planned to direct operations throughout his territory from this base within the Vercors.

It was raining heavily as Descour drove up into the plateau from the west by way of Pont-en-Royans and Les Grands-Goulets. Water streamed down the sheer rock face of the big gorge, flowing on like a river down the tiny mountain road that had been carved from it. The *gasogène* car—converted, like most French cars in wartime, to be driven by a coke boiler fixed to the rear instead of gasoline—labored heavily as it climbed up the massif.

Descour was a little surprised to see no control post at Échevis, a village on the way up Les Grands-Goulets, but when the car was not challenged at Les Barraques, the pass that gave access into the heart of the southern sector of the plateau, he became anxious; for he had expected to find the Vercors already established as an offensive citadel.

Immediately he went in search of Huet, whom he found in his temporary command post in the Hôtel Breyton in St.-Martin. "Why haven't you ordered the mobilization?" he asked.

Huet was slightly taken aback by the question, for he still had received no specific instructions. Chavant, of course, had told him of the assurance he had been given in Algiers and that General de Gaulle had officially confirmed that Montagnards was still "active" as an operation, but no one so far had given him a definite date.

"The plan depends on an invasion of the South," he replied to Descour. "We've had no news of this, no alerts to be ready for it. Allied forces have scarcely established a bridgehead in Normandy eight hundred kilometers [five hundred miles] away. I've had no orders to mobilize."

"We've all had orders," answered the colonel. "There's been a general call to action to the Resistance throughout France."

"But the Vercors is surely in a special category."

"Hervieux," said Descour, using Huet's cover name, "I confirm your orders: you are to mobilize the Vercors as soon as possible. Operation Montagnards is to be set in motion immediately."

So Descour took the crucial decision from which, once the passes were manned, there would be no retreat. He had assumed, as in London General Koenig had known he and others like him would assume, that the Resistance in the South would never have been called to arms without a supporting invasion from the Mediterranean. At this moment, therefore, two days after the date of Koenig's order, he had no doubt that the invasion fleet must be heading for the beaches of Provence. His new orders from De Gaulle were clear: Operation Montagnards was "on."

There is also some evidence that he believed that the signal "*Le chamois des alpes bondit*" had been transmitted by BBC radio—even though in fact it had not been—but he does not confirm this. It is hard to remember the detail of a single message during these crucial days when there were so many signals and so much was happening in the territory.

Yet another factor, according to Beauregard, is that Descour felt partly to blame for a tragedy on the Glières plateau in March when seven hundred Maquisards had been killed by the Germans. In that case, Descour had acted a little too slowly.

This time, with a much bigger and more important operation, he did not want to be too late.

Even Chavant shared Huet's hesitation, but when the Patron went to see Descour later and asked him if he was certain that they should act without special instructions, the colonel was adamant. "General mobilization has been ordered by the commander in chief," he insisted. "How can we ignore the order?"

Huet obeyed his colonel without further discussion. Late into the night, as the rain beat on the windows of the Hôtel Breyton, he sat with his staff writing the instructions that would summon more than two thousand men from the towns all around the massif to join the few hundred Maquisards from the camps. Although he had been hesitant until Descour overruled him, these hours as he actually issued the mobilization orders were deeply emotional. For Huet, as for most regular French officers, the ease with which the Germans had conquered France had been a source of deep trauma. Now, after four years, he was making the first positive move, the first real act of open defiance against a military dictatorship that had broken every moral law in which he believed. The major had been brought up in a family that was deeply religious. One of his brothers was a monk; a sister was a nun. And the command of the Vercors had for him the same kind of strong element of evangelical faith that had motivated the crusaders. The Vercors was one area of France where politics, so divisive elsewhere, were truly not an issue. And even though there were internal conflicts, the sufferings the people had shared had created a binding sense of unity against the enemy—what Huet was to describe later as "a purity of spirit."

Huet was a man who tended to conceal his feelings but, as he signed the complex series of instructions that would mobilize the plateau, in the rainstorm in the Hôtel Breyton that night, his staff could sense his soaring elation.

Soon after dawn, Huet's messengers were on their way from

St.-Martin with the written orders. Some went by bicycle. Others hitched lifts. A few had to wait for the bus. The orders to the Maquis at Autrans in the north of the plateau were taken by the driver of the truck that went up every day to collect the milk churns from the farmers.

Within hours of daylight, with the heavy rain still making rivers of the Vercors roads, there was immense activity both within the plateau and in the towns and villages all around it. The men in the camps, which were mostly in remote parts of the massif, were moved to new positions in the passes. A hotelier at Lans, for example, had to get a message to the bedraggled group of Maquisards that Huet had "inspected" at Plénouze that they were to take up immediate position at the Engins tunnel on the northeast. In Grenoble, Paul Brisac, one of Huet's secret commanders, was at his desk in an engineering works when an order was handed to him: "Mobilize your company immediately. Execute orders already given to you by the morning of the tenth. Send a liaison officer at 0600 to the Pont de la Goule-Noire." Immediately he picked up his phone and set in motion the complex communication process, long planned in detail, for summoning the one hundred and fifty men who formed his company from all over this city. That night they were all waiting at a limekiln at Sassenage just above the ring road for transport to their post in the St.-Nizier pass.

In Villard, Huet's orders to cut the telephone line from the gendarmerie to police headquarters in Grenoble were executed immediately. In St.-Nizier, the switches were thrown on the mountain railroad.

In Romans, the Isère town on the west of the plateau, where the presence of Germans and *miliciens* was much smaller than in Grenoble, three hundred Resistance men climbed into trucks sent down by the Huillier family, openly displaying guns, grenades, and Tricolors. "Now we'll get even with you pigs," they shouted from the overloaded trucks at the *miliciens* who were carefully noting their names. "Our time has come at last." And the vehicles lumbered off slowly along the street in the direction of Royans and the plateau.

By the afternoon the narrow roads of the Vercors, on which normally a walker could stroll for hours without seeing a vehicle, became busier than they had ever been at the height of the vacation season before the war. Buses and trucks crowded with singing men were careering around the steep bends, their horns blaring, on their way to the defense positions. From Bourg-de-Péage, from Die, from Crest, from Voiron, from Tain, even from faraway Lyon in one or two cases, men eager to fight the Germans rallied to the Vercors plateau. Soon three thousand men were waiting ready for attack by the enemy. Many of them had no weapons, for the numbers of Resistance fighters taking up their positions in the passes far exceeded the plateau's arms resources. And most of the guns they did have were light-caliber, whereas what they really needed to hold those twisting roads was mortars and mountain artillery. Buoyant as they were, these inadequacies did not worry the waiting men too much. Proper arms, they were convinced, would be flown in.

At the same time, the support services were being set up. Dr. Fernand Ganimède, a seventy-year-old physician who had headed the Resistance in Romans, established a hospital in an old house on the edge of St.-Martin. Since the hospital had no equipment, the Groupe Vallier, the most famous of the "terror" groups, sent a raiding team down to Bourg-de-Péage in the plain to get what he needed at gunpoint.

Georges Jouneau, an experienced transport man summoned from Lyon by Colonel Descour, established a truck park in St.-Agnan, near Descour's new headquarters, Rang-des-Pourrets, and took control of food supplies. Jouneau's job was to feed the new arrivals on the plateau, the men who had come to fight—in addition, incidentally, to those mobilized in other areas of Descour's R1 region. Chavant's civilian administrators still retained responsibility for supplying the eight thousand residents of the towns and villages of the Vercors, though each group helped the other when needed.

The Germans made little attempt to interfere with the basic supply arrangements. Their policing techniques were based on patrolling columns, temporary road blocks, and brutal punitive reprisals. They also exercised a strange restraint with respect to the wives and families of the men who had rallied to the massif, for these women and children still lived in their homes. It was a delicate consensus that was to be endangered only when a Milice chief, or his family, was personally involved in attacks from the plateau. This was why normally the Vercors leaders were very careful to avoid hurting local VIPs. However, they were always conscious of this aspect of their vulnerability, always fearing that as the conflict grew fiercer their homes were potential targets for reprisal. At one time they considered setting up a communal area on the plateau where wives and children could live, but the sheer numbers would have greatly strained the Vercors resources, which were already under enormous pressure.

Huet's mobilization order had produced a traumatic change in the plateau. In effect, it transformed the Vercors into the first area of Free France. It was now governed by Frenchmen. Soon it would have its own courts, dispensing its own justice within laws laid down by the provisional government in Algiers. If any member of the Milice now tried to enter any of the passes, he would be arrested. Already the Tricolor was flying in all the towns—even though there were Germans on the plain that surrounded the plateau, even though Wehrmacht reinforcements could be summoned if the provocation was seen to be too great, which in due course it must be. For clearly, hard though the Vercors would be to storm because of its cliffs and narrow passes, the Germans could not permit it to remain as a threat to its southern armies—nor as an incitement to other Maquis in the mountains.

CHAPTER 7

At six o'clock the next morning, June 10, Huet stood in the road by the little Pont de la Goule-Noire (Bridge of the Black Gorge) waiting for his commanders in the northern sector to report to him that their companies were in position.

The Gorges de la Bourne, the canyon that the bridge spanned, were not wide—some fifty yards—but they were deep, a huge cleft that cut right through the massif from Royans in the west until it narrowed into a small stream within the mountains of the east side of the Vercors. Tall, sheer cliffs of gray-blue rock leaned toward each other over the gorge, keeping much of the morning light from the bridge, extending the sense of dawn. A hundred feet below, the waters of the Bourne River tumbled white over jagged boulders and rapids. Above, the sky was a narrow curving blue strip, for the rain clouds had gone in the night. The noise of water, however—from the turbulent river, from the dripping onto the road of cliff springs and of excessive rain—was constant and monotonous.

Strategically, the dramatic gorge was of supreme importance, which was why Huet had chosen it as reporting point. From the Pont de la Goule-Noire roads reached north, south, west, and east. The big canyon divided the Vercors into two unequal parts. To the north of it was a triangular sector—the tip of the arrow form of the Vercors—which was smaller than the main broader part of the massif. The high southern cliffs of the Gorges de la Bourne, however, provided an additional wall, creating of the south sector of the massif a kind of inner citadel. The north part would be far easier for the Germans to storm, but they would still have to surmount the big gorge and its high protective wall to reach the main plateau.

Huet did not have to wait long at the bridge. The liaison agents arrived one after the other, all saluting smartly, all as stimulated as he was by the fact that the Vercors was on the offensive. They came from Captain Henri Ullman in the Forêt des Coulmes in the northwest, from the Villard men at La Roche Pointue, the high waterfall on the heights above the Gorges de la Bourne, from Beauregard's Maquis veterans at the Engins tunnel in the northeast. Abel Crouau, one of the five Vercors regional commanders, came himself, but his position at La-Balme-de-Rencurel was not far down the gorge, so he was near enough. His two hundred men, mostly from Romans, were in position, he said, but many were unarmed.

"I know," said Huet. "I'll get you some more weapons as soon as I can."

Some of the liaison agents were women—such as the young blond Lea Blaine, who worked under the orders of Jean Prévost. Hurriedly, out of breath, she pedaled up to Huet on her bicycle along the road from Villard, in her skirt and sweater, her beret on the side of her head. "Company Goderville," she gasped, using Prévost's cover name, chosen from the town where he was born, "is in position."

When Huet had received the last report, he mounted the motorcycle that he had decided was the best means of transport for the Vercors' tunnels and hairpin bends and roared up the road toward St.-Martin, the noise echoing behind him off the hard cliff faces of the gorge. For most of the day he toured the positions in the southern sector, satisfying himself that, even if they had few weapons, the men were at least defending the passes, as they had been ordered. In the wild, high mountains of the southeast, where the Vercors' highest peaks were sited, there were only a handful of men at some of the passes, of which there were several; but in this rugged area of the plateau there were no roads—just narrow mule tracks unsuited to military vehicles. Huet still had to defend them, for the Germans, too, had mountain troops, but he did not anticipate too much of an attack from this direction.

Meanwhile, that morning, Chavant was at work in the Hôtel Breyton as usual when a visitor walked in. Chavant's face broke into a broad smile when he saw him. "Roger!" he greeted him warmly. "Come and sit down." The two men shook hands through the crowd and a place was made for the newcomer next to the Patron.

"Roger," or Francis Cammaerts (his real name), or "Grands Pieds" ("Big Feet") as he was known by many Maquisards, was a handsome man of twenty-eight, with fair hair, a military mustache, and a deep tan from months of walking the mountains in the South of France through spring and early summer. He was also extremely tall and needed his "*grands pieds.*"

Cammaerts, a British agent, had been sent to France some eighteen months before to take over the SOE network operated by Peter Churchill and Odette Sansom, but they had been arrested by the Gestapo almost immediately after he arrived. The network had collapsed and Cammaerts had gone to ground. Then quietly he had begun to build his own organization—the "Jockey Circuit"—and now he controlled more than two hundred teams of secret agents in a vast expanse of France that stretched east from the Rhône Valley and south from the Isère.

Chavant had known Cammaerts for more than a year and they got along very well. Together they had walked across the Vercors' open country, selecting the best sites for parachute drops. Huet's defenders in the passes were very short of weapons, but most of those they did have were mainly due to Cammaerts.

That morning, as the secret agent had driven from Die in the south to enter the Vercors by way of the Col de Rousset, he had been stopped twice by Maquis road blocks, the second time at the tunnel in the pass, and asked to identify himself. Cammaerts had been appalled by what he knew this meant: the Vercors had been mobilized—and, he feared, too soon. For already he had seen the results of a premature stand by the Maquis.

Cammaerts' anxiety was not eased by the enthusiasm that was obvious behind Chavant's quiet, firm confidence—nor by his account of his trip to Algiers. The British agent had traveled across much of France during the four days that had passed since D Day and he already suspected that there were strange circumstances surrounding General Koenig's summons to the South.

"Patron," he said when Chavant finished speaking of Algiers, "I've just come from Barcelonnette. They had the Tricolors flying there, too—*and* the Maquisards waiting bravely at their posts with their Sten guns, and"—he paused for a moment—"well, a lot of them are dead."

Barcelonnette was a little thirteenth-century walled town, surrounded by mountains, in the Ubaye valley, about eighty miles south of the Vercors. Cammaerts had gone there to execute his orders from Algiers to place his network at the disposal of Colonel Henri Zeller, who he had been told would be there. Zeller was the Secret Army commander of the whole of southeastern France and Descour's superior officer within the hierarchy of the FFI.

Cammaerts had found the town prepared for battle. He had also met there a young British staff officer who had just arrived by parachute from Algiers with the news that the Allied invasion of the South was imminent. For Barcelonnette it had not been imminent enough, for almost immediately the town had been attacked from three directions at once by Wehrmacht troops equipped with artillery, and a message came in that a German tank column was approaching from the north.

Cammaerts had slipped away from the town that night by a side road. Even if he had been stopped by the Germans, which he often was, his cover was strong. He carried the papers of a French civil engineer concerned with road works, which gave him a good reason to travel—even, in the case of emergency, by night—and he was, of course, bilingual.

What was concerning the agent on that morning of June 10 when he arrived in the Vercors was that a mistake had been made at headquarters, that the Resistance in his area had in error been summoned too soon. He did not yet know, of course, about the meeting between his own chief, Sir Colin Gubbins, and General Koenig. Certainly he did not suspect that the tragedy he had seen at Barcelonnette was the result of deliberate policy—part of the price that was now being paid for keeping the Germans ignorant of the areas of assault.

Chavant was a little perturbed by what Cammaerts told him about Barcelonnette but he had been personally briefed in Algiers. "We're preparing to receive four thousand paratroopers," he said. "There's a team coming to build a landing strip. General de Gaulle is to set up his headquarters here."

"Then perhaps we shall be able to hold the Vercors," answered Cammaerts. He smiled, but the expression on his face did not reflect his feelings. He was, in fact, furious. The Vercors was the most important Maquis center within his territory. If its mobilization was to be ordered, he should have been warned. He had more than fifty arms dumps within a radius of a hundred miles. He could have supplied many of the weapons that the men in the Vercors so badly needed. Now it would be much more difficult to transport them.

Already he was forming in his mind the blistering signals he would send to SOE headquarters both in Algiers and in London—as soon as he could find his radio operators, or "pianists," as they were known. For safety, both had been ordered to travel separately, with their radio equipment in black leather suitcases lashed to motorcycles, and to meet him at Descour's regional headquarters, which, he learned from Chavant, were near a village called St.-Agnan, at Rang-des-Pourrets. For, like Descour, Cammaerts also planned to direct his network from within the Vercors.

He shook hands with the Patron, walked out of the hotel to the old black *gasogène* Citroën parked in the square, and headed for St.-Agnan.

That day of June 10, when the Vercors plateau had been sealed by thousands of men spread through the passes, was for Colonel Descour one of stimulation and optimism—and, by evening, of acute anxiety.

Rang-des-Pourrets, his new headquarters, was a big forest house, set among firs, on the slopes of the Montagne du Grand Larve. From the window of his office Descour looked up a broad valley—one of the Vercors' giant furrows with forest-covered mountain ridges on either side.

Ever since his arrival on the plateau on the wet evening of June 8, more of his staff had been joining him. With a team of messengers and two radio operators, working from a barn in the nearby village of La Britière, he had directed sabotage operations throughout his big region.

Early that morning Bob Bennes, his cheery senior radio operator, whom he had brought with him from Lyon, had tapped out the report to Algiers that the massif was mobilized. "Remind you urgency to parachute men and arms region Vercors. Mobilization of Vercors completed but armament at present very insufficient. Cannot resist if attacked. Lack light and heavy armament for two thousand men in Vercors redoubt. Urgent to arm and equip them. 'Pencil Sharpener,' 'Paper Knife,' and 'Gummed Paper' ready to receive night and day." The code names, all associated with stationery, indicated parachute dropping grounds.

On reflection, however, Descour decided that this signal did not convey enough urgency, so he ordered young Bennes to send another: "Two thousand volunteers need arming. Initial enthusiasm fading owing to lack of arms. Extremely urgent dispatch men arms fuel tobacco within forty-eight hours maximum. Attack in force possible. Impossible resist effectively under present conditions. Defeat will cause merciless retaliation. Would be disastrous for Resistance this region."

Descour was signaling a man he knew well from before the war. Colonel Jean Constans, who had been so encouraging to Chavant during his visit to Algiers, had been on courses with him at the École de Guerre, the military college. Soon the messages from the Vercors began to assume a personal character. What Descour did not know, however, was the state of utter chaos in which Constans was working. For the rising in the South had been far greater than anyone had anticipated and Constans' department was overwhelmed by the sheer volume of signals—from the Massif Central, from the Haute-Savoie, from Cantal, from the mountains of the Jura, and many other areas as well as from the Vercors, all demanding weapons and support. "The flood of messages that came from the Resistance every day was quite extraordinary," Constans recalls, "and the work that resulted exceeded the imagination . . . each posing a special problem and always urgent. . . ."

Because of this, the peeping of Bob Bennes' receiver in the radio hut at La Britière brought no answer from Constans that day, but by evening a message had come in from London that created crisis at Rang-des-Pourrets. It was a signal from General Koenig, the commander in chief, who four days before had urged the Resistance in such resounding phrases to "drive the enemy from France." He appeared to have changed his mind about the urgency of his earlier instruction. "Curb to the maximum all guerrilla activity," he now ordered the Resistance men throughout the South. "Impossible at present supply you with arms and munitions in sufficient quantities. Break off contact [with the enemy] as much as possible to permit reorganization phase. Avoid large concentrations. Reform in small isolated groups."

When Bob Bennes took the signal to Descour and Dom Guétet, his chief of staff, the two men were appalled. For how could they avoid large concentrations? How could they reform in small isolated groups? They had thousands posted in the passes. How could they break off contact if the enemy attacked —which he was certain to do very soon? The men from the plain could not go home, for they would be arrested at once by the Milice. And even if they did, God knew what the Gestapo would do to the people in the Vercors towns.

Immediately Descour summoned Huet and Chavant from St.-Martin to a crisis conference to consider if there were any options open to them. Grimly the four men "studied the question from every angle," as Huet told a commission of inquiry in Paris after the war, "but we had made the move. The game had been played. We couldn't go back."

One of the most worrying aspects about General Koenig's

signal was the statement that it was impossible to send adequate supplies of arms and equipment—which raised the question, did this apply to the Vercors or was the plateau a special case owing to Operation Montagnards? After all, De Gaulle had only just confirmed that this operation was to be pursued with vigor. It would hardly make sense to leave the plateau bereft of the weapons to execute it. But clearly it could imply delay.

"We may have to wait a few days," said Descour. "The question is, can we?"

"At this moment," Huet answered, "we would be powerless against major attack. We have men in position in the passes but many have no arms. Some have Stens and grenades. Others have old shotguns. If they come at us with heavy weapons, artillery or mortars, then the value of our meager weapons will be limited."

Descour thought for a moment. "The Germans do not at present have many troops in the area to mount a major assault," he mused. "A few hundred at the most."

As they all knew, the enemy could call up reinforcements, but, with revolt throughout the South of France, with the steady withdrawal of troops toward Normandy, there was great pressure on Wehrmacht resources over a very wide area. This must present General Karl Pflaum, the German commander in Grenoble, with a constant conflict of decision. For where should he decide to strike? Clearly, he must regard the Vercors, with its dangerous and contagious defiance, as a priority, but it would need far more strength than any other Resistance area.

"The enemy may not know how short we are of weapons," suggested Dom Guétet. "They'll be aware that we've been reinforced by thousands of men from the plain. It may deter them —anyway, for a few vital days." Dom Guétet always gave an impression of great strength.

"What about explosives?" asked Descour, thinking of the

physical blocking of the passes, a technique that Francis Cammaerts' teams had used very successfully on the Route Napoléon.

"We've got plastic," Huet replied dubiously, which gave Descour the answer to his question, for he knew that plastic was ideal for high-intensity objectives, like blowing up railroad tracks, but dynamite was needed to bring down large areas of rock.

For a few moments there was silence in the room. All four men knew that everything now depended on time. Would the Germans be able to mount their assault on the massif before the paratroopers and heavy weapons arrived from North Africa, and before the Allies invaded the South of France, which Koenig's withdrawal signal suggested might be delayed? There were only two options open to them: to demobilize and face punitive reprisals or to stay posted on the plateau and rely on Algiers. The second course carried more danger, for failure would mean reprisals that would be even more ruthless, but not one of the four people who were faced with the decision would have considered the first. The Allies had vast resources in the Mediterranean, thousands of aircraft, regiments of paratroopers. If the Germans attacked, aid would surely be forthcoming. Even a few bombers could liquidate enemy troops massed in the roads to the passes with no cover.

"We have no choice," Descour said at last. "We can't disperse. We must disobey the commander in chief."

During the next few hours, the most disturbing aspect of their predicament was the complete silence from Algiers. They were indeed a remote outpost, a historical cliché, for so often in past wars men had waited, as they were now doing, for relief or news of relief from headquarters. Indeed, General Koenig himself had been in that position at Bir Hacheim. He at least

should understand the dilemma faced by the Vercors leaders—
if indeed he knew about it.

When by next morning, Sunday, June 11, there had still
been no reply, Descour ordered Bob Bennes to signal Algiers
again, this time appealing to the staff colonel's conscience. The
message reiterated the urgent need for immediate dispatch of
weapons and carried a clear reference to Constans' moral
responsibilities—and to those of others in Algiers. "Mobilization," he asserted, "has been ordered following formal assurance of arms delivery. Failure to execute this promise
immediately will create dramatic situation." The "formal assurance" and "the promise," of course, had been given to Chavant
in Algiers—but even these reminders did not appear to have the
necessary impact. For by darkness that evening there had still
been no response.

At last, on Monday, June 12, after more than forty-eight
hours of anxious waiting, a signal came in from Constans offering the assurance that the "only problem until now has been
bad weather. Will do our best with limited aerial transport." It
was some consolation to be in contact, at least, with headquarters, but they were all conscious how little time they had,
how vulnerable at that moment they were with half the men in
the passes unarmed, how hard it would be to hold a German
attack.

Bob Bennes signaled back to Algiers asking for the maximum
quantity of weapons to be dropped on each landing ground in
the Vercors. "Need machine guns mortars and if possible anti-
tank guns and cannon." It is doubtful if Bennes thought this
would gain anything. He was merely responding to a need to
do something. For he now knew that no weapons could be delivered to the plateau until the weather improved between
North Africa and France.

Soon the weather in the English Channel would not be helping either, for new gales would threaten the supply lines that,

in the case of an invading force, must be maintained entirely from the sea. Meanwhile the Allied armies were holding a narrow strip of the Normandy coast against violent enemy counterattacks. On June 12 it was fifty-one miles long and fifteen miles deep. The Americans were trying to fight their way west toward Cherbourg. On the east end of the line, the British and Canadians were in the early phases of the long agony of the battle for Caen.

On this Monday evening, therefore, the situation in Normandy was absorbing the anxious attention of the Supreme Allied Commander. Planes were held waiting for the weather to improve on the airfield in Algiers. In the Vercors the lookouts on duty were listening intently for any sounds that would indicate the approach of German troops.

That night there were no alerts, but the next morning Huet was summoned to the telephone in the Hôtel Breyton to hear the news that they had all been fearing for three days. An enemy column was approaching the foot of the massif below St.-Nizier.

CHAPTER 8

For Captain Costa de Beauregard and his men in the St.-Nizier pass the worst part that morning was the waiting—knowing all the time that the Germans were getting closer as they came up the mountain toward them, but under orders not to shoot. Most of them could not even see the approaching enemy, for the strategy that Huet and Beauregard had agreed was to set their defense line well back from the lip of the roller-coaster shelf that dipped steeply from the Charvet Hill on the left and sloped up sharply to the foot of the Trois Pucelles obelisk on the right.

"Most of the men," Beauregard recalls, "had Sten guns that are accurate only at short range. The Germans had far better weapons. We knew that if we posted them on the edge so that they could shoot down the mountain, they would be under fire by the enemy before he was within range of our Stens. Almost certainly our Maquisards would start shooting too soon and waste valuable ammunition. So we positioned them at the ideal distance for accurate firing the moment the Germans came over the ridge."

The St.-Nizier pass was the weakest place in the Vercors' outer walls because the side of the massif was less sheer at this point than it was below any of the other passes. For this reason the strategy of its defense, the exact sector of its three thousand feet where the enemy should be opposed, had been endlessly discussed. The decision had eventually gone to the switchback shelf where Beauregard's men were now waiting with grim, taut faces. Almost all were in civilian clothes. Some had berets on. Most were bare-headed, wore sweaters over open-necked shirts, baggy trousers, and mountain boots, and had armbands marked FFI that had been included in a parachute drop. One man was in uniform. The veteran Sergeant Itier, long pensioned from active service with Grenoble's 6th BCA, had answered Huet's summons with the others. He had insisted on wearing the regiment's sky-blue dress jacket that he had worn in the First World War—and on bringing with him his terrier dog. He was old but sprightly enough to handle his bazooka (a weapon that fired shells from the shoulder) with extraordinary precision.

Soon after the lookouts had yelled the warning up the mountain of the approaching enemy column, Beauregard had toured his defense line, studying the final dispositions, satisfying himself that his men were as ready as they could be to sustain the attack, making a few minor changes. It was a long, curving line —with nearly two miles between the extremities of the wings— that dipped sharply in the middle where the zigzagging mountain road to St.-Nizier crossed it near a tiny hamlet called Les Guillets.

On the right of the road, spread through the timber below Les Trois Pucelles with its three gray gnarled fingers reaching toward the sky, were the Grenoble civilians of Paul Brisac's

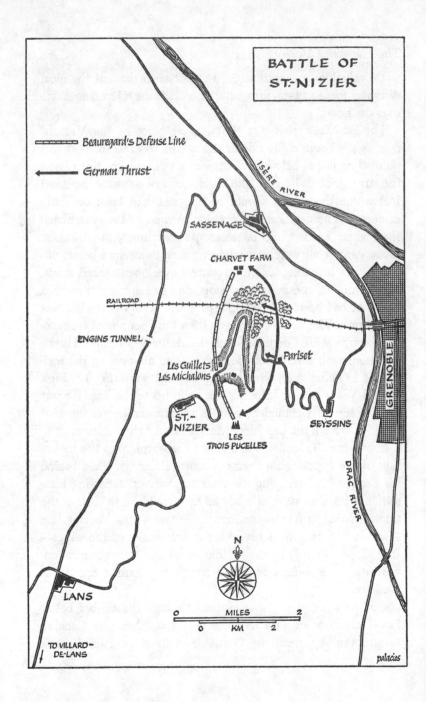

BATTLE OF
ST-NIZIER

======= Beauregard's Defense Line

⟵ German Thrust

ISÈRE RIVER

SASSENAGE

CHARVET FARM

RAILROAD

ENGINS TUNNEL

Pariset

Les Guillets
Les Michalons

ST.-
NIZIER

LES
TROIS PUCELLES

SEYSSINS

GRENOBLE

DRAC RIVER

N

LANS

TO VILLARD-
DE-LANS

0   MILES   2

0   KM   2

palacios

company who had responded with so many others to Huet's summons three days before.

On the left of the road were the men of Jean Prévost's command, mostly locals from Villard. A small lane led from Les Guillets to the farm on Charvet Hill, and Prévost's men were using what cover they could find—the walls of the hamlet, the hedge of the lane, a small wood at one point, clumps of trees, bushes. The solitary mortar was in position near the hamlet itself, where Prévost had established his command post.

Beauregard and Prévost were good friends. They had stayed out of the feuding that had so embittered the people of the plateau, which was one reason why Chavant had asked them both to serve on the Military Committee of the Vercors that Geyer had so scornfully ignored.

Prévost was the Vercors celebrity—a writer who, though barely known abroad, had for years been famous in France, especially among the young intellectuals. A man of thirty-nine, tall, with his hair long as befitted a literary figure, he had joined the Resistance as a romantic, inspired by the pure nonpolitical patriotic concept of the great Resistance leader Jean Moulin, who had been killed by the Gestapo. Prévost was by nature independent but, according to his son Alain, he found in the Secret Army—with its scope for independent action and its emotional dynamic—a cause that totally absorbed him.

The idea of Operation Montagnards, of which he was part-creator, emerged almost by chance. In the late autumn of 1942 Prévost, then living in Lyon, was working on a book about Stendhal, who came from Grenoble. On research trips to the city he often used to stay with his friend Pierre Dalloz, an expert mountaineer and skier, who lived at the Côtes-de-Sassenage on the eastern wall of the Vercors.

On one of these visits to Sassenage, when the meadow in front of Dalloz' farmhouse was covered in deep snow, Prévost had helped his host fell a dead walnut tree. For a moment during their labors the two men had leaned on their axes, resting, savoring the spectacular view of Grenoble and the mountains beyond—and the whole conception of what was to become Operation Montagnards had suddenly come to them. Excitedly they had swapped ideas as different aspects occurred to them: the citadel mountain, the isolation, the strategic perfection of its site.

And now in June 1944 Prévost was an actor, a leading actor, in the drama he and Dalloz had envisaged, even if the reality was unequal to the concept.

Prévost and Beauregard drove up the lane to Charvet Hill in the writer's car, talking to the men, discussing final tactics with Prévost's son-in-law, who, from a post in a small wood, was in charge of one section of the line. They knew how long it would take the approaching Germans to ascend the mountain. They knew, too, that their adversaries were men of the Wehrmacht's 157th Reserve Division—many of them trained mountain troops who had committed the massacre at Malleval and killed seven hundred Maquisards on the Glières plateau.

After the tour of inspection, they returned to Prévost's command post at the hamlet of Les Guillets, where the lane met the St.-Nizier road. Waiting for them beside a small green Renault was eighteen-year-old André Huillier, one of the sons of Victor Huillier who owned the Villard family transport business. "Durieu!" the young man called out, using Beauregard's cover name. "My car is at your disposal. I'll be your chauffeur."

Beauregard laughed and accepted his offer with thanks. He held out his hand to Prévost. "Good luck," he said and asked Huillier to drive him to the villa higher up the road toward St.-Nizier that he had chosen as a command post because from its balcony he could view the whole of his line. It was here that François Huet found him, stayed with him for a while studying the enemy's movements, then raced away on his motorcycle to telephone his staff at the Hôtel Breyton from the café in St.-Nizier.

From the command post the movement of the enemy in their gray uniforms up the side of the mountain could be clearly seen among the trees and scrub bushes. There were no preliminaries, no scattered shots at the leading troops. At one moment, despite the approaching menace, the mountain was enveloped in total quiet and in the next the peace was shattered with appalling brutality by excruciating noise that echoed and re-echoed among the peaks—the short staccato bursts of the Stens, the heavier pounding of the machine guns, the ugly belching of the German 6.3s, "burp guns" as they were called.

The Germans were thrusting for Charvet Hill on the extreme left, exploiting the steep woods beneath it. And Jean Prévost's men held them, drove them repeatedly back into the wood, shooting from the cover of the farm buildings.

Watching through the binoculars, Beauregard suddenly saw two Germans setting up a machine gun between sandbags on an elevated section of the mountain railroad track. Prévost was concentrating fire on it—sand and earth flying as his bullets and mortar shells hit the embankment around the gun.

Just below the gun, behind the railroad track, Beauregard caught glimpses of the helmets of other troops, already positioned for a breakout under cover of the machine gun fire.

Then the gun opened up, its fast thumping echoing off the mountainside. And the heavy 13.7 mm bullets began to take their toll. "Tell Brisac to send a squad to take that machine gun," Beauregard ordered. So far, Brisac, on the right, had not come under attack.

A messenger hurried off down the road, and a few minutes later Beauregard saw the squad crossing the road at Les Guillets on their way up the lane toward Charvet Hill—and toward the railroad track and the machine gun. They were led by old

Sergeant Itier in his antique blue uniform, carrying his bazooka, with his terrier trotting at his heels.

The noise of heavy machine gun fire suddenly intensified. A new 13.7 was in action—this time from high rocks above Les Michalons, another hamlet, down the mountain a little. The two enemy guns were laying down an arc of fire over a whole section of Prévost's line—including his command post in the hamlet.

The Germans tried to use this cover to push some troops up the St.-Nizier road through the defense line, but Brisac's men, posted on the high rocks that bordered the road, stopped this move by dropping "Gammon" grenades on the infiltrators. Canvas bags filled with plastic explosive, these did little damage but detonated on impact with an enormous noise—so much, in fact, on this occasion that the Germans reported later that the Resistance in the Vercors had mountain artillery.

Sergeant Itier—leaping from side to side of his position, followed by his dog, firing his bazooka—forced the machine gun off the railroad track. But the success was only temporary. The Germans got the machine gun back in action on the track and the battle grew far fiercer.

Soon after Huet returned to Beauregard at the villa to tell him he had ordered reinforcements, the command post itself came under fire. "Machine gun bullets were hitting the trees above the villa," says Beauregard. "Branches and leaves began falling on the balcony. Bullets were ricocheting off the wall. It seemed sensible to move, so we went across the road where there was better cover. I ran, of course, bent double, but Huet would never bend. I think he thought it was undignified. He walked across the road, with his head held high. Unhappily he slipped on the tarmac, which rather spoiled the effect."

The Germans launched a new attack—on Brisac's men on the right. The enemy advanced up the mountain using the cover of a long hollow scooped by erosion out of the limestone.

In parts of the woods there was close hand-to-hand fighting. If the Germans succeeded in getting a position on Les Trois Pucelles, they could dominate the whole defense line as completely as they could from Charvet Hill on the other wing, and the battle would be over.

Huet realized that the situation was critical. The Germans were driving at his center and trying to outflank both his wings. Extra support was needed, professional support—and fast. He rode his motorcycle flat out back to the café in St.-Nizier. Within minutes another motorcyclist raced from St.-Martin for Geyer's headquarters at La Rivière, which were not yet on the telephone system. The order he carried was "Send Chabal and his unit." Somewhat slower than the motorcycle, a bus followed the same route—to provide transport.

For Narcisse Geyer, it was hard to control the impatience he felt at La Rivière that morning. He did not agree with Descour's decision to mobilize the plateau at this early stage, believing the whole idea of trying to hold the passes without proper support was ludicrous. He thought that they should still operate as guerrillas, always giving way in the face of serious attack. But naturally no one had asked his opinion. Even so, he yearned for action, which, since the fighting was in the northern sector, was denied him.

When the motorcyclist arrived with the order from Huet to send Chabal, he shrugged his shoulders and sent for the young sergeant.

Chabal was a dark, rather intense, but highly efficient disciplinarian of thirty-four. His company consisted of a mere twenty men—6th BCA mountain troops and a few keen young civilians—but it was a highly drilled shock unit.

Chabal's men were very competitive, with a taste for dangerous games. According to one, Richard Marillier, a group of them were actually playing with a live grenade, one man threatening to explode it, when Chabal came to fetch them.

"You bloody fools!" snarled Chabal. "The next time I find you wasting ammunition I'll break your bloody necks! Get ready to leave for St.-Nizier at once!"

Geyer could stay inactive no longer. He drove to Rang-des-Pourrets to find out if Descour had any information. The colonel, who knew nothing either, was just leaving by car to meet Huet, who was reported to be on his way from St.-Nizier. So Geyer followed him.

Meanwhile Bob Bennes was already tapping out the news of the attack in his barn that served as a radio room—*and* justifying Descour's refusal to obey General Koenig's disperse order. "Are under attack in the Vercors by big forces coming from Grenoble," he signaled. "We cannot consider abandoning without defense a population entirely compromised. Serious situation because we lack arms and munitions. Beg you to come to our aid with big parachute drops on all the Vercors landing grounds. Battalion of paratroopers would help us save the situation." A battalion was only 400 men—10 per cent of the number expected—but Descour believed that Algiers would act faster if he asked for a small force as an advance unit.

Huet had just ridden out of St.-Martin, speeding on his way toward Rang-des-Pourrets, when he saw the two cars coming toward him along the road. He stopped and gave Descour a quick summary of the battle situation at St.-Nizier. It was at this moment that, to the amazement of all, they saw a convoy of covered trucks lumbering toward them along the road from Les Barraques, the pass at the head of the road of Les Grands-Goulets. The vehicles were moving slowly, heavily laden, their chassis close to their axles, and they halted when they reached the parked cars at the side of the road.

A young officer leaped down from the lead truck, his face

creased in a broad, happy grin. He was one of Geyer's men—
Second Lieutenant Perotin. "Do you know what we've got
here?" he said excitedly. "Three 25 mm cannon—*and* ammunition."

"Anti-tank guns?" said Huet, hardly able to believe his ears.
Geyer grinned broadly and embraced his young subaltern.
"Perotin! It's superb. Where did you get them?"

"Chambaran. We ambushed them."

Chambaran was more than sixty miles away. It was an incredible distance for Perotin and his team to have driven these
slow-moving military vehicles across German-controlled territory in which there was certain to be pursuit, but unhappily
when they examined the guns at the roadside, they appeared to
have several parts missing. One of Perotin's fellow officers had
been in an anti-tank regiment and, with the help of a couple of
his men who were good mechanics, they tried to assemble one
weapon that worked by cannibalizing the other two. Then they
set it up in a nearby field and tried to learn how to fire it—
which was not simple, since it still lacked a sight for aiming. It
was several hours before Perotin and his men had with practice
acquired enough skill to risk taking it into action.

Meanwhile a bus came fast along the road, traveling in the direction of St.-Martin. The driver pressed his horn in a long
blast as he passed the parked vehicles. Behind him were Sergeant Chabal and his 6th BCA commando unit. The men
cheered as they went by.

The driver of the bus checked his speed as the road dipped
steeply toward the Gorges de la Bourne—then went even slower
as they ran alongside the deep canyon toward the two short
tunnels in the rock. He sounded his horn urgently as a warning
to any approaching traffic, for there was not enough space in
the tunnels for two vehicles to pass. He drove across the gorge,
climbed the steep, twisting hill into Villard, and pressed the

throttle as they headed across flat open country toward Lans and St.-Nizier.

It was then that one of the men began to sing the "Marseillaise." At first, so Richard Marillier recalls, the soldier sang it softly, almost privately. Then another man took it up, also singing quietly. And another. Soon everyone had joined in and the singing developed an impetus of its own, becoming louder and louder until they were all shouting out the familiar lines in unison while Chabal beat out the rhythm on the back of a seat. As the bus rattled through St.-Nizier, with a blaring horn and the sound of the raucous singing, the people in the streets waved and cheered.

For Beauregard's hard-pressed men, the sound of the "Marseillaise" coming from the mountain road behind them, barely audible or credible at first, then growing in volume as the bus got nearer until there was no longer any doubt, had the same morale-boosting effect as the bugles of the U.S. cavalry had on western pioneers holding off attacking Indians. They had been fighting desperately for more than three hours, and now they felt as though a whole crack regiment had arrived to support them instead of Chabal's little unit of twenty men.

Beauregard did not underestimate their value, despite their small number. They were trained troops and they had a couple of machine guns. As the bus halted up the road from his command post, out of gunshot, he hurried toward it and gave Chabal his orders.

The sergeant led his men at the double along the lane toward Charvet Hill. His objective was the same machine gun on the railroad track that Sergeant Itier had failed to put permanently out of action. He achieved success very fast by making a courageous dash across open country to a small wood and, from this position, attacking the German post with his machine guns from the rear—from the Charvet side of the railroad track. The Germans withdrew quickly to the cover of nearby trees.

Then Chabal, who had suffered only one casualty, tried to gain control of the railroad embankment itself with another dash across open ground. But this was too ambitious. Under intense fire from the enemy in their new position, he lost three more men—two dead and one wounded—before he was forced to order the others to drop back.

The sun was beginning to sink in the sky toward the high horizon formed by the mountains when, to the surprise of the tired Maquisards, the Germans suddenly broke off the action and began to retreat.

From his command position at the roadside villa, Beauregard was watching the Germans' withdrawal toward the little village of La Tour-Sans-Venin, where their vehicles were waiting, when a truck came down the road from St.-Nizier. It was Second Lieutenant Perotin with the 25 mm cannon. "You're a bit late," Beauregard said with a smile, after he had expressed suitable admiration for the size of the gun, "but perhaps there's still just time to knock out some of their trucks on their way home."

He climbed into the cabin with Perotin and they drove down the road to Pariset, where, at the beginning of the attack, the Germans had struck across country toward Charvet Hill. The road wound on in loops below them and, just outside the hamlet, they set up the gun so that they could shoot at the sector between La Tour-Sans-Venin and the town of Seyssins, which the German troop-carrying half-tracks would have to traverse on their way to Grenoble.

"There isn't a sight," explained Perotin a little apologetically.

"So how do you aim it?" asked Beauregard.

"You have to look through the barrel. Then you load it."

Beauregard laughed, for it meant that the targets would have to be very co-operative and stay still while the gunners made their preparations. Nevertheless the German truck convoy lent itself to attack by a gun with these limitations, for all the vehicles would have to pass along the same narrow stretch of road below them.

Perotin and his team of gunners watched the convoy emerge from La Tour, progressing slowly toward Seyssins. With the breach open, Perotin put his eye to the barrel and saw the first truck pass the aperture. He stepped back. "Right, load!" he ordered. His crew slammed home a shell. He watched two more half-tracks across the spot he had mentally marked in the road. The fourth in the line approached the target area. "Fire!" ordered Perotin. The gun cracked loudly, leaping back in recoil. And the shell found its target. The truck slewed across the road but the driver managed to regain control and straighten up. The vehicle had a canvas canopy and the gun did not do much more damage than rip a hole in the fabric and possibly, just possibly, kill someone inside. The military effect may not have been very lethal, but it did much for the gunners' morale. The men on the mountains let out a great cheer that echoed in the evening air.

That night, Huet rode his motorcycle to Rang-des-Pourrets and, smoking and drinking ersatz coffee, he reviewed the battle with Descour and Dom Guétet. The mood in that room was lighter than at their last tense meeting three days before because they could not help feeling some of the elation felt by everyone on the plateau that evening over the German retreat. Perhaps, though, they were less optimistic than the Maquisards in the cafés, for they knew they had only bought a little time. The enemy would clearly return—and in greater force.

"The question is," said Huet, "whether they'll attack at St.-Nizier again or try to take us by surprise from a different direction."

This was the problem of defending a massif. Like an island,

it gave the enemy far more assault choices than they would have in more normal battle situations.

"St.-Nizier," said Dom Guétet firmly. Neither of the others disagreed. The pass presented fewer difficulties and gave scope for maneuver that none of the other passes provided, and the Germans now knew the exact situation of the line of defense.

"They'll come fast this time," Dom Guétet went on, "in strength, and they'll go for your wings, as they did today."

Huet told them he was working on this assumption, moving more men into the pass from other sectors, placing trained troops near each end of the line. "But what can they do without adequate weapons? We've still got only one mortar—one mortar to hold a line two miles long!" He made the beginning of a gesture of opening his hands toward heaven.

Bob Bennes came into Descour's room, grinning broadly. He had good news. "There's to be a parachute drop tonight, sir," he reported. After waiting so long, he had hardly believed his eyes as he had scribbled the two messages on his pad: "*Le petit chat est mort*" ("The little cat is dead"), which meant that there would be a drop at "Writing Pad," the landing ground near Méaudre in the northern sector; and "*Gloire et honneur à ce cochon de popotier*" ("Glory and honor to this pig of a cook"), which was an adaptation of one of the BCA regimental toasts and signaled another drop in the broad flat country near La Chapelle in the heart of the southern sector.

The contact from headquarters was welcome; the fact that planes would be flying in arms from Algiers following signals from the Vercors was even reassuring. But the news they all needed to hear was of the Allied landing in the South, and the meeting was just about to break up when a man who could well be able to tell them walked into Descour's room.

Colonel Henri Zeller was Descour's superior officer in the Secret Army hierarchy, commanding FFI forces in the whole of southeastern France. He was famous throughout the Resistance as "Monsieur Joseph," the organizer of many dramatic coups against the Germans. Several times he had been arrested by the Gestapo and escaped. His wife had also been tortured.

Zeller had arrived with staff and radio operators for, like Descour and Cammaerts, he planned to establish his base in Rang-des-Pourrets, so that the mountain fortress of the Vercors would be serving as a headquarters for the Resistance leadership for a very large sector of France.

Descour grasped him warmly by the hand. "Is there any news of the invasion in the South?" he asked anxiously (so Zeller testified in Paris after the war).

But Zeller, too, had been deceived by Koenig's call to arms. With Cammaerts, he had witnessed the tragedy of Barcelonnette. He shook his head.

"They're certainly taking their time," said Descour.

Later that night, Descour reported the day's events to Constans in Algiers in a signal that reflected both his pride in the performance of the Vercors Maquis and his fears of new attack. "Vercors attacked thirteenth by a battalion. Enemy had to abandon conflict after twelve hours of combat. Await new attack after brief delay. . . . Lack arms. Ask you to redouble your efforts to come to our aid. Population has risen en masse against the enemy. All need more munitions every day. Bazookas are doing marvels."

At three o'clock in the morning the exhausted men sleeping at their posts in the defense line below St.-Nizier were awakened by the sound of the air raid sirens down below in Grenoble. Soon afterward they heard the aircraft. It was a cloudless sky and they could see the shapes of the eight Allied planes clearly enough as they swept over the plateau, once to get their bearings and check the landing grounds, delineated by fires, and then on the second run to drop their loads. From St.-Nizier the men could see the parachutes above Méaudre, drifting slowly toward the ground.

Under Eugène Chavant's personal supervision, the reception teams cut the parachutes loose and loaded onto trucks the heavy metal canisters that contained the weapons. It was already dawn as they drove them to St.-Nizier to begin the long, arduous task of stripping the weapons of the grease in which they were packed and preparing them for use.

St.-Nizier was a busy town that morning. All day trucks and buses were bringing reinforcements from the southern sector and parts of the northern plateau to join the others at the pass. Food had to be taken to the men at their posts in the line, and a great shortage of receptacles for the soup meant repeated journeys back to the village. The weapons that had been dropped by parachute were something of a disappointment to the Maquisards, engaged in the long chore of degreasing them. The Browning light machine guns would help, but many of the canisters contained 8 mm Hotchkiss machine guns made in the First World War. There was not enough ammunition for them and they were too heavy for the easy mobility that was vital for fighting in the mountains. Still, they were all the Maquis had, and they were rushed down to the line as soon as they were ready.

Meanwhile, all day there had been a line of people wishing to pay their respects to the dead who had been laid out in state in St.-Nizier's little Mairie.

Huet repositioned the men in his line. He placed Chabal and his unit near the Charvet farm on the left, to support a veteran Maquisard unit on the wing. He posted a unit high up the slopes of Le Moucherotte, above Les Trois Pucelles, on the right. And he strengthened the line by the road in the center with some 11th Cuirassiers.

That evening of June 14, the Germans opened fire on St.-Nizier with artillery set up in batteries on the edge of Grenoble. Forty shells dropped in or near the town, but astonishingly there was not a single casualty.

Beauregard slept on the balcony of the villa below St.-Nizier. The night was warm and clear. The shelling had stopped, but since reports had come in from Grenoble that the Germans had called in troops from Gap and Lyon, he knew that a new assault must come within hours.

In the plain below, a few lights could be seen in Grenoble and the surrounding country, despite the air raid blackout regulations. Every sound that filtered up to the mountain was noted and analyzed—a truck changing gear on the ring road; a train rattling into the station, which was on the edge of the city nearest to the plateau.

The commanders had urged the men not on guard duty to try to sleep while they could, but they found it hard. Many lay down, but most stayed awake, looking at the stars. Some of them smoked, the ends of their cigarettes glowing in the darkness as they inhaled.

The assault still took them by surprise. At dawn Beauregard was awakened by the sound of gunfire. The enemy was not detected by the lookouts because this time the men did not just approach up the road as they had before. They had come carefully, silently, making straight for the wings, nearly two thousand men, outnumbering the defenders by more than four to one.

They filtered through the woods of Le Moucherotte on the right, to the south of Les Trois Pucelles, and, as Beauregard had expected, they struck hard at Charvet Hill on the left. By the time the sun was rising, they had machine guns mounted on the high hill by the farmhouse. From there they could fire down the line from above it, covering the advance of others.

At the early stages, the men on duty near Les Trois Pucelles heard a familiar call in Dauphinois-accented French: "Don't shoot, comrades!" In the dim early light they saw men approaching them with Tricolor armbands like those they wore themselves. The defenders held their fire, believing them to be

Resistance men from the plain. Then, as they loomed close into view, the newcomers blazed away with submachine guns. They were Milice! And it was the Milice who with the help of this ploy managed to install a machine gun on high ground by Les Trois Pucelles.

By nine o'clock the Germans were behind the defense line on both wings, and Huet, who had joined Beauregard at the villa command post, had no alternative but to order a withdrawal to avoid encirclement. Messengers were sent up the line in both directions. Several units refused to obey. One of Geyer's young lieutenants, commanding a group of 11th Cuirassiers under orders to hold the road, fought a pitched battle for four hours before eventually being forced to drop back with his wounded to avoid being completely encircled. Even then, one gunner remained to cover his comrades' retreat, fully knowing that he was committing suicide.

Chabal, too, refused to withdraw, staying on fighting for more than two hours after receiving the order. Then, when there was a gap of only four hundred yards between the two arms of the enemy behind him, the *miliciens* on one side and the Germans on the other, he called his men to him. "Now listen," he said, so Richard Marillier records. "We're going to break out now—right through that field between the two enemy positions to the wood. Don't panic. Don't turn back. First, they'll be surprised. Second, they'll hesitate to fire for fear of hitting each other. So just run like hell when I tell you to."

Chabal was right—at least he was until the last hundred yards that they had to cover to reach the wood. For by then they were outside the enemy circle and there were no limits placed on the machine gunners. "Faster, you idiots, faster!" yelled the young sergeant, zigzagging as he ran ahead of them. All of them reached the wood except one, and from there they made their way on foot to Méaudre, where a waiting truck took them across the Gorges de la Bourne to the security of the southern plateau.

Another man who failed to obey the order to retreat was old Sergeant Itier, still wearing his sky-blue uniform. Mortally wounded, he refused the instant offers to drag him to safety, knowing he had no chance. "Give me a machine gun," he ordered, for the recoil of a bazooka would be too great for a badly wounded man on the ground. They left him, with his dog licking his wounds, firing the machine gun in bursts until he died.

By late morning, most of Beauregard's weary men were retreating along the road to Villard. As they passed through Lans they were cheered by the villagers. In Villard, too, they were greeted warmly as though they were victorious heroes, as though they had held the pass, whereas everyone knew that the Germans would be in the town by nightfall and no one knew what reprisals they might expect. The Maquisards drank the wine they were offered, accepted the congratulations, for they had done their best against an enemy that greatly outnumbered and outgunned them, and passed on through the town to their preassigned positions. Some traveled on by the Gorges de la Bourne to St.-Martin in the southern sector. Others had been ordered to make for the villages and hamlets of the high country—such as Corrençon and La Roche Pointue, in the mountains that formed the Vercors inner mountain walls. From there they could be deployed fast against the enemy again in the northern sector if that was decided—or join their comrades at St.-Martin.

Beauregard himself had left his villa command post once he had seen that the withdrawal was in progress and set off for Villard through the woods on foot. Earlier, he had told his volunteer driver, André Huillier, to take the car to the town, fearing that the Germans' advance along the road might be very fast once they broke through.

In fact, though, the Germans were in no hurry. From the trees on the high slopes of Le Moucherotte, Beauregard saw the flames licking around the houses in St.-Nizier. The long roller-coaster shelf from which his men, with their pathetic weapons, had tried to hold the pass was obscured from his view by the mountain line, but the enemy was active there, too. By some strange process of rationalization, they saw the Resistance men, who objected to the occupation of their country, as terrorists who merited no mercy. As they explored Beauregard's positions from the Charvet farm to Les Trois Pucelles, they were angry. They killed all the wounded men they found—in some cases by cutting their throats.

They set fire to the houses of Les Guillets and Les Michalons that had provided cover for Beauregard's men in the bitter fighting for the road, as well as the hamlets below them. By afternoon the Charvet farm, too, was in flames.

Then they moved on into St.-Nizier. In the cemetery seven new graves—men who had died on the thirteenth—were well marked with recently turned earth and tributes of still-fresh flowers. The German troops dug up the bodies and dragged them to the town, where they piled them in the square outside the station. They broke open the coffins of other victims of the fighting that were lying in state in the Mairie. These corpses, too, were thrown onto the macabre heap. Deliberately the Germans mutilated the bodies. Some of the soldiers even trampled on them. Then they sprayed gasoline over them and set them on fire. Meanwhile, other troops had begun to burn the little town, as Beauregard had seen from the mountain slopes above. By evening ninety-three houses were smoldering as the embers cooled.

When eventually Beauregard reached Villard he was astonished by the unreal mood of enthusiasm he found there. Despite the agony that was at that moment being inflicted on St.-Nizier, only ten miles away, the crowds in the street were

ebullient. Tricolors were still fluttering from the windows.
Somewhat dazed, the young captain drank the wine he was
offered and even accepted the congratulations, although he felt
they were a little premature considering the course of the day's
events. Then he went to look for André Huillier. He found his
car outside a café where his driver was drinking coffee, and the
sight of the vehicle made Beauregard smile. At one moment
that morning, when they had visited the line, they had come
under fire. Now some humorist had outlined the bullet holes in
the side of the Renault with red paint.

That evening the high spirits of the people of Villard
drained to the reality of fear as the long German column approached across the flat country that lay to the east of the town.
The Tricolors had been removed and the people who had
swarmed into the streets earlier in the day to welcome the tired
defenders of St.-Nizier were now waiting anxiously indoors.
Through their windows they watched the snub gray trucks and
buses grinding noisily toward the square. They heard the
shouted orders in German and wondered if these referred to
the taking of hostages, to the burning of houses, to the making
of arrests.

The Germans did not burn Villard—at least, only the big garage of the Huillier family, whom they knew to be keen Resistance men. They made a few arrests of specific people they already had listed, including Louis Huillier, André's uncle, who
was transported to a concentration camp in Germany. But they
did not submit the town to the punishment that they had
meted out to St.-Nizier and the hamlets—presumably because
there had been no attempt to hold it.

They installed a Gestapo office in Villard, together with a
few troops to secure it. They established more troops in St.-
Nizier. Then the main part of the force of Germans and *miliciens* returned to Grenoble.

The next day, in the Hôtel Breyton in St.-Martin, Huet considered the situation following the harrowing battle for the still-smoking St.-Nizier. In some ways, the Vercors resembled a ship in which the bows were high. The northern plateau was the forecastle deck, the far bigger southern sector being the bridge and upper decks. The similarity is not exact because parts of the northern sector are higher than the southern sector, but the position of the Germans when they gained St.-Nizier and Villard was the same, on a bigger scale, as that of a boarding party that had merely gained the forecastle of a ship. And it was significant that the Germans had not tried to penetrate the southern plateau. Clearly, they saw the Gorges de la Bourne and the sheer cliffs of the mountain ridges that enclosed the sector as obstacles that were beyond a hurriedly assembled attack force of that size.

Chain-smoking, holding his cigarettes as he always did between his thumb and forefinger, Huet discussed his options with Chavant, trying at the same time to put himself in the position of General Pflaum in Grenoble.

Pflaum had to storm the Vercors, but it would need a big, carefully planned operation by a large number of troops brought up from other areas. This must take several days at least, by which time, Huet hoped, the paratroops would have arrived and the invasion of Provence would have been launched. Meanwhile the German general was faced with a sabotage campaign across a huge area of France that was under his command—which was why he had withdrawn most of the troops he had deployed against them yesterday. He was in no position to leave two thousand men in a stalemate position at Villard and St.-Nizier. He needed them for active operations— the same kind of obscene reprisals they had enacted in St.-Nizier—that he hoped would act as a deterrent on the Resistance. He could bring them back for the big assault on the massif when he was ready.

Huet was tempted to consider attacking the few enemy troops that remained in the two northern-sector towns, to re-take St.-Nizier and once more establish his defense line on the roller-coaster shelf. It would have assuaged his pride as a commander, but he had lost nearly fifty men killed and wounded and he had learned the lesson. The broad pass was too vulnerable, given his lack of proper weapons. "What would it achieve?" he said to Chavant. "It'd force the enemy to attack us again immediately and the result would be the same as it was yesterday, except that the reprisals would be even worse."

The Patron needed no persuasion. He agreed with Huet wholeheartedly.

"There's no point in provocation," the major went on. "What we need is time—time to train, to prepare, to organize."

He also needed information—exact information about General Pflaum's plans, about the movement of his troops—and that morning of June 16 two very pretty young girls with dark hair walked into the Hôtel Breyton and offered their services as spies. They were cousins from Sassenage on the northeast of the massif, both eighteen, named Gaby and Jacqueline Groll. Gaby's sister, in fact, was married to Pierre Dalloz.

Huet looked at them with astonishment. "You think you could gather intelligence?" he asked dubiously, perhaps with a momentary thought of the legendary spy Olga Polovsky, who allegedly discovered so many secrets on the pillow. For these were no femmes fatales who would lure officer lovers to talk carelessly in bed. They were two very innocent-looking, fresh-faced young girls.

"That's the point," said Gaby, realizing what was in his mind. "Who would suspect it? That's why two of us are even better than one. If you were a German officer, would you think that two girls bicycling in the country were intelligence agents?"

Huet's face softened. They were right, of course. They were

ideal. They even had a very good contact to suggest: a man who worked for the Syndicat d'Initiative in Grenoble and opened the mail, who therefore knew of train movements and had immediate access to news from other parts of France. Intelligence networks had, of course, long been operated by the Resistance in the towns around the massif, but since the plateau had been mobilized care was needed on the telephones; so couriers with good covers, like the Groll girls, were useful.

Huet sent them to Grenoble on their first mission. In addition to visiting the Syndicat d'Initiative, they were ordered to meet a contact in a café in the Place Victor Hugo. They wore white scarves for identity purposes. They were joined by a man who told them of German troop movements to the south, describing the regiments, the size of the units, and the towns they were passing between. Gaby wrote down the details in the toilet on a piece of paper that she rolled up and concealed in the handlebars of her bicycle, beneath the rubber grip. The next morning they cycled back into St.-Martin and reported to the major. Their information was not of great value, though it formed a part of the mosaic of information flowing to the plateau from various channels. However, Huet thought the girls' potential merited a role for them on his staff. At his suggestion, they moved to St.-Martin and were given a room in one of the village houses.

From that first trip to Grenoble the Groll cousins also brought back a declaration by the German command that had been posted in the streets of the city. Huet had already heard of it, for it had been broadcast on the radio, but the sight of it in cold print was chilling. It warned Resistance men that, if they were captured, they would not be treated as soldiers but as "francs-tireurs" (terrorists). Quoting Article 10 of the 1940 Franco-German Armistice Agreement, which dealt specifically with Frenchmen who continued to fight on against the German Reich, the statement declared that rebels who fell into their hands would face automatic sentence of death.

There were no good omens on that morning of June 17. For another signal to the southern Resistance had just come in from General Koenig in London. It emphasized that all air resources were needed in the battle areas and ordered that the Resistance should avoid assembling unarmed groups around armed units—which, of course, was the exact situation in the Vercors.

Although the Hôtel Breyton was alive with activity that morning, Huet could only have felt a cold, consuming loneliness. Although he had declared the flat country of the northern plateau a no man's land, which meant that the Germans could move through the villages as freely as they chose, he had troops stationed in the mountains to the north and the west of the sector—especially to the west, for a road snaked through this range through the pass of the Col de Romeyère from St.-Gervais at the northwest foot of the massif to Rencurel, which lay close to the Gorges de la Bourne and the Pont de la Goule-Noire. From the north this provided the best access to attack the southern sector. But, tactically speaking, those northern mountain positions were merely outposts. The line of Huet's northern perimeter was now formed by the cliffs of the great Bourne canyon that divided the massif.

Effectively, the commander had withdrawn his forces into the Vercors inner citadel. And, apart from preparing his military organization, all he could do was wait.

CHAPTER 9

The one event that was critical to the fortunes, and even to the lives, of the people of the Vercors was the invasion of the south coast of France. Without that assault from the sea, no paratroopers in force would be dropped into the massif. And the fact is that by June 18, as Huet and his men were waiting tensed within the Vercors southern plateau after the trauma of St.-Nizier, the date of the operation had not even been settled.

Eleven days before, on June 7, General Sir Henry Wilson had signaled Eisenhower that, owing to the progress of the Allied advance in Italy, he could now proceed with preparations for the delayed landings on the coast of Provence. This message was radioed to London barely forty-eight hours after the Resistance in the South had been summoned into action believing the invasion to be imminent. But one sentence in particular in Wilson's signal would have horrified the Vercors leaders had they known of it: "The target date at which I am

aiming is August 15." In two months' time! Always, from the
very beginning of the planning of Operation Montagnards, it
had been accepted that the longest period that the defense of
the Vercors could be maintained without paratroopers was three
weeks, and already eight days had passed.

There was yet another factor, concerned with global war
strategy, that was vital to those men and women waiting in the
isolated mountain fortress. In that third week of June, despite
Wilson's signal to London about his preparations, the key
question in top Allied circles was: Would the assault in the
South take place at all? Eisenhower and the U.S. chiefs of
staff were firmly in support of it, believing that France should
be used as a solid base to strike straight up through Western
Europe at Germany—and they needed for this the big deep-
water port of Marseille to bring in troops from America. By
contrast, Churchill and his Cabinet were vehemently opposed
to it. The British Prime Minister, with his wary eyes on the
Russian advance westward, was utterly convinced that instead
the Allies should strike north from Italy through Yugoslavia to
eastern Germany.

So while Huet waited anxiously in St.-Martin for a signal
warning of the arrival of paratroopers in force, the men directing
the war were in bitter deadlock about the role the Southern Sector of France should play in the fight against Germany. This
top-level struggle, however, was highly secret and known to very
few people indeed. In Algiers the planning staff, who had been
working on Operation Anvil since January, were proceeding on
the assumption that the attack would be launched. And although the Vercors commander was anticipating the arrival of
troops in their thousands, he would have been slightly encouraged if he had known how prominent the massif was in the
arrangements in progress in the old Moorish city.

Major Longe and his Mission Eucalyptus, which Jacques

Soustelle had mentioned in the crucial order that Chavant had taken back to Colonel Descour in France, was at this moment waiting in Algiers to be parachuted onto the plateau. So, too, was an American OSS combat team. Also, Soustelle had ordered a group of French officers to stand by to fly to the massif —in particular an engineer who was to supervise the construction of an air strip in the Vercors so that planes could land there with troops and heavy armament that were difficult to drop by parachute.

However, Huet's greatest hopes would have lain in a quaint but imaginative project named "Operation Patrie" that was being promoted by Fernand Grenier, the skinny, gray-haired Minister for Air in the French provisional government. Grenier, a dedicated Marxist, was one of the two Communist Party members that De Gaulle had been forced to include in his Cabinet as the price of co-operation by the important left-wing Resistance groups within France. With a formidable record as a Resistance fighter, Grenier had been arrested in France by the Gestapo, had actually faced a firing squad—his execution being deferred at the very last moment—and had succeeded eventually in escaping from the infamous prison camp at Chateaubriant.

It was not strange that the communist Grenier and Jacques Soustelle, De Gaulle's close lieutenant, should be in conflict. Both claimed authorship of Operation Patrie, and both accused the other of opposing it for party political reasons. Without question, it was an idea that could be vitally important to the Vercors. It was born in the fact that the sheer size of the Allied air forces in the Mediterranean, with their thousands of aircraft, made them cumbersome and inflexible—geared to the mass bombing of major targets but ill suited to supply and attack operations at short notice over mountain territory.

Operation Patrie was to consist of a squadron of French aircraft that were no longer in operational service—notably some antiquated bombers that had long lain unused in Syria and some training aircraft that had been employed for teaching French pilots in air schools in Morocco. These veteran planes, it was suggested, could be deployed to aid the Resistance in such places as the Vercors in between the big Allied air force operations that required time to plan and schedule.

Whoever thought of the idea, there was no question that it was Grenier, as Air Minister, who had the responsibility for seeing the project through; and certainly no one challenged the man he placed in charge of it: Lieutenant Colonel Morlaix, one of France's most famous air aces, who held a senior post in the Air Ministry.

Morlaix took on the assignment with great enthusiasm. On June 18 he had a long meeting with Colonel Constans to discuss the problems. He gave orders for the old planes to be flown in from Syria and Morocco. He set up an emergency plan to fit them as fast as possible for operational use, and he began co-opting young pilots, most of whom, while expressing doubts about the machines' capacity to fly, agreed to do their best to help their comrades in the Maquis.

By June 22 Operation Patrie was sufficiently far advanced for approval to be sought from the Allied High Command, for this was needed before the planes could operate. The matter was referred first to De Gaulle at a meeting of the top-level Committee of Action in France, of which Soustelle was secretary, and it was received with warm enthusiasm.

For the Vercors, where time was so crucial, this squadron of vintage planes would be vital, both for supply purposes and, even more important, for bombing the enemy in the passes and other places where they formed a threat—as was emphasized only too vividly that very day.

For as Soustelle and his committee were in session discussing the project, a signal came into Colonel Constans' office from the massif calling for immediate help against a grave new

1. The cliff walls that enclose the Vercors (*A.I.G.L.E.S. Paris*).

2. Jean Prévost.

3. Pierre Dalloz, who with Prévost conceived the idea of transforming the Vercors into a fortress.

4. Lieut. Colonel Marcel Descour, commander of the Secret Army's Region 1, with Dom Guétet. ˙

5. Eugène Chavant, the "Patron" of the Vercors.

6. Captain Narcisse Geyer.

7. Lieut. Colonel François Huet

8. General Pierre Koenig
(*Photo A.F.P.*).

9. The Gorges de la Bourne
(*Editions Arthaud, Paris.
Photo by H. Paillasson*).

10. The Grands-Goulets
(*Editions Arthaud, Paris.
Photo by A. Trincano*).

11. Major Francis Cammaerts.

12. Yves Farge.

13. Sergeant, later Lieutenant, Abel Chabal.

14. Jacques Soustelle (*Photo A.F.P.*).

danger: "Request extremely urgent bombing Chabeuil airfield where at present there are sixty aircraft. . . ."

The moment, on that morning of June 22, when Huet looked at the slip of paper that had been handed to him in St.-Martin and saw the words "sixty aircraft" was by far the worst he had experienced since he had arrived in the Vercors. For Chabeuil airfield lay near the southwest sector of the ring road that encircled the massif. By air it was only a few miles from the interior of the plateau.

The news was no surprise, for the danger of Chabeuil had been obvious from the earliest moment of planning. It was more in the category of a nightmare dread. Of all the weaknesses in Huet's defenses, the airfield held by far the biggest menace. The facilities he possessed to hold the passes against ground assault were fairly minimal, but he had no means at all of protecting his men against attack from the air—no anti-aircraft guns, no fighter cover. It was because of the potential threat of the airfield that it had been watched extremely closely by one of the Resistance intelligence networks, which had three members living locally.

Until a few days before, there had been only a few light planes on the field, used mainly for reconnaissance. Then more aircraft began to arrive. That morning one of the network's Chabeuil observers had been shocked to discover how many new planes had landed overnight and now lay on the field. Immediately he had hurried to Romans by bicycle and reported the new situation to his contact in the organization's hierarchy. The news had been phoned at once to La Chapelle, where Huet's newly appointed intelligence officer had set up his office close to the plateau telephone exchange. The officer scribbled a note to Huet, which was rushed over to St.-Martin by bicycle, and asked Romans for confirmation of the report. For sixty aircraft was an enormous number for so small an airfield.

Huet had little chance to speculate whether the Vercors was the target of the planes. Soon after midday, some of them were in action—not within the plateau itself but in the southwest foothills of the massif.

Until two days before, the farm of the Belle family at Combovin, a village that lay on a mountain ridge about a thousand feet above Chabeuil, had been the headquarters of the Maquis of the Drôme Département, which was responsible for the defense of the Vercors southern slopes as well as a big stretch of country that the slopes dominated. However, the commander and his staff had moved south and all that remained was a team of radio operators.

That morning of June 22, Lilette Lesage, an attractive twenty-year-old girl who was one of Descour's couriers, had been sent by the colonel on an errand to the farm in the old ambulance she drove as cover because, in the event of being stopped by German patrols, it provided her with a good reason for traveling.

She was inside the farmhouse when she heard the explosions as thirteen aircraft from Chabeuil swooped on the ancient villages of Plan-de-Baix and Beaufort, a few miles to the south. As Lilette rushed out of the house, the planes turned for a second run over the villages, dropped their bombs, and headed directly for Combovin. They attacked a large house that served as a Maquis base—then flew straight for the Belle farm. As usual, the German information was superb.

The farmhouse was shattered by bombs and several men were wounded. Then, to her horror, Lilette saw a German armored column approaching up the mountain road below Combovin. Realizing that the troops were certain to visit the farm, she managed with the help of others to lift five wounded men into her ambulance and drove the vehicle farther up the mountain by a cart track.

Her plan was to find somewhere they could be concealed

until the Germans had left. With her assistance, the wounded men crawled behind some bushes at the side of the track. But the pilots of the planes circling above the farm could see what was happening and directed the ground troops by radio.

The Germans killed Lilette's wounded, set her ambulance on fire, and left her for dead with a bullet in her thigh. They shot everyone they found in the farmhouse, as well as seven villagers, and threw the radio sets down a well. In all, there were eighteen casualties. That evening, after the raid was over, Lilette, the sole survivor at the farm, was borne up to Dr. Ganimède's hospital in St.-Martin.

Combovin, with its ominous new element of aircraft, was the crisis point of the anxious week after the St.-Nizier battles. Twice, during the days following Huet's withdrawal south of the Gorges de la Bourne, German columns had approached the canyon from different directions. Each time they had been fought back fairly easily for, as Huet knew, these were not really attacks—merely reconnaissance operations, preliminaries to a strike in force. These probes were to become a regular pattern after a few days, like the presence of planes every day circling slowly over the passes. Huet was only too conscious that in Grenoble some officer, with a map of the Vercors in front of him, was recording the information that the units and aircraft brought back to him: the strength and positions of the defense, the geological features of the passes, exactly where the bends and tunnels were, at what points the cliffs overhung the roads. At the same time, reports were coming in to St.-Martin of major enemy forces, including tank divisions, on the move to the south of the massif.

Throughout that anxious week, Huet was conscious of a sense of ever-growing threat, but never was the feeling so stark as on the evening that a Resistance man, who had come to the plateau from the south, was brought into his office. The man was in a state of shock, and shaking. The skin on his face was gray, his eyes bloodshot.

"I've come from St.-Donat," said the Maquisard, lighting with trembling fingers a cigarette that was offered to him. "I've never experienced anything like it."

St.-Donat was a small town about ten miles south of the Vercors southern cliffs—in Drôme Département territory where the Resistance had been exceptionally active since D Day. The Germans had selected it as an example to deter other towns and villages that harbored "terrorists."

"It started with planes," said the Maquisard. "They dived low over the town, machine-gunning everyone they saw. There were people in the streets screaming, running for the cover of the shops. Then they brought in the Mongols."

The Mongols were a special punitive corps of Russian prisoners of war captured in the fighting on the Eastern Front. As an alternative to confinement in the POW camps, they had been incorporated into a unit in which a native cruelty could be exploited. They had arrived in a long convoy of twenty trucks that rumbled noisily into the town and parked in rows in the square. As the shocked people of St.-Donat watched anxiously, these strange-looking men with their flat faces and slightly slanting eyes had leaped down from the vehicles.

Under the orders of German SS officers, they swept through the town shooting people at random. They ransacked stores and set fire to a pharmacy. They lined up eighty-six hostages against a wall and toyed with them, killing some, beating up some, torturing some.

"Finally," said the Maquisard, "they raped every female they could find in the town—including old women and young children. It was a terrible day that the people of St.-Donat will never forget."

For a few moments after the man had finished, Huet said nothing. He sat, as he often did, with his hands on his desk, his fingertips together, his face impassive. He was not a man to whom emotional words came easily and what possible comment would have been adequate to what he had just heard? At last he said very softly, "My God!" And everyone in that room knew what he was thinking. This was what the Vercors could expect if the Germans succeeded in storming the southern plateau, if the paratroops and heavy weapons did not arrive in time.

Throughout the week, in the barn that served as a radio shed near Rang-des-Pourrets, Bob Bennes and the other operators had been waiting to hear from Algiers. On the day that St.-Nizier was burned, Colonel Zeller, hoping his seniority would add weight to Descour's earlier pleas, had signaled Constans: "Are under heavy attack. Implore you to act fast. . . . You have created for us a catastrophic situation, for our ammunition is exhausted. You are responsible. . . ."

There was no answer. The days passed, with German probes into the passes, with the horror of St.-Donat, with the reports of major enemy forces moving north, and there was just no answer from Algiers.

On June 21 Descour sent yet another message to Constans: "Vercors about to be attacked from northeast and south. Impossible to hold out unless we are sent immediate aid."

The next day, when the news of the build-up of planes at Chabeuil reached the plateau, a signal came in at last on Bob Bennes' receiver from Constans. "Know the importance of the Vercors. Everything is being done to aid you. You will be supplied as soon as weather conditions permit. . . . Congratulations on your wonderful stand in the Vercors."

The message, when Descour read it before sending it to Huet in St.-Martin, did not encourage him. It sounded too much like the kind of soothing palliative that so often emerged from headquarters when nothing was being done. Then Descour heard about the planes at Chabeuil, and the signal from his

comrade of the École de Guerre seemed intolerable. Angrily, he
ordered Bob Bennes to send a message urging the immediate
bombing of the airfield and, within an hour after coding it, just
about the time the aircraft were taking off to attack Combovin,
the radio officer was tapping out the urgent message in his
barn.

During those anxious days after St.-Nizier, the people of the
Vercors lived consciously under conditions of great menace—as
indeed do front-line troops—but their anxieties were combined
with a zest for action, with a pride in the isolated fortress role
for which they had been selected. Certainly they were famous.
The news of the fighting had rippled through central France
like a summons. From the moment the plateau had been mobilized, a few men had walked, cycled, and driven up through the
passes from the plain to offer their services to the Vercors command, but now the trickle of volunteers became a flood of hundreds a day.

Technically, of course, St.-Nizier had been a defeat for Huet
and his men, but the fact was that they were still there in the
mountain fortress, defying the occupying power. The Tricolor
was still flying in St.-Martin and La Chapelle and Rang-des-
Pourrets. So to those Frenchmen living under German rule in
such places as Lyon and Grenoble and Valence, it seemed like
a victory for the Resistance.

By June 20, only five days after Huet had ordered the withdrawal behind the Gorges de la Bourne, he had under his command some four thousand men—in addition to those whose
homes were on the massif—and the stream of recruits arriving
at the four access points to the southern sector of the plateau
showed little sign of easing. Some, indeed, came from as far
away as Paris.

The numbers were far greater than they had ever expected.
Chavant had assured the headquarters staff in Algiers that

there would be twenty-five hundred men to hold the passes and service the paratroopers when they arrived. Soon, clearly, there would be double this figure.

All the newcomers were welcomed and conducted under guard to St.-Martin, where Captain Pierre Tanant, Huet's lugubrious chief of staff, had set up an interrogation center in the schoolhouse. There his officers questioned the new arrivals, probing carefully to detect any signs that they might be spies, before allocating them to one of the five areas into which the Vercors was now structured for military purposes.

Jean Prévost's command region had been changed when Huet had withdrawn his main force behind the Gorges de la Bourne. The writer was now in charge of the northeastern corner of the major's "inner citadel"—the walls being formed by cliffs of the Gorges de la Bourne and by two of the parallel mountain ridges that reached south down the interior of the plateau. In a white farmhouse set in the open meadows of Herbouilly between these two ridges, the writer spent his evenings working on a critical study of the poet Baudelaire when his duties as a commander permitted it. Sometimes, too, he would have long discussions with his men about philosophy and, in particular, about the kind of Europe that would exist after the Germans had been defeated.

Huet had now moved out of the Hôtel Breyton and set up his headquarters in the Villa Bellon, a large timber Alpine house in the higher part of St.-Martin. There he began to build a headquarters staff in the traditional regimental manner, in four different departments or bureaux, each concerned with different aspects, such as personnel or intelligence. Soon there were no fewer than fifty officers in the villa and other buildings helping him direct the Vercors forces.

For all of them it was a heady experience. For the first time since the fall of France in 1940, these career officers were working to shape the nucleus of a French fighting force. They were under grave and imminent threat of attack, but there was scope for glory and much historical precedent of other beleaguered garrisons with which to identify.

Huet encouraged the emerging sense of military pride. He introduced some traditional military ceremony. The colors were hauled down at night to the sound of a bugle. Officers and men saluted each other smartly. Recruits were seen drilling. Uniforms began to appear—not many to start with, and often just a jacket, because they were not easy to obtain.

In the officers' mess in the Villa Bellon, the meals began to be as formal as those at any regimental base. From his place at the head of the table, Huet would propose the traditional toasts that French officers had been enjoying for years. The company would respond with the familiar words in noisy unison.

The one officer who was absent, of course, was Narcisse Geyer. In fact, Huet did unbend a little toward him, perhaps realizing that the situation between them was a little absurd, and suggested that he should move his southern-sector command post from his farmhouse at La Rivière to St.-Martin so that he would be closer to headquarters. But Geyer declined. Although he enjoyed military ceremony and played a prominent role in the parades that were to become a regular feature of Vercors life, he believed Huet with his big regiment ideas and enormous staff was courting a disaster of appalling proportions. Surely the lesson of St.-Nizier would now be learned, he argued, for the Germans had taken the pass with great ease once they made a serious effort. "I was not *au courant* with my chief's intentions," he wrote a little acidly in his account of the Vercors conflict, "but after St.-Nizier I was horrified to see that once more regular army tactics were to be employed instead of guerrilla methods of combat. Was this," he queried incredulously, "the time to speak of lines . . . of the fortress and free republic of the Vercors?"

The captain wanted to have no part of Huet's new establishment and Huet appeared to accept this with a strange temerity that was in striking contrast to the impression of moral strength that he imparted to many of the people who worked closely with him. It was a strength that certainly made no impact on Geyer, who could barely address his commanding officer without a sneer.

For Huet, Geyer must have had the quality almost of a ghoul, always warning him of the enormous danger of the inevitability of overwhelming assault when, sure as God, he knew it well enough. His instincts were toward formal dispositions; moreover, his orders were to hold the passes, which, for practical purposes, meant formal lines of defense. If he had adopted Geyer's ideas, he would have been disobeying the orders that were a basic part of Operation Montagnards. Yet why did he not point this out to Geyer? Why did he not order him, as his superior officer, to move his command post near the headquarters in St.-Martin, which would at least have been logical? Was it because he was afraid Geyer would resign, as Descour had warned? Or did he merely want to avoid a scene? Often, as one of his staff officers has described, Huet would mentally shelve unpleasant action. He would nod and pass on to other matters. His volatile captain, who commanded the interior citadel of the Vercors, was perhaps in this category, in his mind, but this friction between the two men could only threaten the efficient control of the plateau defenses.

Geyer's reluctance to move to St.-Martin was not only because Huet was there. He remembered only too vividly the Germans' swoop on the plateau in March, when he had only just got his men and his horses away in time, and he was convinced that a town was an unwise site for a headquarters in terrain like the Vercors. By contrast, La Rivière was well positioned for escape and the captain suspected that, when the enemy attacked, he would once more be leading a fast withdrawal into the thick Forêt de Lente in the west.

So he had La Rivière wired into the Vercors telephone system by the plateau engineers, who were extremely adept, and stayed where he was, still controlling the troops who manned the passes and most of the professional units—apart from Chabal and his men. After their courageous performance at St.-Nizier, Huet had placed Chabal under his personal command.

The taste of Huet and his officers for the revival of military tradition was not very popular with the civilians. At first the veteran Maquisards in their ragged sweaters and baggy trousers mocked the soldiers for their saluting and their ceremony. Then the joking developed into something more serious. Some of the soldiers began to hint that St.-Nizier had been lost because of the poor showing put up by the nonmilitary units— which, of course, was most of them. Had there been troops stationed on the right wing by Les Trois Pucelles, it was suggested, the Germans would never have been able to outflank the pass so easily.

Eugène Chavant heard the talk and glowered angrily at his table in the Hôtel Breyton. When Francis Cammaerts dropped in to have a *pastis* with him, the Patron asked him to help. "They're creating a very awkward situation, Roger," he said, "brandishing their swords and behaving as though they were on the parade ground at St.-Cyr."

Cammaerts discussed it with Beauregard, who, like Geyer, preferred not to be part of the headquarters setup in St.-Martin. He had a small command post in St.-Julien, the nearest village to the northern sector. The captain was as concerned as Chavant and insisted that everyone at St.-Nizier had fought very well. On his suggestion, Cammaerts went to see Huet in the Villa Bellon, but he did not get very far. The major fixed him with his cold eyes and noted what he said. Bilingual secret agents operating under civilian covers in the section of the SOE for which Cammaerts worked were not popular with French military men, who suspected with good reason that they were not too bothered about the politics of the underground groups they helped. There was therefore little hope that any suggestion Cammaerts made to Huet would be received with sympathy.

So the seeds of a new feud between the civilians and the soldiers, which could so easily have been checked at this stage, began to grow. In a short time they would flower into crisis.

Meanwhile, the life of the plateau as free French territory developed a momentum and style of its own. The Vercors went onto the offensive, in a reaction to the growing menace of major attack. There was nothing to lose, and needs to be satisfied. Raids on the plain became a daily occurrence—on food stores, freight trains, road transport. If anything was required, it became common practice to go and take it at gunpoint. One Maquis group, for example, returned grinning triumphantly from the ring road with a huge wine tanker destined for a German barracks.

At Chavant's request for transport, the Groupe Vallier, the most famous of the independent militant units, set up a holdup point near St.-Lattier on route N 92 from Grenoble to Valence and, aiming their submachine guns, waved all traffic that suited their purpose to a stop. They took possession of nine trucks and four cars, one of which, they discovered to their concern, was being driven personally by Valence's chief of police. As the officer stood in the road with a gun pointed at his stomach, the group held a hurried discussion on whether or not to let him drive on. It was normal practice to avoid unnecessary personal provocation of VIPs, since they could retaliate against the families of the Vercors defenders, but at last the leader decided, "We'll keep the car." And the police chief had to walk.

The Germans were soon alerted to what was happening at St.-Lattier and a busload of troops arrived at the hijack position—but by then the Vallier men were hurrying back to the Vercors in the transport they had acquired.

Sergeant Chabal sent down a five-man team to raid a water-works at Pizançon, near Romans, where the engineer of the installation had sent word he had both oil and gasoline in his store. The problem was that there was a gendarme post at the works consisting of six policemen. "They lunch at midday," Chabal briefed his men, "so that's when you'll attack." It was a high-risk operation, for Pizançon was only two miles from the German barracks at Romans.

As planned, with guns at their hips, the unit stormed into the guardhouse where the astonished gendarmes were having their meal. "Don't make a move! Hands on the table!" ordered the team leader, so Richard Marillier records. They handcuffed the policemen together with their own handcuffs—then, for his own safety, held up the engineer who had tipped them off. They drove back to the Vercors with 200 liters of gasoline and 80 liters of oil—a small haul for so dramatic an operation, but they were vital commodities in desperately short supply.

Old scores were paid off during this period, too. The Vercors men based in the southwest carried out a series of executions of collaborators through whom they had suffered. They also raided the post office at St.-Jean-en-Royans just below the Vercors' western cliffs, ordered the cashiers to hand over all the money in the till, and shot four men who tried to intervene.

The Vercors had been outlaw country since Chavant and his comrades had first made it into a refuge, but now the restraints that he had always placed on his Maquisards, the low profile on which he had always tried to insist because of the fear of retaliation, had been removed.

The emotions of the people living on the plateau were strangely mixed. They lived in constant anxiety of the big attack that they knew the Germans were preparing but they assumed—at least, most of the time they assumed—that the Allied paratroopers would arrive before the enemy. This combination of ever-growing danger and the new joy of living on free French soil produced a mood of lawlessness among a gun-carrying community.

At the same time, the overwhelming daily surge of new recruits onto the plateau—with all the problems of allocating them to sectors, feeding them, and supplying them with equipment and weapons—only added to the enormous task with which the administrators were faced. Instead of coping with hundreds, they now had to meet the needs of thousands. In theory, Chavant and his old group of Vercors leaders—who by now had also moved from the Hôtel Breyton and taken over part of the St.-Martin school—were responsible for feeding the residents of the plateau while Descour's transport chief, who had set up a base for his fleet of trucks at St.-Agnan near Rang-des-Pourrets, was in charge of supplying provisions for the fighting men who had rallied to the massif since D Day. In practice, the two systems merged—and with the merger came accusations that some of the truckloads of food were being diverted onto the black market. The sheer volume of traffic made this very possible, but it was never proved.

Feelings ran high, too, about the allocation of clothing, cigarettes, and chocolate that were included in the parachute drops. For the distribution of these was under the control of Huet's staff, and some of the veteran Maquisards from the camps alleged that their share was being withheld in favor of the military men. It only served to fan the growing resentments between the two groups.

And every day the people of the Vercors eyed the skies for bombers from Chabeuil—or from North Africa—and talked in the streets and the cafés and the shops about the latest rumors, about the latest enemy probes, and about St.-Donat.

With militants taking summary revenge, with growing internal conflicts, with thousands of newcomers to the plateau, with the problems of food distribution over which there was inadequate control, the Vercors was threatened with chaos, and both Huet and Chavant knew that something had to be done to prevent this.

Almost certainly Huet was more conscious of the difficulties inherent in mixing civilians with soldiers who needed to refind their pride than he had cared to admit to Francis Cammaerts, for the man he entrusted with the job of establishing law and order was the only senior man he took onto his staff who was not a career officer. Vincent Beaume, a lanky forty-five-year-old, had far more in common with Chavant's veteran administrators of the plateau than he had with Huet's young officers in the Villa Bellon. Like the Patron, he too had been a sergeant in the First World War and had emerged with left-wing views. A schoolteacher by profession, from Romans on the plain, Beaume had long been head of a local intelligence network and knew the Vercors and its people well.

Huet made Vincent Beaume head of his Second Bureau, which meant that he was in charge of the police, the prison at La Chapelle, the military courts, security, and intelligence. It was his duty both to keep out German or Milice spies and to curb the tough independent groups such as the Groupe Vallier, who did not see the need for formal trials before executing known traitors. In a way, his role was not unlike that of a marshal in one of the tougher towns of the American West—except that he had Huet and Chavant to support him if real crisis arose. But it was Beaume who had to handle the in-fighting.

The task he faced was formidable and he flung himself into it with immense enthusiasm. From a headquarters near the prison in La Chapelle, he issued an edict in Huet's name warning that information about the manning of the passes or other defense positions—which until now had been openly discussed in the cafés—was to be kept rigidly secret. "Trust no one," he ordered. "Remember the eyes and ears of the enemy are constantly alert." At the same time, he set up an information network throughout the Vercors villages so that he could be informed immediately of any pessimists who might forecast the disaster that was only too probable if the Germans attacked too soon. Morale, Beaume was convinced, was a vital element to the survival of the Vercors, and anyone who was too gloomy about the prospects they all faced soon had a warning that it would be wise to stop that kind of talk—if he or she wanted to stay out of jail.

Beaume's officers set up censorship of all mail leaving the plateau and issued everyone with passes that had to be shown at the control points on leaving or entering the plateau.

Beaume's main energies, however, were directed at establishing a special military tribunal to hear the many cases of crime—crime, that is, as defined by De Gaulle's provisional government in Algiers—and at accommodating the enormous number of prisoners who in due course were brought to him. For the fact that the Vercors was under free French control had led the Resistance in the plain to make arrests—or kidnaps in areas where the Milice or German presence was strong—of suspected collaborators and to send them onto the plateau for trial. One evening, for example, a convoy of vehicles from Die, the Drôme River town under the Vercors southern cliffs, arrived in La Chapelle with no fewer than eighty-five prisoners, including twelve women and eight Germans, whom Beaume had to accommodate.

The most serious suspects were held in the cells of La Chapelle's gendarmerie. The rest were housed in school buildings that had been empty since before the war when the plateau was famous as a vacation and education area for children.

Women were segregated from the men, but from the start they were the source of trouble—not least, on the first day, because of a resentful immodesty. Beaume saw two of them wandering to the bathroom, their breasts bare, along a corridor of the school where they could clearly be seen, but not approached, by male detainees. "Do that again," Beaume warned them, "and you'll be in military confinement for a week!"

Soon Beaume had no fewer than three hundred prisoners in his care and, as the concentration camp grew, the lack of dishes, flatware, cooking utensils, and bedding became a big problem—a problem that Beaume solved, as everyone in the Vercors solved their problems, by sending a team down to the plain to get what he needed at gunpoint.

Then one of his officers came to him with a difficulty of a somewhat delicate nature. The women prisoners had been brought up to the plateau from Die with no toilet equipment at all. There was an urgent need for sanitary napkins, which Beaume did not consider merited the risk of men's lives by yet another raid in the plain. He thought for a moment. Then his eyes brightened. "The parachutes!" he exclaimed. The one item of which they had ample supply was the parachute silk from the airdrops of munitions.

Vincent Beaume's prisoners did not come only from the towns around the massif. Throughout the Vercors, arrests were made every day, often with little foundation. In that anxious atmosphere, with the Germans preparing to attack, with enemy columns probing the passes, suspicions flowered easily. Personal resentments were rationalized into charges of collaboration with the enemy, whose intelligence of the plateau interior was demonstrated repeatedly to be extremely sound. So who was passing this information? Somebody was—somebody who was there in the streets and the cafés, somebody who was walking about the towns.

Beaume set up a Commission of Inquiry, consisting of two

officers, to investigate the suspects prior to trial. They faced an enormous problem. Often in the case of people sent up from the towns around the massif, there was no dossier and the interrogators had to ask the prisoners themselves on what charges they had been arrested. In other cases, the evidence was so flimsy that there was clearly no case. Every release, however, was deeply resented on a plateau that had endured much suffering, and poor Vincent Beaume soon found himself facing strident criticism for what was seen as soft treatment of traitors.

Beaume was a man of some charm, with an acute, rather impish sense of humor and demoniacal energy. With his long, lanky figure, steel-rimmed glasses, and bald head from which a few hairs stuck up in untidy disarray, he was a familiar sight in the Vercors towns pedaling his bicycle ferociously. For he was always in a hurry.

In the new command structure of the Vercors, he was something of an odd man out and, quite apart from his leniency with prisoners, he was not really very popular with anyone. The civilians and the veteran Maquisards, accustomed to the relaxed life on the plateau in the past, resented his law-and-order regulations, which smacked far too much of all the military innovations that Huet was bringing in—and Beaume was, after all, on the military staff. At the same time, the officers at St.-Martin, enjoying their military muscle-flexing, tended to look down on him a little because he was a civilian and resented his constant criticism of the deficiencies in their organization.

In his daily meetings with Huet, Beaume would produce a stream of new ideas or grim warnings of what would happen if corrective action was not taken in one aspect or another of the plateau command. Many of Beaume's suggestions were sound, but Huet was under great pressure, working late every night in his office in the Villa Bellon at the mammoth task of creating a fighting force from very raw material. He was not always too receptive to the ideas of his Second Bureau chief.

Within a few days of his appointment, however, Vincent Beaume instigated an event that had the approval of everybody. He knew that there was a great need for revenge in the Vercors, though, being a democrat, he was convinced that this urge should not be satisfied outside the proper course of law. In particular, the executions by the Milice in April, only two months before, were especially vivid in everyone's mind—including Beaume's, for one of the victims had been his friend. So he lost no time in staging the first trial of Free Vercors: of three *miliciens* who had been among the big group of prisoners brought to the plateau from Die.

Unlike many of the cases that the military tribunal heard, the penalty for the crime of association with this collaborationist police force, under specific instructions from Algiers, was death. Since the three accused did not deny their association with the Milice, they were guilty by definition. Even so, Beaume was determined that justice should be seen to be done.

The tribunal—consisting of a president, who was a lawyer, and two military officers—took their places at a long table in the La Chapelle schoolroom. Behind them, displayed against a cloth of black velvet, were the words *"La République Française —Le Tribunal Militaire du Vercors"* and two Tricolor flags. A typist, sitting at a desk, transcribed the proceedings.

Since there could be no real defense, the trial did not take long. At the end of it, the president nodded to an officer, clad in full dress uniform. Following the custom of French military courts, he turned stiffly toward the accused, his sword held rigid, point-upward before his face. The soldier guards standing behind the prisoners responded by leaping to attention with a noisy click of heels. The court rose to its feet and three times, as was traditional, the president passed sentence of death.

The next day, in the presence of a crowd that included Descour, Huet, and Chavant, the three men stood against a wall opposite the Hôtel Allard in Vassieux—in the exact spot where the three Resistance men had faced the Milice execution squad in April. One of the condemned men had asked permission to see his father, also a prisoner, before he died, and the older man had been brought over from the prison in La Chapelle. His doomed son embraced him. "Adieu, Father," he said, according to Beaume. "I allowed myself to be deceived—and I'm paying for it."

The older man was led away in tears. For the second time in two months, an order was given to fire. The noise of the shots reverberated off the buildings of the town and the fading echoes were reflected back from the sheer sides of the Grande Côte that formed the west border of the open country of Vassieux.

In spite of the Milice action in April, it was rough justice, for two wrongs never made a right. Even today Vincent Beaume wonders if it was fair to one of them at least who was charged only with collaborating with the Milice. After this, Yves Farge, the political area chief appointed by Algiers, ordered that future trials should be heard only by a five-man court of regular officers under the presidency of a general, with the defense in the hands of a practicing attorney. The incident was obviously open to criticism. It was a ritual bloodletting but, after all that the Vercors had suffered at the hands of the Milice, it was not, perhaps, unnatural.

These were strange days for the waiting defenders of the plateau and, in response to the Germans' activity or news from the plain, emotions ranged sharply from exultant, optimistic joy to deep and anxious depression. By June 22, sixteen days after the Resistance had been summoned to rise in Koenig's call to arms, some of the Vercors chiefs were beginning to wonder if the paratroopers would come. It was not done to say so—except for the skeptical Geyer, who told his men, "I'm like St. Thomas. I believe what I see"—but it was apparent at the

end of tired and anxious days in remarks about the time that
Algiers was taking to dispatch the troops and about the lack of
signaled information. Only Chavant had no doubts at all.
"They will come. There can be no doubt. There is just a
delay." He remembered only too vividly the staff officers' asser-
tions: Not twenty-five hundred. Four thousand.

Paratroopers were much spoken of, for that was how the people of the Vercors could calm their fears of German attack. It
was therefore a highly excited Bob Bennes who rushed into
Descour's office on the evening of the twenty-second with a second signal that had come in from Colonel Constans in Algiers
a few hours after the earlier soothing message of congratulations that had irritated them so much. For it promised action. "Sending you team of parachutists on landing ground
'Gummed Paper' night 23-24," the signal read. "Password:
'Here is the Trojan Horse.' Your reply: 'The end is near.' "

At last it seemed that Operation Montagnards was starting.
It was timely, for by now Descour and Huet had heard about
the air attack on Combovin and the colonel had been to visit
his wounded courier, Lilette Lesage, in Dr. Ganimède's hospital in St.-Martin.

The next night, the twenty-third, Chavant's reception team
waited in the darkness near Vassieux, the site of "Gummed
Paper," ready to light the flares as soon as they heard the engines of the aircraft; but no parachutists fell from the sky saying "Here is the Trojan Horse." As the dawn light came with
no sign of Allied aircraft, the waiting men walked sadly home.

By and large it was not a reassuring morning. Within three
hours, the Vercors defenders were under attack by the biggest
force they had faced since St.-Nizier. The enemy was driving
for the Col de Romeyère, high in the northern sector. It was a
distant pass, but it was the route that provided the best access
to Huet's inner citadel.

CHAPTER 10

That morning of June 24 was cold, for, although it was light, the sun had not yet risen above the Vercors peaks to the east and the road was still in shade. However, from the Renault with its bullet holes still ringed in red, which André Huillier was driving as usual, Beauregard could see the shadows cast by the trees on the ring road in the sunshine, three thousand feet below.

The Route des Écouges is a long, straight stretch of mountain road that descends gently from the high pass of Romeyère, passing through a cut in the rugged heights until it reaches a tunnel in the Vercors' outer northwest rim—at the head of the sheer cliffs that look so gaunt and forbidding from the plain. From there, a tiny road that has been carved out of the rock face curls down extremely steeply to the town of St.-Gervais at the bottom.

The view is overwhelming. The vast, flat plain of the Rhône

Valley reaches away from the foot of the Vercors cliffs for miles toward Lyon—until the patchwork of fields and woods blurs in the far distance.

Beauregard had chosen that morning to review the measures to hold the pass because, although the road from St.-Gervais was probably the steepest of the routes into the Vercors and the danger of attack there was doubtful, it *did* lead to Rencurel —and access to the Pont de la Goule-Noire that spanned the Gorges de la Bourne was easier from Rencurel than from anywhere else. Furthermore, the Germans clearly knew this, as their recent probes toward the Gorges had indicated.

With Beauregard was Henri Ullman, one of the Vercors' five regional commanders, who was in charge of the sector. As the car emerged from the closeness of the mountains, Beauregard asked Huillier to stop. With Ullman, he got out and looked down the steep cliffside, pondering once again if the defense was well enough placed, whether in their planning he and Ullman had missed any sector of the road that the Germans could possibly exploit.

It was formidable country in which to launch an assault. The heights had been eroded into strange shapes, set at unusual angles to each other, often sheer, with outcrops of rock. There was plenty of cover for defending troops and little scope for an attacking force to deploy its numbers—for the defile was very narrow and exposed. This was no St.-Nizier, with slopes at the side that troops could climb. Off that slim road, everything was sheer.

It was as the two men were studying the cliffside so intently that they discovered that their assumption that attack was unlikely was wrong. Way below them they saw a long gray column of trucks moving steadily up the lower levels of the mountain road. There were some twenty vehicles, which meant three hundred troops. This time, though, there was a new factor that had not existed in previous attacks. They had mountain artillery.

The main defense position covering the approach from St.-Gervais was behind the cover of boulders at one end of the Pont Chabert, a bridge across a small river that overlooked the tunnel in the rock through which the road passed on its way down the mountain. It was also in direct line of fire with a lower level of the snaking road that passed over another bridge skirting a waterfall, which was called for this reason the Pont de la Cascade. The gunners could therefore put down lethally concentrated fire on three narrow sections of the road along which the German trucks could approach only singly—the tunnel and two bridges.

At dawn the duty picket had changed. The machine guns, an American Thompson and a World War I French FM 24/29, were now manned by two Russians named George Morosov and Paul Borisov. They were Red Army soldiers who had been taken prisoner on the Eastern Front and drafted into the German Army—though, unlike the Mongols, into ordinary field battalions. A few weeks before, when their Wehrmacht unit was on the move in the plain, they had deserted and had sought refuge in the Vercors. Both Morosov and Borisov were seasoned troops, well accustomed to handling machine guns under battle conditions, so they were a valuable acquisition.

As soon as the lookouts had reported the approaching column, Morosov had left his gun to alert their commander, Cadet Francisque Troussier, who hurried down to the Pont Chabert with all the reinforcements available to him—five Maquisards armed with rifles. So, like Horatio on the Tiber bridge, these eight men prepared themselves to defend the Vercors against three hundred German troops, supported by mountain guns.

Borisov, the older of the two Russians, was at the Thompson. He had only four belts of ammunition, so he knew he

BATTLE OF
PONT CHABERT

N

ISÈRE RIVER

RING ROAD

ST: GERVAIS

PONT DE LA
CASCADE

TUNNEL
PONT CHABERT

FRENCH
DEFENSE
POSITION

Autrans

MÉAUDRET RIVER

COL DE
ROMEYÈRE

Méaudre

Germans

ROUTE DES ÉCOUGES

0   MILE   1
0   KM   1

Rencurel

TO VILLARD-
DE- LANS

must conserve it, and he had calculated very carefully the moment he was going to open fire. From the defense position, any vehicle approaching the Pont de la Cascade on the lower level of the road would be concealed by a bend until it was some thirty yards from the waterfall. But for this short stretch as it neared the bridge, it would be beautifully positioned as a target—well within range and approaching in a straight line so that it could be held steady in the gunner's sight. It was as the first German truck came into view around that bend that Borisov planned to start shooting.

Sounds travel far in mountain altitudes and, as the defenders waited, the noise of the convoy grew steadily louder. The two Russians were under orders not to fire at the same time. The FM tended to overheat and often jammed. Both, anyway, would be out of action for reloading. By shooting alternately, one of the two guns could be firing all the time.

When the snub hood of the lead truck came into view Borisov hesitated for a few seconds, holding the approaching vehicle in his sights. Then he opened up. The noise of the loud staccato cracks of the heavy machine gun was exaggerated by the angled faces of the mountains, echoing and re-echoing, the reflected sounds of past shots merging with those of the new. At that range with a steady target, accuracy was not difficult. From the bridge, they could hear the scream of bullets as they ricocheted off the metal of the trucks. Others were going through the canvas canopy—as was quite obvious when the troops leaped out, like "jumping jacks," as young Troussier described them, diving for what cover they could find.

Then the Germans brought their own machine guns into play, shooting up at the Pont Chabert, though it was hard for them to see exactly where the defense position was sited behind its cover of boulders.

Two field guns were manhandled around the bend and set up behind the cover of the truck. While Borisov reloaded the

Thompson, Morosov took over with the French machine gun, firing at the artillery crews, switching his aim sometimes to check the troops, lying at the side of the road, from making a dash across the bridge. Meanwhile, choosing their targets carefully, the five men with rifles were shooting steadily.

Then the first shell howled over their heads to burst with a deafening explosion higher up the mountain. It was soon followed by others. At first they were wide of each other, as the gunners laid down a pattern, searching for the target they could not see among the rocks.

By trial and error, the German gunners found the defenders above the Pont Chabert. Shells started dropping very close, exploding below and above them, and it was hard to keep up the same rate of return fire. Enemy troops began to move across the bridge at the waterfall—one at a time, making a dash.

It was a crucial moment in the attack—and it was made even more critical by the fact that at this moment the French machine gun overheated and jammed. At almost the same moment Borisov exhausted the last belt of ammunition for the Thompson. Even the men with rifles had very few rounds left. To all intents and purposes they were defenseless. There was a sudden sharp increase in the rate of enemy fire. Shells dropped all around them, showering them with earth and chips of rock. Machine gun bullets were striking the boulders that were providing them with cover. "They're going to attack," said Troussier.

He was wrong. It was a farewell burst. The few troops who had managed to cross the Pont de la Cascade returned to their half-tracks. The field guns were rehitched to their vehicles. The long column moved off down the road back toward St.-Gervais.

Astonishingly, despite the shelling, there had been no French casualties at the bridge and it was with a sense of deep satisfaction that the watching men saw ambulances turning off the ring road, presumably responding to radio calls to meet the returning convoy. Troussier, so he commented later, was convinced that they had killed or wounded at least fifty of the Germans.

Beauregard, from his position on the Route des Écouges above, was relieved when he saw the enemy withdrawing, but he knew the Germans had not been very determined. As always with these probes, the purpose was to gain information.

He drove to St.-Martin and reported to Huet, whose feelings were mixed, as they had been after the first day at St.-Nizier. He was pleased with the performance of his men, but the size of the German force made him anxious. It emphasized how little time was still left for aid to arrive from Algiers.

That afternoon Francis Cammaerts drove back into the plateau with information that made them even more concerned. At an airfield at Montélimar, about thirty miles to the southeast, he had seen German gliders making practice descents. What had struck the British agent as ominous was that, instead of just circling down in the usual way, they were using parachutes to check their speed. Why? To get down fast under fire? To land in restricted spaces such as there were within the Vercors cliffs?

By the next day, no further word about the nonarrival of the parachutists had come in from Algiers. Even more important, as new air attacks on Beaufort and Plan-de-Baix in the southwestern foothills were reported, was the fact that the airfield at Chabeuil had not been bombed.

Zeller, the FFI commander of southeastern France, added the authority of his new appointment as a general to support Descour's urgent signal of two days before. "Repeat request for urgent and repeated bombing Chabeuil," he radioed Colonel Constans in Algiers. "Fifty to sixty aircraft permanently on the ground or in nearby woods . . ." adding the latest intelligence that had just come in to the Vercors: "Have news of assembly of 120 troop transport trucks at Valence next Monday but since the assembly point is in the town you must avoid bombing." But a few hours later, he had decided the risk was worth it and sent another signal with exact information: "One hundred and forty trucks assembling Champ de Mars Valence at 1630. Bombing must be executed with precision to avoid townspeople."

Cammaerts, too, did his best to add pressure by signaling the SOE in Algiers, accusing the High Command of leading the FFI chiefs into thinking that the landings in the South would follow within fifteen days of the Normandy invasion. Nineteen days had already passed without any signs of the promised assault. Now the Maquis felt they had been duped into premature action. Unless big supplies of arms and equipment were delivered to them, Cammaerts warned, "the whole Resistance organization in the southeast will collapse."

He was in a good position to know because, of course, the plateau was the headquarters of Zeller and Descour, who were directing Maquis operations throughout an enormous sector of France. In fact, it was because of their links with the neighboring territory that they learned of yet another German purge, this time against the Maquis in the Ain mountains to the north. The details of the SS techniques—and the ominous reminder of what would almost certainly happen in the Vercors if help did not come soon—made the lack of response from Algiers especially chilling.

Isolated as the people of the Vercors were, cut off, it sometimes seemed, even from radio contact with Algiers, the BBC news bulletins about the war assumed an intense importance. In the morning and the evening, the broadcasts were listened to most carefully and the contents repeated immediately in the cafés. Over the past ten days the fighting in Normandy had reached its crisis. The Germans had counterattacked fiercely at several parts of the front and the weather had become so bad that the landing of Allied supplies had ceased entirely for twenty-four hours. But by June 22 the heavy gales had begun to ease. U.S. troops were already in Cherbourg, the big port on the west of the peninsula. The battle for Caen on the eastern extremity was still in progress, but slowly the British and Canadians were gaining ground.

At Rang-des-Pourrets, Descour, Zeller, and Huet discussed the implications of the Normandy fighting. It was going well, but the battle was not yet won and it was obvious that until that first stage of the invasion was completed, Normandy would absorb the resources and energies of the Allied commanders. Since Colonel Constans appeared to be impotent to do anything to aid them, the Vercors leaders were considering the possibility of help from England. Francis Cammaerts, one of whose radio operators communicated all the time with London, was sending repeated messages to SOE headquarters—and in fact, though this was unknown yet on the plateau, action was being planned there concerning "the urgency of the Vercors." Meanwhile, at Rang-des-Pourrets, in view of the situation in Normandy, London did not appear a likely source of aid. "I think we must accept," said Descour, "that our hopes have got to rest mainly with Algiers."

In that city, meanwhile, Fernand Grenier, De Gaulle's communist Air Minister, was puzzled by a delay in the formal approval of Operation Patric, his squadron of vintage aircraft. On June 22, the day when the crisis signal about the build-up of planes at Chabeuil had come in from the Vercors, the important Committee of Action in France had welcomed the project. After the meeting, Soustelle, as secretary of the committee, had phoned Grenier and asked him to prepare an official memorandum of recommendation involving two formal documents, for De Gaulle to sign. Grenier had acted immediately. By the next morning the papers were on the General's desk awaiting his signature, without which the operation could not proceed. When three days had gone by and the General had not returned the documents, Grenier began to suspect that something was happening in De Gaulle's inner circle that he did not know about. What concerned him even more was the agenda for the June 26 meeting at the top-level National Defense Committee. For although this included various minor matters, there was no reference to the important issue of his squadron.

Grenier had been giving a lot of thought to Patrie and was considering ways of developing it. Before the Defense Committee meeting, therefore, he wrote to De Gaulle urging that it should be discussed at the session and posed the possibility of extending the concept of this all-French unit. Would not the Allies allow them to attach to the operation 1,800 French paratroopers who were at that moment awaiting orders in Trapani, in Sicily? There was also a French squadron in the Middle East that was not currently in action. Could this not be assigned to Patrie, too?

By now the story of the Vercors was being promoted by the French government public relations men in Algiers. The picture of the brave people of the isolated mountain fortress defying the Germans surrounding them was indeed romantic, and soon it was being featured prominently by newspapers around the world—as well as by French radio services beamed to France. But one vital point was omitted from these glowing tributes to the courageous patriots. They had transformed their plateau into an area of Free France only because they believed that they were going to be reinforced by thousands of trained paratroopers, that Allied forces would be landing on the south coast. If no paratroopers arrived, if the southern invasion was postponed too long, then they were doomed. The press stories contained no hint of doom. They portrayed a picture of glorious success, which, it seems, despite all evidence to the contrary, many leading figures in Algiers and London came actually to believe. However, it did dawn on one general at

Mediterranean headquarters, Gabriel Cochet, who was to play a significant role in the saga of the Vercors, that this type of heroic publicity might provoke the Germans in France to attack the massif sooner than they might otherwise do—and he deployed his powers of censorship to stop it.

At any rate, the anxieties of Fernand Grenier about his squadron of old planes were soothed after the National Defense Committee meeting. He was informed officially that "the proposals of the Air Minister concerning Operation Patrie are approved." But the project still needed De Gaulle's signature—and the Allied commander's consent—before any of those antiquated aircraft would be permitted to fly.

In the Vercors, Sunday, June 25, was a very special day. There was to be a memorial service in the church at St.-Martin for those killed in St.-Nizier, to be followed by the first of the big parades to be staged since the plateau had been declared free territory. The occasion was eagerly awaited and reflected the strange dichotomy of life on the massif. Despite the dissensions and jealousies, everyone was conscious of facing a common danger from a common enemy, of sharing the same hopes of support from Algiers, the same grief for the dead, the same immense pride in the Vercors' new sovereignty.

It was a glorious sunny day with a cloudless sky, and it began with a spectacular event that was completely unexpected. At nine o'clock in the morning, thirty-six heavy Liberator bombers roared over the mountains, the noisy throbbing of their engines causing alarm at first in the villages, followed by relief as the U.S. markings were seen on the wings. Eight hundred containers, suspended by parachutes of various colors, fell slowly onto the open country near Vassieux. The planes had come from England in response to Francis Cammaerts' signals.

Chavant was taken by surprise, since the usual warnings had not been radioed, but within minutes hundreds of men were driving every truck that was available toward the landing ground. Everyone knew that the Germans at Chabeuil would have seen the bombers, and they feared an immediate air attack to destroy the material on the ground before it could be recovered. But no enemy planes came and, to everyone's relief, none of the containers had opened on the descent. For this was a worrying aspect of the air drops from Algiers, where the arms were packed carelessly by reluctant prisoners of war, with devastating results. Weapons that hit the ground without protection were always broken by the impact. Only that morning Bob Bennes had signaled Algiers angrily that nearly all the light machine guns that had been parachuted to them the previous night were useless owing to faulty fastenings on the containers.

Following the big air drop from England, the people who at 10:45 crowded into St.-Martin's square and the approach roads were happy and elated, although they were too many for everyone to find places in the pews of the old church. Those who could not sit stood at the sides or crowded into the entrance at the back.

Lilette Lesage, wounded at Combovin, insisted on being present, and the obliging Dr. Ganimède arranged for her to be carried on a stretcher and laid on the flagstones between the altar steps and the front pew where her chief, Colonel Descour, was standing with the other Vercors leaders—Huet and Dom Guétet and Zeller and Cammaerts and Geyer and Beauregard and, of course, Chavant and the principal civilian administrators.

The mass was read by Father Tixier, the old curé of the village, too old to be one of the fighting priests of the Vercors but a man of courage nevertheless—as he had demonstrated by hiding Father Vincent for several months when the abbé was high on the Germans' list of "wanted men" and dared not go near his own village of Corrençon.

The people of the Vercors knelt in the old church of that

mountain town and, with Father Tixier chanting the Mass in
Latin, mourned the death of the men who had died in the first
pass they had so far tried to hold with their Sten guns and their
sporting weapons and the First World War machine guns.
Then they got to their feet and sang—and their voices could be
heard across the valley in the villages of the high woods on the
slopes of the Roche Rousse.

After the service, everyone filed out between the big wooden
doors of the church and the troops formed up in the little
square that was truly too small for such occasions. There were
enough uniforms to give the parade an air of realism, though a
number of men lacked matching trousers or proper boots. The
6th BCA men were in blue jackets and berets. The 11th Cuirassiers were in khaki. Also, there were some nurses from Dr.
Ganimède's hospital at the edge of the town, who, in their
starched caps and aprons, provided a pleasant feminine contrast.

Geyer was mounted, of course, and in full dress uniform, his
bared sword held in a white-gloved hand. Flanking him was a
soldier bearing the blue silk regimental standard with its fleurs-
de-lis. Even the forelegs of his horse were swathed in smart
white bandages as they would have been in a parade before the
general in the barracks at Lyon. His men stood behind him in
ranks, although, as one civilian observer mocked later, there
was so little space in the square that the rear line had their
backs crammed against the wall of the Mairie and the troops in
the middle of the front rank had their faces flicked by the
swishing tail of their commander's horse.

Huet, not to be outdone by his flamboyant junior, was also
in uniform—though unmounted and in modest battle dress.
The civilians, too, displayed an expected sense of occasion.
Chavant and his civil chief wore hats and dark suits.

Le Barbu, Geyer's big bearded fighting priest, executed the
religious rites of the parade and formally blessed the standard

of the 6th BCA. The heroes of St.-Nizier were honored. Huet, who had just been made a colonel, pinned the Croix de Guerre to the breasts of Chabal and his men, and announced to cheers and clapping that the sergeant had been promoted to the rank of lieutenant.

Gilbert Joseph, a teen-ager who had been a member of one of Chavant's Maquis camps for a long time, watched sourly from the crowd as the soldiers were decorated. "The civilian companies who had fought back the first assaults [at St.-Nizier] with severe losses were given nothing," he was to write later in a highly critical book. He had a point, and it did not help the growing tension between the Army and the Maquisards.

That day, however, was colored by military ceremony. To the soaring notes of a bugle, the Tricolor was slowly hauled up a mast that had been erected in the square. Orders were bawled. The troops presented arms. Geyer slashed his sword downward in salute.

Then the band struck up and the parade began and not even Chavant objected too much to the sight of Geyer at the head of the column, with his horse reined in so that it stepped out with pricked ears, followed by the Chasseurs with their standard; and the 11th Cuirassiers with the ancient blue silk flag that their commander had taken from Lyon; and the Maquisards bearing the Tricolor and the Cross of Lorraine, Joan of Arc's emblem that De Gaulle had adopted as a symbol of the Resistance. They marched to the bottom of the town—then turned and paraded back up again through the main street to the square, passing on the left a beaming Mme Breyton among the crowd in the doorway of the hotel, and on the right, General Zeller, taking the salute, with Descour and Huet standing stiffly at his side. As the column reached the edge of the town, the wounded in Dr. Ganimède's hospital waved to them through the windows. Anyone watching that morning scene in the little mountain town would scarcely have believed that the plateau was under serious menace of German attack. That Sunday, for a brief while, the people of the Vercors were able to forget for a moment the enormous threat they faced. They were happy and even confident, but very little would be needed to shatter that fragile, illusory sense of security.

These parades were to become frequent not only because they were popular with the soldiers, but because they also stirred the patriotic pride of the civilians.

Geyer, who now kept himself remote in every other way from the military command, was always eager to play the star role in the processions. Strangely, no one ever sought to stop him. He did, of course, have possession of the only suitable horses, but Huet could easily have suggested that, since no one else was mounted, it would be more desirable if he were to lead his men in the parades on foot. Still, it seemed, Huet was unwilling to have the confrontation that would have been welcomed by his disapproving junior officer.

Meanwhile, the zest for raiding the plain, for setting up dramatic coups, that seemed to infect everyone on the plateau during that last week of June extended even into Rang-des-Pourrets. Marcel Descour himself was closely involved with the planning of one of the most ambitious schemes of all.

It was, in fact, the idea of Georges Jouneau, Descour's transport chief, that they should send a team all the way to Lyon to kidnap fifty-two Senegalese prisoners who were employed as orderlies in the German officers' mess. Lyon was some ninety miles from the Vercors, so this was not some quick raid onto the ring road to hijack a gasoline truck. Even if the operation was successful within the city, getting back without being intercepted would be hazardous.

Even so, the suggestion had much appeal for Descour. The Senegalese were part of an elite unit of the old French colonial army—massive men from the African west coast. Each stood

over six foot three, had enormous shoulders, and was a first-
class shot. Not least, from Descour's point of view, the stealing
of these men right under the Germans' noses in their headquarters town would be great for morale.

Jouneau planned the operation with great care. The Senegalese did not sleep in the German barracks where they worked
but were kept in confinement at the La Doua university cam-
pus on the north side of the city. They were transported by bus
to the barracks every morning before the end of curfew. Clearly
that would be the time to stage the coup.

The next afternoon two brothers, Pierre and André Grosset,
each driving a truck to transport the Senegalese after the kidnap, left the plateau by way of Les Grands-Goulets and headed
for Lyon. They had been chosen because their father owned a
small transport business in Villeurbanne, the district of the city
in which La Doua was situated.

On the outskirts of the city, the Germans had set up a road
block and were stopping all traffic. Both the Grosset brothers
were wanted men, so André, who was driving the leading truck,
slowed down as he neared the block—then, as a German soldier
waved him to a halt, he trod on the accelerator. The truck
leaped forward, almost knocking the soldier over as it passed
him. There were yells—then bullets as the Germans opened
fire. Since the troops' attention was fixed on the first truck
careering fast up the road away from them, they did not notice
the second vehicle approaching the barrier. Pierre adopted exactly the same technique as his brother. He slowed down, then
at the last moment raced through the road block, past the Germans, with submachine gun bullets slamming into the body-
work of the truck.

Both men knew that a search for them would be ordered,
but their vehicles were soon off the road and under cover in
their father's yard.

That night an officer of the Lyon Resistance called at the

Grosset home to give them their final instructions. "Everything is settled," he told them. "You're to be waiting tomorrow morning at 0445, with your engines running, in the Rue Marguerite. The bus carrying the Senegalese will pass the end of that street. As it does so, they'll overwhelm their guards. There aren't many of them and they know the Senegalese to be good-natured, so they won't be expecting any trouble. The men will join you in the trucks and you'll get out of the city as fast as you can."

The next morning the Grosset brothers drove through the dark streets of Lyon to the Rue Marguerite and parked with their engines running as they had been ordered. It was a small sidestreet, and their father, who had traveled with them, stood backed up against the wall near the corner of the main road so that he could warn them when the bus was coming.

Meanwhile a second part of Jouneau's plan had been executed. The principal danger of the operation was that the Germans would learn of the raid too soon—and organize the pursuit before the Grosset brothers' trucks had been able to disappear into the country lanes between Lyon and the Vercors. For this reason, a cover party, led by Le Barbu, the priest, had left the plateau a few hours after the Grossets. Now, as the brothers waited tensely in the darkness in the Rue Marguerite, Le Barbu and his group took up position at a crossroads at St.-Priest on the eastern fringe of Lyon, on the escape route to the Vercors. Pursuit could come along either road, and Le Barbu's Maquisards were lying behind machine guns aimed to fire on the two arcs—west to south and west to north—at any Germans who might be chasing the kidnap trucks.

The plan worked with amazing perfection. The Grossets' father signaled his sons that the bus was coming and in two minutes the big Africans were running up the street and clambering into the back of the trucks. The Grossets drove fast out of the city, which was still deserted because of the curfew.

At St.-Priest, Le Barbu and the cover party, waiting tensely behind their guns, saw "two vehicles looming out of the grayness of the morning." Their fingers tautened on their triggers, but there was no one in pursuit. So they loaded the machine guns onto the truck that had brought them and drove off after the Grosset brothers into the network of lanes that had been selected as the safest route back to the Vercors.

The Germans reacted as expected. They closed every road out of the city, but by then it was too late.

Descour was delighted at the success of the operation. When the Senegalese arrived at Rang-des-Pourrets, he welcomed them personally and made them his guard. With their round red caps, smart blue uniforms, and noisy leaps to attention every time an officer passed, they gave the forest house the atmosphere of a military headquarters—which provoked the inevitable sneering among the civilians to whom the raid seemed an enormous risk for remarkably little return. The Senegalese were placed under the command of one of Geyer's officers, Lieutenant Yves Moine, and when they were not doing guard duty at Rang-des-Pourrets, they lived with the rest of Geyer's men in the farm buildings at La Rivière.

Descour, of course—unlike Huet, who was commanding the plateau—was directing a wide-ranging campaign against the Germans for many miles around. On June 26 he reported the results of the Resistance operations in a somewhat jaunty signal to Algiers: "Isère Département reports total stoppage railroad traffic on lines Grenoble–Chambéry, Grenoble–Valence, Grenoble–Vienne, Grenoble–Lyon. Enemy has had several killed and wounded during operations. All telephone and telegraph communications cut."

Although the colonel was reporting the results of attacks on the Germans outside the Vercors, these were vitally important to the massif. They meant that no German troops could be brought up by rail for the assault on the plateau. Road transport was the only means available and that, too, was highly vulnerable.

The menace of Chabeuil, however, grew greater every day. By June 27, no less than five days after the first request that it should be bombed, the airfield had still not been attacked by Allied planes. Nor for that matter had any parachutists arrived speaking of Trojan horses.

To the Vercors chiefs, the situation seemed absurd. More planes were arriving at the airfield every day and they were impotent to do anything about it other than send signals that met no response. This acute sense of frustration was obvious in an angry message sent to the SOE headquarters in Algiers by Francis Cammaerts. "You must immediately bomb Chabeuil aerodrome," he insisted. "It is absolutely certain that there are 110 planes . . . with a lot of equipment. The planes are in the woods around the airfield. . . . Vercors is menaced from there. This is absolutely essential. Very big stock of bombs not yet placed in the woods. Positively demand aircraft over target."

A few hours later, Bob Bennes reported to Descour, who was in conference with Zeller. The radio officer had just decoded a signal from Constans that he knew would not please them. "Chabeuil airfield and the Champ de Mars in Valence," the staff colonel advised, "are included in the MAAF [Mediterranean Allied Air Force] program. Action will be taken from here within several days. . . ."

"Several days!" repeated Francis Cammaerts when Descour sent a message asking him to join them in his office. "What in hell does that mean? Next week? The week after?" Cammaerts of all people had grounds for complaint. In February he had been recalled to London for discussions, and during these he had emphasized that the maximum period the Vercors could be expected to hold out was three weeks.

"Think of those hundred and forty troop transports lined up

in rows in the Champ de Mars in Valence," complained Zeller unhappily. "If they're still there." It was already June 27—some twenty-four hours after the 1630 assembly time he had signaled Algiers. By now the trucks—which would have made so easy a target massed together in the Champ de Mars—might have been routed elsewhere. Almost certainly, since the railroad tracks had been sabotaged, they would transport troops that would be used in the assault on the Vercors. The need for Fernand Grenier's Operation Patrie squadron of old planes could not have been better demonstrated.

There was little opportunity for the Vercors leaders to forget Chabeuil. The next morning, soon after dawn, the lookouts of a small Maquis enclave at La Rochette, a village in the massif's southwestern foothills, not far from Combovin, saw a German column of ten trucks—which meant anything up to 150 troops —moving along the ring road from Valence. Flying above it was the usual plane whose pilot, conforming with the German air-to-ground tactics, would be studying the country ahead.

The lookouts awakened their comrades and the Maquisards hurried to the cover of bushes on either side of the mountain lane below the village. There was still doubt about the destination of the enemy convoy, but when it turned off the ring road and headed up the mountain route for La Rochette, there was no longer any question of the Germans' target.

The noise of the approaching column grew louder as the Maquisards waited beside the lane. Deliberately, they allowed the two motorcyclists at the head of the convoy to pass by them unchallenged. Then they lobbed grenades at the first truck and the mountainside was devastated by noise. For a moment a sheet of flame concealed the vehicle. Then it was revealed, shattered into burning, smoking pieces. Everyone in it was killed—including the commander of the column, as the Maquisards later learned.

The French had struck the first blow, but now they had to

pay for it. The German troops attacked. Junkers Ju 88s
swooped over the Maquis positions bombing and machine-gunning.

The Maquisards dropped back into a wood, which gave them
some concealment from the air. The Germans attacked on
both sides in an attempt to surround it, but the French had
mortars and were able to hold them.

Soon after midday, more enemy troops were brought up
from Valence and the battle grew fiercer. They were supported
by a tank, but the Maquisards to their delight succeeded in
putting it out of action with a well-aimed mortar shell.

All the time, planes were flying low over the wood as their
pilots tried to note the exact positions of the flashes from the
French weapons and other signs of movement that could be
seen through the trees—and passed the information by radio to
the troops. Gradually the Germans were gaining ground on
each side of the wood, and at last the Maquisards had no op-
tion but to withdraw to avoid being surrounded. They left the
wood, hugging what cover they could, and, moving quickly
through La Rochette, they made across country for Cobonne to
the south, where it was hard for the Germans with their road
transport to follow. Remembering the fate of the wounded at
St.-Nizier, the French took with them the two who had so far
been hurt in the fighting.

As usual, the Germans took their vengeance on the village
that had harbored "terrorists." Soon eleven houses in La Rochette were in flames.

From the air, of course, the movement of the Maquisards
across the mountainside toward Cobonne was easy to detect,
even though there was plenty of cover in the form of beech
shrubs and bushes. Planes dived on them in repeated attacks,
their machine guns hammering.

Then suddenly the Maquis won another small success. Other
French groups posted near villages in those southern foothills

joined in the attack on the planes as they circled for their attacks. From a position near Gigors, ten miles farther up the mountain, a machine gunner opened up on one of the Junker Ju 88s as it turned for a second assault on the men who were trying to escape to Cobonne—and, to his astonishment, he actually hit it! With smoke streaming from its tail, the aircraft made for its base. But it did not reach the airfield. It crashed into the mountain—the Montagne de la Côte Blanche—near the village of Ourches. From there in the last moments, as the plane lost height, the pilot, Lieutenant Stefan Ulrich, would have been able to see the Chabeuil runway, tantalizingly close ahead of him. He died with all his crew as the bomber burst into flames on impact.

That night one of Constans' irritating signals of congratulations—but nothing else—came in, peeping in Morse, on Bob Bennes' receiver in the barn. "Bravo your splendid result reported the twenty-sixth [about the Isère Maquis attacks on the railroad tracks]. We are proud of you. Repeat my friendship and trust in you."

The next day, planes from Chabeuil were in action again. Descour had ordered fifty Maquisards to come to the Vercors from St.-Donat in the south and they had traveled in a little convoy of three trucks, passing on the way through the towns of St.-Nazaire-en-Royans and Pont-en-Royans, both close under the massif's western cliffs. Presumably the local Milice reported the fact because the two towns were selected for punishment by bombing. In St.-Nazaire a hundred and thirty houses were damaged in the attack, though no one was badly hurt. In Pont-en-Royans, where there was not so much damage to property, there were twelve casualties, including two children, who were brought up to Dr. Ganimède's hospital in St.-Martin.

That day, Descour signaled to Constans the results of the attack on La Rochette, reporting one dead and four wounded, and again asked for "action against Chabeuil airfield." Colonel

Zeller sent a signal, too: "Repeat request bombing Chabeuil airfield, east of Valence, already called for three times."

As Zeller testified at the Paris inquiry after the war, "Chabeuil became an obsession" with the Vercors leaders. As a threat, it was colossal, dwarfing all other dangers. They felt as though they were living without means of escape beneath an active volcano that was certain to erupt within days. For the fact that the Germans had not yet launched an air attack in strength on the towns within the plateau, limiting themselves to small operations in the foothills of the massif, was merely because they had not chosen to do so; there was nothing to stop them. The planes were at Chabeuil. So, too, were the bombs. Reconnaissance aircraft flew low over the Vercors towns and passes every day and aerial photographs must have provided the Germans with fairly accurate information about Huet's defenses. So why were they waiting? As Huet and Descour and Zeller puzzled over this strange restraint, the issue was also being studied in German headquarters in Grenoble.

CHAPTER 11

From his office in Grenoble Barracks, General Karl Pflaum, commander of the German 157th Reserve Division, could see the Vercors massif. Those enormous gaunt cliffs reaching away south into the distance were a constant reminder of the formidable task that storming the plateau was going to prove.

The 157th had been responsible for controlling southeastern France ever since the Italians had been withdrawn on the signing of the armistice with the Allies in July 1943. Since then "terrorism"—as the Germans styled it—had steadily become more violent and more organized—especially from the Vercors. However, the general had responded to the challenge and his division was now experienced in dealing with "terrorists" and well equipped to do so. It included a regiment of Alpine troops and two batteries of mountain guns and had the use of tanks and also of engineers for repairing sabotage damage.

The Allied landings in Normandy, and the national uprising that had coincided with them, had forced a change in the general's policy. Previously he had spread his forces across the large area he had to control—in some cases, in relatively small units. But after the invasion these were too vulnerable to attack by the Maquis and he began to consolidate his forces in strong groups, using mobile columns to execute punitive operations against the "terrorist" bases.

As an objective, however, the Vercors was in a class of its own and the general did not underestimate the problems inherent in assaulting it. The attack was to be the biggest operation the German army of occupation had ever launched against the French Resistance. Furthermore, Pflaum did not intend merely to take the plateau. He was only too aware of the guerrilla practice of withdrawing and reforming later, and he planned to destroy any possibility of the Vercors being used again as a Resistance base.

By the end of June the German general's plans were well advanced. Intensive reconnaissance, still in progress, had begun to produce a detailed picture of the plateau. Colonel Schwehr, who was in charge of the operation, had already concluded where the main weaknesses lay in the defense system: not in the main passes, though he would need to push the main body of his troops and transport onto the plateau through these, but in the high mountains of the southeast where there were no roads.

Schwehr spent a long time studying this wild territory on the large map of the Vercors in his office. In the arrow shape of the massif, the area he was studying was the east flange. In fact, ruled on the map, the distance from the ring road to the interior of the plateau was only about ten to fifteen miles, but this rugged terrain was all mountains and deep valleys. It contained Le Grand Veymont and Mont Aiguille, the Vercors' highest peaks, and the actual distance Schwehr's men would have to traverse, since much of their progress would be upward or downward, rather than forward, was probably more like fifty miles. Nevertheless, the colonel did not believe that his Alpine troops, his Gebirgsjägers, would have too much trouble advancing along the network of mule tracks or in fighting their way through the weakly defended passes in this area.

The basic concept of the assault plan was to get troops into the interior of the plateau as fast as possible. They would not have heavy guns, but they could attack the defenses from within and in this way make it far easier for the main column on the roads to blast their way through the passes. The first assault stage of the operation, therefore, was to be achieved by the use of airborne units and mountain troops.

There is nothing in the German records to suggest that Pflaum or Schwehr ever considered the possibility that the Allies might drop a force of paratroopers into the Vercors—which is strange, since this would have greatly prejudiced the success prospects of the assault. Perhaps they believed that they could act before the Allies, or maybe they discounted the whole idea since the Vercors was so far from the coast. In no other way, however, was Pflaum prepared to take any chances. The attack he was preparing was to be launched with no less than twenty thousand men—backed up by tank and armored divisions.

First, however, Schwehr needed more information—especially about the vital range of mountains in the southeast.

As the German Colonel Schwehr was preparing his attack in Grenoble, François Huet was working enormously long hours, both at his desk at the Villa Bellon and also on his motorcycle, roaring across the plateau between the passes, in an attempt to organize an adequate defense against the assault when it came —although it is doubtful if he yet foresaw the scale on which it would be launched. Certainly, engrossed as he was with the enemy, he had no time or energy left to involve himself with domestic disputes within the Vercors. Yet suddenly, on June 28, he was faced with nothing less than civil war.

The events that led up to the arrest of Eugène Chavant, the Patron himself, and of the counterarrest of Captain Geyer— poor Captain Geyer, whom no one in the top echelons of the plateau wanted even to talk to—were so bizarre as to be barely credible. There are still so many conflicts in the drama that the motivation has never been completely clarified, but certain facts are unchallenged. Some of these involve Vincent Beaume, Huet's Second Bureau chief.

Since Beaume was in charge of discipline and security, Huet had ordered him to take charge of the "wild men"—the *groupes francs*, who really did conform with the German description of "terrorists," although their motives were fiercely patriotic. The most important of these was the Groupe Vallier, who were famous throughout the Grenoble area for a whole campaign of imaginative coups. They had, for example, blown up the Milice headquarters in the Place Victor Hugo; they had destroyed a printing works that was producing propaganda wall posters; and, clad in stolen Milice uniforms, they had raided the Gestapo prison in the St.-Joseph sector of the city and released some comrades who were held there. They had exploded ammunition dumps, raided motor transport convoys, and shot German soldiers.

Then their fortunes had changed. In March their leader, Paul Vallier, had been killed in an ambush, and four days later his two main aides had died in a shoot-out with the Gestapo in St.-Nizier. The rest of the group, shattered and desperate for revenge, had consolidated and prepared to fight on, retaining Vallier's name in honor of their dead chief. Numbering about twenty men and three girls, they lived in a house just outside La Chapelle.

They claimed to have no leader, taking their decisions jointly, but when Vincent Beaume called on them to convey Huet's wish that they should come under the control of the Second Bureau he was confronted by a tall, lean man who looked a little overwhelming. For he had tried to dye his hair red in an attempt to change his appearance, but something had gone wrong with the coloring agent and his hair was now streaked with different shades of blond and henna.

Indignantly, the Vallier spokesman rejected Beaume's suggestion of control, insisting that the group had always taken its orders directly from Algiers, and abruptly ordered the Second Bureau chief to leave the house. When Huet heard what had happened he put the tips of his fingers together, nodded his head to indicate that he had heard, and passed on quickly to other matters. There was nothing he could do. He knew that if he ordered the arrest of the Groupe Vallier there would be a revolt.

Beaume accepted this situation until the next day, when, to his fury, he discovered that the group had abducted one of his prisoners at gunpoint from his prison at La Chapelle—a woman schoolteacher who was under pretrial investigation as a Milice spy. According to Beaume, the Vallier militants were impatient at his legal formalities and, convinced of her guilt, tried to torture a confession out of her by putting hot coals to the soles of her feet.

It was an extremely angry Vincent Beaume who returned to the Vallier house outside the town, this time with a large posse of gendarmes, and, in the name of the Military Tribunal of the Vercors, demanded the return of the teacher.

He was confronted by the man with the dyed hair, who insisted, "She's a traitor."

"Perhaps she is," answered Beaume, "but in the Vercors we now have the rule of law. Her guilt will be decided by the tribunal."

"Because of people like this, Vallier died," argued the militant. "You make me sick with your tribunals and your law!"

Beaume remained quite cool. "It's not your responsibility to interrogate prisoners," he said. "That's been vested in the Second Bureau. For you to act in this way can only diminish the immense prestige of the Groupe Vallier. Now will you please hand over my prisoner."

The Vallier man hesitated. He realized he was on weak ground. Through the line of command from Algiers, through Descour to Huet, Beaume was an appointed free French official. After pausing for a moment, he answered, "She'll be delivered to your gendarmerie later today."

"Unharmed," insisted Beaume, who did not yet know she had been tortured.

The other man nodded. "I'd advise you," he said carefully, "to see that she's put on trial without delay."

Later that day, the Vallier group delivered the girl by car, as they promised. It was their first move toward accepting that times on the plateau had changed, that some kind of organization was needed in the general cause. They continued to insist on their independence, but they agreed to co-operate with Huet and in due course served him with great loyalty. Later, investigations revealed that the schoolteacher was innocent.

Beaume had only just emerged from this searing confrontation to find himself involved with another militant in a strange drama that was to have far greater repercussions. "Little René" was not in the same league as the Groupe Vallier, but he had the same hankering for action. His name was a joke because he was, in truth, very tall. He dressed with melodramatic effect like a stage gangster, with a belted raincoat and a broad-brimmed hat pulled low over his eyes, and he always wore a couple of guns in his belt. He claimed credit for sixty-eight killings.

On the afternoon of June 27, René called at Vincent Beaume's office at La Chapelle and, on the pretext that Geyer wanted to see him at La Rivière, persuaded him to get into his car, in which two other men were already waiting. As soon as the vehicle moved off, René drew a gun and informed the astonished Second Bureau chief that he was under arrest. Furthermore, Beaume gathered, they were now on their way to Vassieux to capture Chavant, whom René believed to be attending an investigation in the schoolhouse.

In fact, Chavant was not in the Vercors that day, and at Vassieux, while René was out of the car, Beaume succeeded in escaping. But he was by now a very anxious man. For René was under the command of Geyer and, since both the Patron and Beaume himself were socialists, Beaume was convinced that they were targeted together as victims of a right-wing military plot. Geyer responded with alarm when he heard by phone what had happened and immediately drove over to La Chapelle to assure the anxious Beaume that he had never given such orders to Little René, who was clearly unbalanced anyway. But Beaume remained suspicious—especially in view of Chavant's experience the next day.

The next morning the Patron returned to the Vercors by way of Les Grands-Goulets. His car was stopped at a Maquis road block at Échevis, a hamlet halfway up the mountain. "Your pass, please!" said the sentry on duty.

Chavant did not have a pass, assuming in view of his position in the Vercors that it was unnecessary. However, there were now thousands of new arrivals on the plateau who did not know him, and the duty guard, who had orders to let no one proceed without a pass, was one of them.

"I'm Clément, you fool!" snapped Chavant. "I'm civil chief of the Vercors. Ask anyone you like in the village. They all know me."

The guard now looked even more determined to carry out his orders than he had before. He called his sergeant. "This man has no pass," he explained. "He says his name is Clément and that he's civil chief of the Vercors."

"Clément, you say?" queried the sergeant. "Is your name Clément?" he asked Chavant through the car window.

"Yes, of course it's Clément, you idiot!" shouted the Patron, who was now growing very angry. Unhappily, this only made matters worse, for all the posts had been warned to arrest a man named Clément who was suspected of being a spy for the Gestapo.

"I must ask you to hand over your weapons, please, monsieur," said the sergeant. To Chavant's horror, he was disarmed and conducted by motorcycle escort to the main control point farther up the road at Les Barraques. There the reception was no better. The officer of the guard insisted he did not know him, though Chavant was sure he did, and placed him in custody. On Chavant's angry insistence, word was sent to Geyer at La Rivière, and another officer who had long been on the plateau and knew Chavant hurried down to Les Barraques. He confirmed that the Patron was not a Gestapo spy.

All this took several hours, and naturally, since the men involved were under Geyer's command, the furious Chavant suspected that it was a conspiracy directed against him by this arrogant young captain, his old enemy.

Like Vincent Beaume, he could not quite see what the plot would actually achieve but, given the lawless mood that colored the whole plateau during those tense days, the possibility that the intention was a political execution did not seem completely out of the question. Both men, therefore, were very scared. Beaume had slept the previous night away from home in case of an assassination attempt. Now Chavant, when eventually he traveled to St.-Martin after his release, was escorted by a second car crammed with grim Maquisards, guns thrust through the windows, at the ready.

The Patron was badly shaken and was not satisfied by Geyer's explanation. He distrusted the story of the Gestapo agent who also had the name of Clément, and he was determined to investigate it further.

That day, Geyer and one of his officers went to lunch with a friend who had a house near St.-Julien. The journey from La Rivière involved passing through St.-Martin. On their way home, as the car entered the town, a couple of armed Maquisards stepped into the middle of the road and waved the driver to stop. The two officers were ordered to get out of the car and were conducted at gunpoint to one of the administration offices on the upper floor of the Hôtel Breyton. There they found themselves facing a tribunal under the presidency of a glowering Chavant, who, with his shoulders hunched and his gray eyes dangerous, that day truly did resemble a boar, as he was nicknamed. In his deep, rasping voice, the Patron accused Geyer of instigating a Royalist plot against him.

Geyer was so astonished by this charge that he could hardly believe the scene in which he was taking part. "That's absurd," he answered, "as indeed is this whole masquerade. Tell these men to release us at once."

"Oh no," growled Chavant, his eyes fixed on the fleur-de-lis badge embroidered on Geyer's tunic. "Look at that. Do you deny your obsession with the fleur-de-lis, the crest of the Bourbon monarchs? Do you deny that it's depicted on a flag on the wall of your office?"

"Of course I don't deny it," answered Geyer. "It's the standard of my regiment."

Meanwhile, Geyer's driver had raced to La Rivière with the story of what had happened. Immediately a team of Geyer's alarmed men set off in trucks for St.-Martin to release their commanding officer. Lieutenant Moine, who was in charge of the Senegalese, ordered them to start marching toward the town, since there was not enough transport for all of them. In turn, news of the approaching men reached the civilians in the town. When the first of Geyer's troops arrived in St.-Martin there was a defense force waiting.

In the square outside the Hôtel Breyton the two groups faced each other. Insults were shouted. There were threats, even jostling. One or two blows were struck. The only reason that a pitched battle did not break out was the lack of leaders—but there was clearly great danger that this explosive situation could flare into serious bloodshed.

It was at this dramatic moment that Huet arrived in the

square, having been hurriedly summoned from the Villa Bellon. He pushed his way through the crowd. "Lieutenant Moine," he snapped angrily, "you will order all military personnel to return to La Rivière at once. The rest of you," he declared to the crowd, "will disperse immediately."

After watching the reluctant withdrawal he went into the hotel and climbed the stairs to the room where the interrogation of his southern-sector commander was in progress. "I must insist, Clément," he said, "that these officers are released at once. I will personally conduct an immediate investigation into the whole distressing business."

Back at the Villa Bellon, Huet told Geyer to admonish his officers at Les Barraques for a tactless excess of zeal and ordered the arrest of Little René—but the gunman had disappeared and, although there were reports of his being sighted from time to time, he was never taken into custody. Vincent Beaume saw this as evidence that the military authorities viewed these strange events with a certain tolerance, and he still harbored a suspicion that there had indeed been a plot that had somehow gone wrong. In reality, though, Huet was probably just too busy to pursue the issue.

General Zeller drove over to St.-Martin that night to have a placatory drink with the Patron and asked Jean Prévost, whom he knew Chavant liked, to join them. "Perhaps," suggested Prévost as they discussed the sensitive matter of Geyer's fleurs-de-lis, "we should abandon regimental flags. Could not all units march under the Cross of Lorraine?"

Geyer would never have agreed to give up his 11th Cuirassiers standard but he, too, made a gesture of peace and extended an invitation to Chavant to join him and his men for a camp dinner at La Rivière—to which the Patron responded by accepting and even appearing to enjoy the evening.

The trauma of that dramatic day, however, was dwarfed by other events. The arrival of parachutists was signaled once more. There was skepticism in St.-Martin about whether they would truly arrive. "Here is the Trojan Horse" had become something of a slightly bitter joke among Chavant's reception teams following their abortive all-night wait a week earlier. But soon after midnight, the men waiting on the ground in the open country near Vassieux heard the first of the Hudsons, lit the landing lights, and flashed the identity signals. Fifteen parachutists—the American OSS combat team—jumped from the bomber. A few minutes later, as a second plane flew over the plateau, four more parachutes, bearing Major Desmond Longe and his SOE liaison team, opened and floated downward.

There was champagne waiting—and a welcome that would keep the tired parachutists up until the dawn was lightening the sky behind the eastern peaks of the plateau. For the people of the Vercors, who saw the new arrivals from Algiers as an advance party that had come on ahead of the main body of paratroopers, this was the best day they had known since the German occupation.

CHAPTER 12

In Algiers that day, June 29, Fernand Grenier, the Air Minister, was growing increasingly anxious about the slow progress of Operation Patrie. For still De Gaulle had not signed the documents needed to activate the project.

Repeatedly Grenier phoned the General's office, to be told each time "You will have them tomorrow," but he never did. By July 1, when he knew there was another meeting scheduled for the Committee of Action in France, his suspicions became acute that De Gaulle was masterminding some kind of political maneuver that involved his vintage squadron. The next day he was left in no doubts, for the committee issued a public statement: Colonel Billotte, a well-known figure in top French circles, had been ordered to create a special French force—designated Force C—to establish "an interior front" within France. "It will consist of paratroop units, the FFI, and air forces of which the composition will be decided later," said the statement.

Ever since D Day, De Gaulle had been determined that the role of French troops in Operation Anvil, the invasion of the south coast of France, should be far greater than it had been in the Normandy assault, where, because of its huge size, they had played a relatively small part. In fact, the Anvil planning staff had included a whole French army in the scheme for the attack —but De Gaulle sought more. His demand that the invasion forces should be directed by a French corps commander had been rejected by Sir Henry Wilson in favor of the U.S. general Alexander Patch, so this operation, too, only partly met his aims. What he wanted—and what he felt France needed after the humiliation of occupation—was a strong identity. Frenchmen should be liberating France, not just helping the Americans and British to do so.

It was for this reason that for weeks Jacques Soustelle had been working on the Caiman plan—known as Operation C—to drop a force of paratroopers into the French mountains, where they would be joined by large numbers of Resistance men and supported by all-French air squadrons.

Superficially, this seemed identical to the Vercors plan—and it may have developed from the same roots—but Operation C was not a military concept designed to exploit a unique mountain fortress. It was political—and, from this aspect, the Vercors was too far east.

The communists had agreed to co-operate with the General in fighting their common enemy, but already the conflict had started over who was to rule France after the war—the left-wing parties or the Gaullists. So the site that was marked for Force C was the Massif Central, the huge range to the west of Lyon that had none of the citadel advantages of the Vercors but was positioned in the middle of France. With a base in the Massif Central, the General would be well placed geographically to extend his influence throughout the country, to ensure that

Gaullists liberated as many towns as possible, or, at least, were close on the heels of the Allied troops who did so.

As soon as Fernand Grenier saw the announcement, he realized that he had been duped. The reason that the General had delayed signing his documents was that he wanted the Patrie squadron to be part of his Force C. And indeed the Allied headquarters files record that, two days before, General Marie Édouard Béthouart, De Gaulle's chief of staff, had called at the St. George's Hotel for a meeting with the U.S. major general Lowell Rooks, Sir Henry Wilson's deputy chief of staff. The French general asked permission to use some old planes they had to fly aid to the FFI in the Massif Central. He asked, too, if the Allies would consider releasing the French squadrons that were operating from Sardinia and Sicily—an adaptation of Grenier's suggestion to De Gaulle on June 26. Rooks was non-committal. He would, he said, consult the appropriate departments.

A few days later, De Gaulle finally severed Grenier's connection with Operation Patrie. He returned to him his documents of authorization with a scribbled note in the margin: "Not sufficiently detailed."

Grenier was not the only person now convinced that De Gaulle was playing politics. On July 10, in a personal message to General Rooks, Eisenhower himself warned that "the main preoccupation of Colonel Billotte [the commander of the projected Operation C] has been in forming a Gaullist political party in France rather than concentrating on defeating the enemy." Sir Henry Wilson signaled London that he regarded De Gaulle's idea of Force C as "of no assistance to [Operation] Anvil."

The situation in those first days of July, therefore, was that De Gaulle and his staff had killed Operation Patrie in order to reserve the planes for use as part of Force C in the Massif Cen-

tral. It is also a fact that there were French paratroopers standing by awaiting orders in Trapani in Sicily and at the Staouelli
base near Algiers—paratroopers that, according to testimony in
the Paris Vercors hearings, were so frustrated by their lack of
action they had coined a sarcastic nickname for themselves:
"Les Paratouristes." But they, too, were unlikely to be going
anywhere except the Massif Central.

Meanwhile, the crisis in the Vercors grew daily more acute,
with five thousand men awaiting the arrival of the expected
paratroopers, awaiting the Allied bombing of the enemy squadrons at Chabeuil, awaiting a massive German assault.

De Gaulle's concept of an interior front no doubt had much
merit, but without question he had approved the mobilization
of the Vercors massif at the end of May. And even if Colonel
Descour had responded prematurely to this approval, the
French authorities in Algiers had been fully informed about
the critical situation of the people on the plateau for more than
three weeks. Surely, at the very least, Descour and Huet should
have been warned that no paratroopers would be coming for
more than a month—if they came at all. Surely some attempt
should have been made to help them extricate themselves and
the Vercors population from their dangerously exposed position. Francis Cammaerts, for example, believes that it would
have been possible to evacuate the whole plateau by moving
both residents and fighting men to the higher Alps. No one in
Algiers, it seemed, gave the problem much thought.

By July 6, however, the struggle between Churchill and the
U.S. chiefs of staff over whether there would be a southern invasion at all was over. The British were overruled by the senior
partner in the alliance and Eisenhower formally ordered Sir
Henry Wilson to proceed with the operation—offering him all
the facilities he needed from the West European Theater. In a
bitter note to General Hastings Ismay, the chief of staff in the
Cabinet, Churchill said, "I hope you realize that an intense im-

pression must be made on the Americans that we have been ill-treated and are furious. Do not let any smoothings or smirchings cover this fact. . . . The Arnold, King, Marshall combination [the U.S. chiefs of staff] is one of the stupidest strategic teams ever seen. . . ."

However, for the men and women in the Vercors who knew nothing of this high-level conflict, the question still remained: Could they hold out until the troops landed on the beaches of the South of France?

In the Vercors, as soon as the parachutists had been given the chance of a few hours' sleep, Huet held a conference with them in the Villa Bellon. He was as pleased as everyone else on the plateau that they had arrived, for although they were hardly a regiment of paratroopers, Major Desmond Longe and his liaison Mission Eucalyptus would give him direct radio contact at a relatively senior level with headquarters in Algiers and London—not only with the French but with the American and British commanders whose hands were on the levers of power. The OSS team was a highly trained combat unit, well equipped with weapons of which he had high hopes.

"When may we expect the paratroopers we've been promised?" Huet asked as soon as all the introductions had been completed, only to be met by blank faces. In the briefing sessions in Algiers there had been no mention to Longe or the Americans of paratroopers. "And the invasion of the south coast?" Huet queried. Again, he was given no adequate answer. They knew an invasion was being planned but had not received the impression that it was imminent.

"Then we must proceed as best we can," said the colonel, surveying the new arrivals.

Desmond Longe was an exceptionally tall man of twenty-seven who wore a military mustache and, unlike Francis Cammaerts—who worked for a rival section of the SOE and as a secret agent often dressed as a civilian—had arrived in British battle dress. His group consisted of two radio officers, a Frenchman and an American, and an English second-in-command, who was also a close friend, Captain John Houseman. Two other French officers were to join the team in a few days' time.

The American, Andre Paray, was of French extraction and, since he spoke the language fluently, also served as an interpreter for Longe.

The landing of the mission had not been very successful. Longe had been unable to stop himself swinging beneath his parachute and had hit the ground so hard that he had broken his dental plate, hurt his head, and dislodged a vertebra in his neck. Paray ended up on a rocky road with his feet thrust through a barbed wire fence and his right hand, vital for tapping out signals, badly torn.

To cap it all, the driver of the car who had been assigned to transport them to Vassieux became so expressive with his description of experiences on the plateau that he had driven into a ditch and overturned the vehicle. They had to clamber out of the windows, feeling, after two accidents, like nothing less than the welcome, with hugs and kisses and constantly refilled glasses of champagne, that awaited them at Vassieux.

The OSS team of eleven Americans and four French Canadians was led by a very young southerner—First Lieutenant Vernon Hoppers from South Carolina—with a Texan, also a first lieutenant and equally inexperienced, named Chester Myers, as second-in-command. The team had been training in the Mediterranean for six months, but this was their first operation. Their briefing was to tutor the Maquis in the use of the weapons that were being parachuted to them, to try to prevent them acting prematurely—although they were now rather late for this—and to provide a boost to the morale of the people of the plateau, since it had at last dawned on someone in Algiers that they "were getting discouraged, feeling that they had been forgotten."

In this last aim, there was no doubt about the success of the new arrivals. The surge of morale on the plateau was overwhelming. As they were driven to Huet's conference at St.-Martin, under the escort of Narcisse Geyer, they were mobbed as they passed through La Chapelle. The crowd stopped the cars, presented them with flowers, and submitted them to joyous and extravagant hugging and kissing, which both Hoppers and Longe found embarrassing.

The two men were astonished, too, at the situation in the Vercors. They had both arrived expecting a few scattered camps of disorganized Resistance men. As Hoppers put it in his official report, knowing nothing yet about the Groupe Vallier or Little René, he discovered that the Vercors "was no longer a Maquis headquarters but the headquarters of a republic with an organized army of 5,000 men." With wonder, he described how the plateau was divided up into sectors with a commander responsible for the defense of each.

The false idea about the Vercors of Longe and Hoppers only reflected that of headquarters. Even though signals had been dispatched daily from the massif giving the precise position with exact numbers of fighting men, there was a strange failure in Algiers to comprehend it.

Huet's briefing of the new arrivals at the Villa Bellon lasted all day—so Paray reported. Standing beside a large map of the Vercors in the sitting room of the villa, which served as an operations room, the colonel explained his defense system. Smoking all the time—Camels, an unexpected bonus presented by the Americans—he outlined the various areas of command, described the nature of the huge massif, and detailed his enormous range of problems. "The Boche attack us somewhere almost every day," he declared. "Mostly they're not very determined. They're testing our defenses. They're bombing the

villages in the foothills to discourage them from giving help to
the Maquis. Up here on the plateau they haven't bombed us
yet, but reconnaissance planes fly over the area constantly and
it can only be a matter of time. Probably they're holding back
until they're ready to launch their main assault on the ground."

"You're convinced they're going to attack?" asked Longe.

"Without question," answered the colonel. "We have intelligence reports every day. Clearly they cannot allow a Free Vercors to remain unchallenged. Its effect on French morale is
enormous. That's why our numbers are growing all the time.
According to our information, the Boche are moving troops
north from southern areas. Aircraft are being massed at Chabeuil—which, as you can see"—he tapped the map—"is very
close. Repeatedly we've asked for the airfield to be bombed.
We've been promised that it would be, but so far nothing has
happened and all the time more planes are being flown in.

"All our men are now armed but only with light arms—Stens
for the most part, and a few light machine guns. We are in desperate need of heavy weapons—especially mortars, which are
vital for holding the passes."

Huet spoke of his men—mostly young, many still in their
teens, few with any military experience. "They can fight hit-
and-run actions," the colonel went on, "but they find it hard to
stand up to combat for a sustained period. We lack almost
every item of equipment you can think of—blankets, raincoats,
boots, warm clothing. As you've discovered, it's cold at night
up here in the mountains even in summer. Many of the men
still have no shoes. They're forced to make moccasins out of
parachute silk. It's not the best way to fight a modern army like
the Wehrmacht."

Huet outlined his defense plan. He spoke of his immense
line, in all some forty miles, and the problems of holding the
passes—not just the main ones, but also the small cuts in the
mountains. He talked of his engineers, who had mined the

approaches, especially in the woods, and had made plans to blow up the tunnels and such important bridges as the Pont de la Goule-Noire when the attack came.

At one stage, Longe asked him, "If you got all the equipment you need, how would you rate your chances of holding the plateau?"

Huet hesitated for a moment. "I think," he said, "providing we got the equipment, we could fight off a division—say ten to fifteen thousand men. If they come at us with more than a division, well . . ." He broke off, so Paray reported, and forced a wry smile. "Then I think it will be dubious."

Huet invited the officers of both teams to take their meals with him in the mess at the Villa Bellon. Hoppers, however, politely declined. He wanted to keep his unit compact and independent, a little apart if possible from the French forces. Huet appeared to understand this, and the American lieutenant was provided with a house at Tourtre, a hamlet about two miles from St.-Martin, where the officers and men lived together. Responding in kind, after learning that the Vercors commander was a coffee addict, Hoppers presented him with some genuine product. It was the first time Huet had been able to drink real coffee, instead of ersatz, for four years.

Longe and the officers of his mission accepted Huet's offer to join his mess and were fascinated to witness the formal dinners, with the toasts and traditional ceremony, that were enjoyed every day in this remote threatened outpost in the mountains. They were allocated a cottage in St.-Martin. Andre Paray, needing higher ground for his radio antennas, took over a loft of a cattle shed—which was often full of cows—at a farm above the town. His first action, as soon as he got his set working (it had been damaged in the parachute drop), was to transmit the list of equipment Huet needed and request that it should be dispatched without delay—in addition, of course, to a plea for the bombing of Chabeuil.

Four days later, a signal about Chabeuil came in from Colonel Constans in Algiers. Allied aerial reconnaissance, he said, could trace only ten aircraft on the ground at the airfield. At Rang-des-Pourrets, the anger that this produced in Zeller and Descour was so deep that they truly felt helpless. Quite clearly no one in Algiers understood the danger that faced the people of the plateau. They had already said repeatedly that most of the planes were camouflaged in the woods surrounding the airfield, so obviously they would not be detected by cameras from the air. General Zeller signaled back in sarcastic tones: "Regarding the bombing of Chabeuil, which has been requested at least six times between June 23 and July 3, this is the reply we get . . ." and he repeated Constans' message word for word in despair before demanding he should be permitted to fly to Algiers—presumably to enable him in person to shake some sense of reality into the heads of the headquarters staff.

For once, Constans answered immediately. The RAF would be bombing the airfield, he said, but the "FFI must consider planes dispersed around airfields as targets" for attack on the ground.

By then a desperate Huet was already working on a plan to attack Chabeuil from the Vercors. It seemed an ideal task for young Vernon Hoppers and his OSS combat team—and Hoppers had eagerly accepted the assignment. The day after his arrival on the plateau, while his men were sent in pairs to give weapons training to the civilians, he and one of his corporals had driven to the airfield perimeter on a reconnaissance trip.

The next morning, he took the whole unit, together with eight Maquisards, who knew the country. On the way, however, they were tipped off that a small German convoy of an armored car and two troop-carrying half-tracks was on its way up the road from Chabeuil to La Vacherie, a small town in the Vercers foothills.

Although Hoppers was under no orders to attack Germans, he could not resist the temptation to stage an ambush and positioned his men on a high bank. As the German vehicles passed beneath them, they tossed grenades into them and opened up with Sten guns. The first two trucks were blown to pieces with deafening explosions. The third was far enough back along the road to reverse fast out of danger and escape. All the same, it was not a bad strike. They had killed eighteen Germans and destroyed two armored trucks. "We wanted to save the flag on the lead vehicle as a battle token," Hoppers reported happily, "but the largest piece was only two inches square."

The OSS men spent the whole of the next two days surveying the perimeter of the airfield through field glasses, trying to work out a plan to attack it with the Maquisards who had been assigned to work with them. But as a target it presented enormous problems. First, it was quite big—about four miles wide by five miles long. Thirty-six of the aircraft were parked on the field itself, in three groups of bays, dug out of the ground and surrounded by bomb blast walls eighteen feet high, each group being in a different part of the airfield. Other aircraft were, of course, under camouflage nets in the woods on the far side of the field.

The Germans had anticipated attack on the ground. Defenses had been constructed in depth with heavy machine gun posts in relays. The entire airfield was a zone forbidden to the public and vigorously guarded by a total force of two hundred troops. Any attack, therefore, would have to penetrate this formidable cordon of protection before it could reach the targets that were widely dispersed in a vast open area where, since visibility was unrestricted, there was no cover.

Quite clearly, as Hoppers reported to Huet on his return, it was a task either for a major attack by hundreds of men—and the open ground made even that dubious—or for some clever sabotage operation. The Germans were conscious of this last danger. The passes of all Frenchmen working there were renewable every month and only after careful review.

Nothing was more urgent than the destruction of the planes at Chabeuil but, after Hoppers' report, Huet himself concluded that the only way of attacking it was from the air by low-level precision bombing. Meanwhile, he had other problems. Every day he received reports of enemy movement in one section or another of the vast line he had to defend. Twice during the past week, German columns had probed the Col de Gresse in the wild mountainous country in the southeast of the plateau. This enemy interest was puzzling to the colonel since there were no roads through these mountains that were suitable for vehicles, and to Huet the idea that the enemy might attack the plateau by means of a few mule tracks appeared so unlikely as to be impossible. He knew that, to assault the massif successfully, the Germans would need to get a great many troops onto the plateau, and he had planned his defense on the assumption that the enemy effort would be concentrated on the main passes, for this was the only way they could drive the necessary numbers through the Vercors' mountain walls.

Huet's five-thousand-man defense force was much larger than he had anticipated, but his line was extremely long and distribution of his troops needed careful calculation against the attack dangers—especially since the rugged nature of the terrain, with its few roads, meant that it could take hours to move men from one sector to another if reinforcements were needed. The colonel decided, therefore, that the tiny shepherd routes through the southeastern mountains merited only a handful of troops at each cut. But the thrust of the German reconnaissance in the area demanded an aggressive response to indicate that it was much more strongly defended than it really was.

On the day Hoppers reported to him about Chabeuil he had received intelligence that offered him the opportunity he was seeking. In two days' time a big German convoy of troop trucks was scheduled to travel along the ring road to Grenoble from Aspres in the south. It would pass close to the foot of this southeastern range. "Lieutenant," Huet told Hoppers, through one of his team's French Canadians who was acting as interpreter, "I want to destroy that column."

The next day, the OSS team—with the exception of the unit's radio operator, who was regarded as too valuable to expose to action—left the plateau in trucks, together with twenty Maquisards, and headed for the network of lanes in the foothills in the southeastern corner of the Vercors arrow. For security, they covered the last few miles to the ring road on foot. That night they all slept in an unused railroad station near the village of Lus-la-Croix-Haute just off the highway.

Hoppers planned to place his men on a thirty-foot cliff that dominated a three-hundred-yard horseshoe bend in the road— which he dubbed the "death trap." The idea, like many ambushes depicted in Westerns, was to wait until the column had passed into the trap, then to blow up the vehicles at the front and back so that the road would be blocked and escape would be impossible. At this stage the ambush force would rake the convoy with machine guns, bazookas, and grenades.

At seven o'clock the next morning the thirty-four men were in position, waiting concealed on the cliff above the road. Half an hour later they heard the convoy approaching. It came into view, an armored truck at its head, moving steadily into the horseshoe bend below them. As the men nearest to it watched anxiously, their fingers on their triggers, they could see that the convoy was made of various types of vehicle: a couple of buses, some open half-tracks, one or two trucks with canvas canopies.

Hoppers had placed one of his best men, a New Yorker named Sergeant Nathan Richman, at the north end of the bend with orders to block it at the precise moment that all the vehicles in the convoy were within the "death trap." The convoy slowed down to take the sharp bend and at first, since

Richman was on the extreme left and the column was concealed by the bend, he could not see it. He waited, his eyes at the sight of his bazooka. As the lead truck came into view, he followed it with his weapon, training it slowly left, resisting the impulse to start shooting. He had already marked the point where the truck had to be stopped—where the road began to straighten out from the sharp curve.

By now he could see some of the other vehicles behind it out of the corner of his eye, but the line of his sight was held steady on his target moving steadily toward the exit from the trap. As it reached the spot he had mentally marked, he opened fire. The range was close. A bazooka shell exploded the truck into flames and the burning vehicle slewed across the road—but it did not quite block it. The driver of the second truck tried to overtake the helpless leader, but his truck, too, was stopped by heavy machine gun fire.

Now, all the way along the line of the bend, men were firing or lobbing grenades and the noise, reverberating between the cliff faces, was enormous. The third truck and the fourth vehicle, a bus, were stopped by heavy fire.

Hoppers, however, had underestimated the length of the convoy—which was more than the three hundred yards of the trap. At the moment when Sergeant Richman opened up with his bazooka, the rear trucks had not entered the bend. The troops on board these leaped for cover, mounted a mortar and a machine gun, and launched a counterattack in which the small party of OSS and FFI men were outnumbered and outgunned.

For twenty minutes they fought on, shooting no less than three enemy teams off the machine gun, so Hoppers reported, but the mortar was better placed. At last, with mortar shells exploding all around them, Hoppers ordered the withdrawal.

A fall-back assembly point, deep in the mountains, had been arranged. The Americans, unused to climbing, found the going difficult, and the Frenchmen, who had lived in the area all their lives, helped them by carrying some of their equipment. They were on the move for twelve hours before they reached the rendezvous; when Hoppers conducted a check of the weary men, he found that, although there had been no OSS casualties, two of the French were missing. One had been shot dead during the battle, but the failure of the other to arrive was the cause of enormous concern that he might have been taken prisoner. The anxiety was not misplaced. When a party of men went down to Lus-la-Croix-Haute the next day to investigate, they found the body of their comrade. The villagers had been forced to watch while he had been tortured to death—as a warning to "terrorists." His eyes had been gouged out. The bones of his fingers, his arms, his toes, his legs had been shattered slowly one by one. There were twenty carefully placed bayonet wounds in his stomach and chest. When his body was brought up to the plateau, together with that of the man who had been shot, his face was so mutilated that even his brother could not recognize him.

The two men were given a formal funeral, in state. The coffins were brought from Dr. Ganimède's hospital to the graveyard by the little church in a procession led by Narcisse Geyer on his horse, followed by the controversial regimental standard with its fleurs-de-lis. He was followed by Chabal's BCA mountain infantry, his 11th Cuirassiers, and other units, including the OSS team, all moving in slow march, with their weapons reversed. The crowd of civilians was large, for in addition to those who lived in St.-Martin, many had come from other towns and villages on the plateau to pay their respects.

Huet, as the dead man's commanding officer, delivered an emotional tribute at the graveside. It was colored with the optimism of a man of faith for whom death was not a tragedy. "Be happy, not sad," he declared. "The ears of corn have ripened and the wheat has been harvested. . . . There, where your comrades have fallen at St.-Nizier or at Lus-la-Croix-Haute, the soil will be richer and the crop more prolific. From now on, the Germans must reckon with you, and they know it. Men of the Vercors, I am proud of you!" There was no simmering conflict this time between the civilians and soldiers. Everyone was deeply moved.

As the bodies were lowered into the graves, a squad of BCA men fired their rifles in salute. Le Barbu read the final prayers. And even though Desmond Longe was greatly touched by this ceremony in the little mountain town, he could not help smiling when the big priest bent down to pray. For as he did so, his short surplice rose a little up his back to reveal the belt packed with grenades.

The previous night more parachutists had arrived on the plateau—in a high cross wind that made it hard for the pilot of the Hudson to hold the plane on course. Fortunately, Captain Tournissa, the engineer under orders to supervise the construction of the air strip, reached the ground without mishap. But one of the four French lieutenants who came down with him hit the ground so hard that he broke his shoulder and had to be taken off by truck to Dr. Ganimède's hospital in St.-Martin.

Christine Granville, a replacement for one of Francis Cammaerts' assistants who had been captured by the Gestapo, was blown so far off course during her descent that a full-scale search had to be mounted for her. She was found eventually in daylight in the Forêt de Lente with a damaged coccyx. "Pauline," as she was code-named, was a vivacious dark-haired girl of twenty-nine who was Polish by origin and fluent in five languages. An expert skier and rider, she had been in the Resistance from the earliest stage of the war, beginning by operating escape routes out of Poland. Cammaerts was to find her an immense help and an invaluable companion.

For Huet, of course, Captain Tournissa was by far the most important of the new arrivals. Once the air strip was built and planes could land, heavy weapons could be flown in—as indeed could troops without the use of parachutes.

Vincent Beaume, as conscientious as ever, organized huge working parties to make the strip as soon as Tournissa decided the site—which the captain did within hours of his arrival, opting for the flat open country near Vassieux, where he had spent the night in a hotel. By the afternoon the labor teams were at work. They included a colony of Poles who had settled on the plateau before the war and some of the prisoners in Beaume's camp who volunteered to help. One of these was a German officer, an ardent Nazi, who had been captured by Resistance men in the plain. He always refused to answer Beaume's questions when summoned for interrogation. Instead, he would leap to attention, his arm outstretched, declaring "Heil Hitler!" Eventually Beaume had broken through the man's reserve by making him laugh. He still declined to answer questions but proved to be a keen and able worker.

Another useful group working on the landing strip was Beaume's Discipline Section. This was made up of a nucleus of teen-agers who had been sent to him on a charge of stealing eggs—a serious crime in food-deprived France. In view of their age and physical fitness, Beaume decided not to jail them but to use them. He put them in charge of Sergeant Major Bernstein, late of the Foreign Legion, who soon reported that they were making great progress. In the labor teams on the air strip they kept the work pace high and, with songs and humor, helped the morale of the workers as well.

On the first night, Tournissa signaled Algiers that work had already started on a runway, 1,150 yards long by 150 yards wide, that would be ready to receive aircraft in six days' time—by July 14. He suggested that Hudsons, instead of Dakotas, should be used for the first mission since they could land on a shorter strip, but within hours this proposal was countermanded by an order from headquarters: the runway must be big enough for Dakotas, since Hudsons would not always be available and were not as suitable, anyway, for the purpose required of them.

This was bad news because it meant that the strip would take longer to build—and time, as everyone on the plateau was only too aware, was running out. Obediently, however, Tournissa signaled back his compliance and Beaume scoured the plateau for more workers for the labor teams, who started digging soon after dawn and stopped only when it was too dark to continue.

Colonel Constans, anticipating the completion of the strip, sent a message offering to dispatch some American 75 mm mountain guns if they had anyone who could operate them. "If they had *anyone?*" queried Huet indignantly as soon as he heard about the signal. They now had an artillery regiment. It had no weapons, but the men were yearning for action— especially for the kind of action that, in those narrow passes, would enable them to stop the advance of enemy armor.

The effect of all this activity on the morale of the people in the Vercors was buoyant. Although Huet welcomed it, he also worried about it sometimes. One evening he told Chavant, "It's unreal of course. Our position is no different from what it was. Until we actually get heavy weapons—and some more trained troops—we'll never be able to hold the plateau if the Boche come at us in force, which they're obviously planning to do."

Chavant smiled. "You'll get your heavy weapons—and your troops." His memory of his visit to Algiers was still vivid and, despite the delays, he had not lost faith in the staff officers who had been so enthusiastic about Operation Montagnards.

As the days passed, as the time available to them drained steadily away, Huet believed it was increasingly vital for them to capture some VIP hostages. General Zeller had urged this

from the moment he had arrived on the plateau on the theory
that it might give them some leverage if the Germans retaliated
against the families of Vercors men on the plain. Now that an
attack on the plateau was far more imminent and punitive operations would almost certainly follow if it succeeded, leverage
seemed even more important.

Huet had assigned the task of obtaining hostages to Vincent
Beaume, who in turn had asked the Groupe Vallier to help
out, but after their conflict relations were not good between
them. So Beaume sought assistance from another militant
group who called themselves "Les Hommes aux Chapeaux
Mous" ("The Men in Soft Hats"). There were four of them,
all dressed like Chicago gangsters, with a cheerful audacity that
made them resemble the Three Musketeers more than a terror
group. Viewing the whole business of sabotage as a kind of
sport, they never took any security precautions at all and their
survival was a constant source of surprise to the Second Bureau
chief.

All the same, they worked hard to execute his assignment
to capture hostages, operating usually with one of Beaume's
officers. But somehow fortune was not with them. They
planned to raid a secret meeting of Milice chiefs at a big house
at St.-Marcellin, only to arrive an hour after the conference had
ended. They swooped on a senior Gestapo officer in Villard,
only to choose the wrong moment when he was surrounded by
SS men, and just managing to get away by car at full speed with
bullets hitting the metal. They tried to abduct from his home a
Romans professor, a close friend of the local Milice chief, only
to find he was out. By the time he returned, he had been
warned they were waiting for him and he was accompanied by
German troops. This was the narrowest escape the group had
yet experienced, and even their sense of humor temporarily
deserted them, but they succeeded in shooting their way out

and returned to the Vercors to report yet another failure to
Vincent Beaume.

Meanwhile, as hundreds toiled on the runway and Tournissa
spent hours every day peering through his surveyor's sextant,
Huet and Vernon Hoppers were planning more ambushes. For
although the operation at Lus-la-Croix-Haute had been darkened by the shocking tragedy of the tortured man, it had been
a great success in military terms. They had killed sixty Germans, severely wounded another twenty-five, and destroyed a
number of vehicles. Huet now planned to set up a special ambush force, and since Hoppers had staged two successful operations within a week of his arrival, he was clearly the right man
to run it. His men were allocated to various French units to
give special training in OSS ambush techniques.

At the same time, the raiding of the plain from the plateau
was intensified. Some of the coups were daring in the extreme,
some were bizarre, some produced vital hauls. When information reached Huet from the railroad men at Crest that a train
of food for German troops was coming through, he gave orders
for it to be derailed outside the town by men of Geyer's headquarters at La Rivière. As a result, thirty tons of sugar as well as
a carload of tobacco were brought up to the plateau.

Then poor Desmond Longe was having trouble with the dental plate he had broken when he landed badly in his parachute
drop. There was a dentist on the plateau who explained that
the plate would be simple to mend, but that he had no cement.
So a raiding party was sent down to get some from the German
Dental Center in Romans. A few days later, Longe's plate was
returned to him repaired and tied up with blue ribbon.

Then there was the strange attack on the gendarmerie at St.-
Marcellin, on the ring road to the northwest of the massif. All
the gendarmes at the post wanted to join the Vercors forces,
but they feared reprisals against their homes and families. So,

obligingly, Huet gave orders for the police station to be attacked and its occupants taken by force.

Captain Tanant, Huet's chief of staff, organized a raid on a warehouse in Grenoble where he knew many uniforms were stored. The raiding party was stopped on the way back at a German road block, but, after routine questioning, was allowed to continue.

Uniforms had suddenly assumed great importance. This was partly psychological, a desire that had grown from the whole concept of the Vercors as a base for aggressive action. The civilians, too, began to feel a little shabby beside the soldiers, who were becoming smarter every day. It did not really matter what uniforms they wore. Jean Prévost's men, for example, were all dressed as police.

The traditional ritual of the meals in the officers' mess in the Villa Bellon became more elaborate. Every night at dinner, Huet, in his seat at the head of the table, would call for silence —so Desmond Longe recalls—and propose the regimental toast that BCA officers had been drinking to for more than a hundred years: *"Gloire et honneur à ce cochon—qu'il en crève."* It was a mocking gesture to the enemy. "Glory and honor to the swine—may it choke him!" And his officers would bawl back, *"Gloire et honneur à ce cochon—qu'il en crève!"* and raise their glasses to their lips. "It was so formal," comments Longe, "so much a tradition of a base regimental headquarters that it was sometimes hard to believe that we were living on a remote Alpine plateau in grave danger of imminent attack, that the planes at Chabeuil only five minutes' flying time away could blow all those pretty little Vercors towns out of existence at any moment the German commanders felt inclined to give the order."

CHAPTER 13

In Algiers, during those first two weeks of July, the Vercors had acquired a new ally who was fully alert to the danger faced by its people. He was General Gabriel Cochet, who from July 15 was to be responsible to General Koenig in London for FFI operations in this Southern Sector of France—at least, he was in theory. For the powerful Jacques Soustelle had little time for Cochet and, although he acknowledged his technical position, he tended to ignore him—as indeed did the other Soustelle men such as Colonel Constans.

In fact, Cochet now had no jurisdiction over the Vercors. For the line dividing the Northern and Southern sectors of France passed *through* the massif, roughly along the course of the Gorges de la Bourne. When this absurdity was at last realized, for everyone accepted that the homogeneous nature of the Vercors demanded single control, General Koenig ruled that the plateau should be included in the Northern Sector that he administered personally from London—which was just as absurd, since the FFI leaders there were directed and supplied from Algiers. So Cochet, alert as he was to the Vercors' danger, ignored Koenig's order.

In addition, therefore, to all the other menaces faced by the Vercors, another adverse factor in its fortunes was developing: a quarrel between two generals about which of them commanded the massif.

When Koenig found out that Cochet was not obeying his ruling about the plateau, he sent him a sharp signal reminding him that all orders concerning the Vercors were to emanate from London. When this did not appear to have the desired effect, Koenig sought the aid of Soustelle, who promptly issued an instruction to all senior officers within his command orbit, including Colonel Constans, that they were to accept no orders from General Cochet concerning the Vercors.

This feuding was highly dangerous to Huet and his threatened force, who already had problems enough. Cochet, however, persisted in striving in Algiers to get aid for the Vercors—and, in particular, in pressing the Allied High Command to bomb Chabeuil. At the end of June he had sent a note to the American general Benjamin Caffey, the Allied officer in charge of special operations, emphasizing the number of requests received for bombardment of the airfield. At headquarters everyone believed that one raid had already been carried out on Chabeuil resulting in the destruction of eight aircraft and a fuel store—although, in fact, the aircraft must have attacked some other airfield, for no bombs had fallen at Chabeuil.

On July 11 Cochet had a long meeting with Caffey to urge more bombing, for quite clearly the first raid had not achieved enough. The U.S. general was responsive, for he, too, was very anxious about the Vercors. Aerial reconnaissance had just revealed that the Germans were moving forces north toward the plateau. "It looks as though the Vercors is the target," he told Cochet.

Then Cochet left Algiers for Corsica, the headquarters of the Mediterranean Allied Air Force Command, with more than five thousand planes under orders. He was determined to get more air support for the Vercors and other Resistance enclaves. On July 14 he sent a personal signal to De Gaulle confirming that the Allied commanders had agreed to provide the necessary air support. One or two details, however, still remained to be ironed out. By then, as far as the Vercors was concerned, there was so little time left that the new arrangements were academic.

One important event had occurred on the plateau in early July: the Vercors had become respectable. It had been given formal recognition as a sovereign state by De Gaulle as the President of the French provisional government. And, being a state, it naturally had a head of state, equipped with official powers.

This somewhat Ruritanian concept was brought into being by Yves Farge, one of the most famous Resistance chiefs in the South, who had been largely responsible for the acceptance of the whole idea of Operation Montagnards by the underground movement directed from London. Farge, too, had now acquired official status. He was one of the commissaires de la République, appointed from Algiers as civil chiefs of the various regions into which France was divided. At this moment, when most of the country was still under German control, these commissaires remained working underground, but they would, of course, assume their functions openly as soon as their territories were liberated.

Farge had been placed in charge of southeastern France, the same area in which Zeller was military commander, just as

Chavant was civil chief of the plateau while Huet was in charge of its defense.

Like Zeller and Cammaerts and Descour, Farge planned to set up his headquarters in the Vercors, and his arrival on July 3 was eagerly awaited. Like so many others, he thought of the Vercors as the home of a few Maquis camps—as it had been the last time he had visited the plateau. He was surprised, therefore, to see the military presence at the road blocks in the passes and astonished on arrival at Rang-des-Pourrets to find fifty-three Senegalese, in full uniform, formed in ranks as a guard of honor to receive him. A young officer, with his sword drawn, stamped up to him and invited him to inspect the guard—which Farge did with some embarrassment since, unaware of the new situation, he was carrying a bundle of dirty laundry under his arm.

Farge was a middle-class revolutionary—a poet and painter, similar in many ways to Prévost, except that he was more political in motivation. He knew Chavant well and the two men greatly admired each other. When Chavant greeted him, his gray eyes mocked as he said, "So it's Monsieur le Commissaire de la République now, is it?"

In the name of the French government, Farge established the Free Republic of the Vercors and created a Committee of National Liberation that, under the presidency of Chavant, would govern it.

The new committee would, in fact, sit in the same schoolroom in St.-Martin where previously Chavant and his comrades had administered the plateau, but it would take itself a good deal more seriously. It would have ministers—such as Father Johannes Vincent, who had so anxiously supervised the first meeting between Chavant and Huet. He was to be the Minister of Justice. There were plans for issuing postage stamps of the Free Republic of the Vercors and even of minting coinage, although these last projects were curbed by a lack of production facilities. The eager Vincent Beaume even started a newspaper under the title *Vercors Libre*.

As for Chavant, the socialist victim of alleged military plots, the first act he took in his new formal role as President was to send a message to General de Gaulle affirming the allegiance of the Vercors to the French provisional government in Algiers.

The new republic was officially established in yet another parade in St.-Martin's little square. The members of the Committee of National Liberation stood together under the old lime tree while Yves Farge declared the creation of the republic. Then Chavant stood up, his eyes shining, to issue his formal declaration as the ruler of the plateau that would be displayed later in posters in all the Vercors villages.

"People of the Vercors," he declared in his thick, strong voice. "Today, the third of July, the French Republic is officially restored in the Vercors. From today, the decrees of the Vichy government are abolished and all the laws of the [former] republic are restored. . . .

"Our plateau is in a state of siege. The Committee of National Liberation, therefore, asks the people to do everything possible, as it will itself, to help the military commander . . ." He paused and looked at Huet, who was standing rigid in his uniform, showing no overt response to Chavant's words. ". . . to help the military commander," the Patron continued, "who has the crushing responsibility of defending us against a barbarous enemy.

"Citizens of the Vercors, it is in *your* home that our great republic is reborn. We can be proud of it. We are certain you will fight for it."

Again he paused. Then he shouted, *"Vive la République Française!"* Immediately the crowd of soldiers and civilians in the little square responded with a roar, *"Vive la République Française!"*

"*Vive la France!*" cried Chavant. "*Vive la France!*" they echoed.

"*Vive le Général de Gaulle!*" declared the Patron. "*Vive le Général de Gaulle!*" they yelled and the sound of their voices echoed back across the lush valley below the town from the sheer craggy sides of the Roche Rousse.

Huet stood up to respond to the Patron's generous appeal to the civilians to support him and assured them that the Army would do its duty to the best of its ability. There was the usual parade led by the mounted Narcisse Geyer, and afterward dinner at the Hôtel Breyton, at which Yves Farge sat between Chavant and Huet, as the guest of honor.

The creation of the Free Republic of the Vercors as a kind of sovereign state touched the pride of civilians and soldiers alike and gave them a sense of great common purpose. Shortly afterward Huet fanned this new spirit by a declaration that, in effect, co-opted everyone into the Army. There were no longer to be any civilian companies. There were just six traditional regiments, with their standards flying. Some of the old Maquisards grumbled, of course, but even they began to respond to the new atmosphere.

Meanwhile, Beaume's problems with his prison camp were growing. The sheer number of inmates was beginning to produce conditions of overcrowding, and Beaume ordered one of his officers to find a new site—a site, what was more, the Second Bureau chief ordered, that was remoter than La Chapelle, for he knew the Germans would attack soon.

As was seen with the kidnapped woman teacher, the women prisoners who were accused of collaboration were more resented than the men. One of them had been a night club singer in Grenoble and was reported to have socialized regularly with German officers. But the charges against her were imprecise and Beaume kept her in the camp more on hunch than on good legal grounds.

Then he arrived one morning in his office in La Chapelle to discover that a girl named Mado, a waitress from Romans, had been brought into the prison during the night. Beaume was furious, for everyone knew that she was the mistress of one of the local Milice chiefs, a man named Arnaud who was greatly feared. Sure enough, by midday news reached the plateau of Arnaud's response to the capture of the girl. Orders had gone out for the arrest of the wives of six men, including Beaume himself, who were known by the authorities to be in the Vercors. These women were still living in the plain, and fortunately they had all been warned in time to escape, but the clear fact that Mado's powerful lover was determined to retaliate made her a dangerous liability, badly though the Vercors needed hostages.

Beaume, with his own wife in danger, had as good a reason as anybody for setting the girl free, but the decision was not easy. The men who had captured her had ignored the most important of his strict security rules: all prisoners brought to the plateau must be blindfolded.

Because her eyes had not been covered, she had had ample opportunity to see the whole military setup in the Vercors. Also she had recognized many of the men from Romans in La Chapelle and had learned from other prisoners vital information about conditions on the plateau. "It's too dangerous to release her," Beaume insisted when the husbands of the threatened women came to see him. But they complained immediately to Huet, and later that day Pierre Tanant phoned Beaume and ordered him to have her escorted back to Romans. Beaume feared the results of this decision, which he believed would have imminent repercussions, but he had no alternative but to obey Huet's instruction.

Mado was not the only sensitive prisoner in his hands. A Milice leader who was particularly hated in the town of

Saulce-sur-Rhône in the south had been brought to the Vercors for trial. Following the new rules, he was to be tried by a five-man court, but the hearings were delayed pending the arrival of an attorney from Paris to defend him.

On July 12 Descour received a signal from General Cochet in Algiers warning that German troops were moving north toward the Vercors. "Please report any indications of this threat and provide attack details for air operations that are now being prepared." This kind of message from headquarters, following the signals that Bob Bennes had tapped out day after day from his radio shed, always exasperated Descour and Huet, even though they went through the motions of supplying what information they could from local intelligence regarding the forces that were threatening them.

The same day a signal arrived from General Koenig in London. It was lavish with praise of them but indicated that he had little idea of their true situation. "For three years you have prepared yourself for conflict in the rough life of the Maquis. On D Day you took up arms, heroically resisting all enemy assaults, and hoisted . . . the flag of liberation on a corner of French soil. To you, fighters of the FFI, to the brave people of the Vercors who are supporting you, I send my congratulations and my wish to see your success spread quickly through the entire territory."

The two colonels smiled at each other a little sadly as Descour finished reading out the signal. They had both been in the Army long enough to know what the other was thinking. It was good to receive recognition and congratulation from the commanding general, but it hardly solved the immediate practical problem.

That evening, July 12, Cochet's warning from Algiers of approaching troops was sharply underlined. They were accustomed to the sight of German planes flying over the plateau, studying the passes, noting the troop positions, and, over the last few days, photographing the beginnings of the runway. Always the aircraft flew low, their black Swastikas deeply etched on the underside of their wings—so low, in fact, that as they passed over the little valley below St.-Martin they were level with the Villa Bellon. Huet could see the pilots, goggled in their cockpits, as they passed by his office windows.

Once a German pilot sent a message to Huet that he wished to join his ranks and put his aircraft at his disposal. He would, he said, fly up and down the plateau three times on a certain day and wait for a signal indicating to him where he was to land. From his office, Huet watched him fly past the windows but no signal was given to him. It could have been a ploy, the oldest trick in the world, to get information. And even if it was genuine, Huet did not want him. He had no time for traitors. Anyway, there would be nowhere to land until the strip was finished.

At 8:00 P.M. on July 12, however, a single aircraft flew over La Chapelle and it was obvious that this time the pilot was not taking photographs or planning to desert. As the lookout gave the alarm, the plane dived toward the little town and dropped a stick of bombs on the main street. Vincent Beaume, who was responsible for the defense of the town, had ordered trenches to be dug to provide air raid cover. And as the plane turned to make a second run, the townspeople leaped into them. Another stick of bombs exploded. The plane swooped on the town a third time, now with its machine guns firing.

There were only four casualties. One of them was the town's grocer, who, despite a tourniquet quickly applied by the mayor, died on the journey to Dr. Ganimède's hospital in St.-Martin.

Vincent Beaume was certain that this air attack was a direct result of the release of Mado, the *milicien*'s mistress. Because she had seen several administration offices near the prison camp in La Chapelle, she had thought that this was the headquarters town. The pilot believed he was bombing the Vercors base.

The event caused a deep shock throughout the massif. It was the first air attack on a town within the heart of the plateau, the first sign that the Germans were almost ready for their assault, that the days of mild probes into the passes were nearly over.

CHAPTER 14

The next evening, July 13, German aircraft from Chabeuil attacked again, this time in greater strength. A few minutes after seven o'clock, when the sun had dipped below the heights of the Forêt de Lente in the west, a small squadron of Focke-Wulf Fw 190s flew low over the trees of the forest and dived on Vassieux. They killed five people, wounded fifteen, blew the windows out of the shops in the main street, and partly destroyed the church.

The planes flew on to La Chapelle and strafed the streets of the town. Vincent Beaume's duty defense team responded with three machine guns that normally would have been poor weapons for fighting attacking aircraft, but the Focke-Wulfs were flying so low that they made good targets. One plane wheeled away, heading back toward Chabeuil, black smoke streaming from its tail. Only one bomb was dropped, presumably all that was left on board after the attack on Vassieux, but it was a big one. It landed in the cemetery but fortunately failed to explode.

Later that night, Beaume pedaled over to St.-Martin on his bicycle for one of his regular meetings with Huet. For the colonel, now haggard with overwork—as indeed were most of his staff—his keen Second Bureau chief was clearly becoming more of a trial. He was efficient and worked hard, but the accounts of their meetings suggest that Huet was finding it increasingly difficult to control his irritation. For Beaume, once he was on a line of investigation, would follow it with the tenacious determination of a terrier.

Just recently there had been the case of the spy who Beaume was convinced was signaling important statistics to the enemy in a letter that had been spotted by the censors about the dimensions of rabbit hutches—which it so happened coincided with certain troop figures. Since the writer had signed the letter only with his first name, Beaume's investigators had not been able to track him down—or, for that matter, anyone who kept rabbits.

Huet, it seems, was thoroughly exasperated by the whole subject of rabbits and Beaume's keen sleuthing, yet the fact remained that Beaume's warnings were often very soundly based —as he demonstrated clearly during this evening meeting of July 13.

Two reports had come in from Beaume's agents on the plain that German officers had been heard boasting, "They'll certainly remember July 14 in the Vercors!" What was worrying Beaume was the parade planned at La Chapelle for the next morning. July 14, of course, was Bastille Day and the occasion was to be marked by the biggest display that had yet been organized on the plateau. It was to be attended by all the Vercors leaders and the site for it had been chosen more for its suitability for parading than for security—in flat, open country just outside the town with nowhere to take cover if German planes attacked.

"Our plans for the parade are common knowledge in the plain, Colonel," Beaume explained. "Royans have even asked permission to send a delegation to take part. Without question we must change the venue." Beaume wanted it moved to another site alongside a wood—which would, at least, provide some cover if this should be needed. The Second Bureau chief also told Huet anxiously that one of his men had come up onto the southern plateau through the steep woods at Valchevrière, which overlooked Villard from the south, without seeing any sign of any defending troops. The lane that passed through Valchevrière was an obvious attack point, for it gave access to the south sector of the plateau. Huet can have had no doubt that Jean Prévost, who was in command of the area, had the lane properly covered. He nodded in his usual noncommittal way and Beaume realized the interview was over.

Even though Huet appeared to be unimpressed, he acted on Beaume's suggestion. He gave orders for the La Chapelle parade site to be altered, and he sent Chabal and his unit to Jean Prévost, the sector commander, with the suggestion that they should be stationed at Valchevrière.

That night, on the eve of Bastille Day, Bob Bennes tapped out a signal to Algiers about the growing signs that the German attack could not now be long delayed. He reported the air attacks during the day, the fact that the German garrisons at Valence and Romans had been increased sharply, that there were now seventy planes at Chabeuil.

If the signal lacked the stridency of earlier messages, if there was no demand for paratroopers, it was because a certain sense of resignation had settled over Rang-des-Pourrets, despite the parachute arrivals and the emerging runway. For Chabeuil had still not been bombed, and by comparison nothing else truly mattered. It was against air attack that the plateau was utterly defenseless.

July 14 was a brilliantly sunny morning—as was fitting, for this was the first Bastille Day since the Allies had invaded France, since the Resistance had risen against the aggressors, since the creation of the Free Republic of the Vercors. And this was warmly acknowledged in a signal to the president, Eugène Chavant, from "your friends in Algiers," urging him "on this July 14, the festival of liberty . . . to give all those around you our admiration and good wishes"—which was pleasant enough even if it did not destroy the planes at Chabeuil or announce the invasion or herald the arrival of paratroopers or anything else that might do something to ameliorate the appalling danger that they all faced.

Beaume's intelligence about the German plans was accurate. The controversial parade at La Chapelle never took place, for by then the participants were all far too busy trying to survive.

The day started with another spectacular like that of June 25—and a noise that threatened to shatter the eardrums of the population. No fewer than seventy-two Flying Fortresses, the biggest bombers in the Allied air forces, roared low over the Vercors peaks, flying in rows of twelve, attended by fighter escort. Then, holding tight formation, they turned slowly and flew back over the plateau, the roar of their 288 engines seeming to vibrate the Vercors cliffs to their foundations. In every town and hamlet on the plateau, in St.-Martin, La Chapelle, Vassieux, Autrans, thousands of people were watching as the planes began to drop containers of arms and equipment from their bomb doors—more than eight hundred of them held by mushrooming parachutes in red or white or blue. Against the clear sky, the effect of the three colors was fantastic.

Later, at the Vercors inquiry in Paris, it was stated officially that the facts that the colors were those of the Tricolor and that the day was July 14 were coincidence, since the shade of the parachute merely indicated the contents of each container; but to the people of the plateau that sunny morning it was a dazzling national display that brought tears to the eyes of many and pride to the sourest of the Maquisards. Even Huet and Chavant, watching through the windows of their offices in St.-Martin, were deeply moved—although they knew the dangers that this immense delivery might provoke.

And it did. The reception teams raced in trucks out of Vassieux, intending to gather the containers and rush them under cover. For they had been dropped on and around the landing ground where the runway was being constructed. But unlike the last big daylight drop on June 25, this time they never had the chance. They had barely started before German aircraft were attacking, flying low over the half-constructed runway, their machine guns hammering. The teams of men loading the containers flung themselves flat to escape the stream of bullets. Desperately in between attacks they tried to cut loose the white parachutes in particular, since these were exceptionally conspicuous from the air.

At La Chapelle, while the enemy attack appeared to be concentrated at Vassieux, arrangements proceeded for the big parade—mainly because no one actually suggested that they should be stopped despite the German raid. The two previous bombings had been relatively brief and there was a kind of unspoken hope, therefore, that it would all soon be over. Enemy planes still hovered over the runway and dived with machine guns firing on anyone who went near the containers on the ground, but there was little bombing.

At La Chapelle's Hôtel Bellier, in a room decorated with the Stars and Stripes and the Union Jack as well as the Tricolor, a formal but early lunch began as scheduled. At one stage Vincent Beaume stood up, as arranged, to make a speech. He held the lapels of his coat, looked around the table expansively, and began, "*Mesdames et messieurs . . .*" An enormous explosion drowned his voice as the first bomb dropped on the town.

There was no rush to the door. On mutual impulse, everyone

just stood up and began to sing the "Marseillaise." The last note was lost in the noise of a second bomb. For an hour the attack on the town continued. Every time the planes dived on their bombing runs, the machine guns of the defense opened up on them.

The Groupe Vallier, in their house just outside the town, had three Thompsons lashed to the railings of the garden and fired at every plane that swooped over them. Then the aircraft began to attack the machine gun posts. The Vallier house came under heavy attack. Again the defense secured some direct hits and experienced a marvelous sense of elation as several planes streaked for home with smoke pouring from their tails.

That day, nowhere in the southern sector of the plateau escaped. Vassieux, La Chapelle, St.-Martin, Rousset, and almost every hamlet was bombed. As cars or people moved along the roads that connected them, planes swooped on them from the sky, raking them with machine gun bullets.

At St.-Martin, Desmond Longe and John Houseman, one of his officers, arrived for lunch at the mess in the Villa Bellon while planes were attacking the town. To their surprise, Huet and his officers were behaving as though they could not hear the explosions and the howling of the diving planes outside. The colonel sat at the head of the table as usual, chatting calmly. He did not, in fact, hold up his glass and propose *"Gloire et honneur à ce cochon—qu'il en crève,"* but he gave the company a number of other toasts to drink to.

Longe and Houseman watched the events at that luncheon table incredulously. Bombs were exploding all around them. Enemy planes were swooping past the windows of the villa so close that sometimes they almost touched it with their wings. And here was Huet offering toast after toast as though he were at a regimental dinner.

"Vive la France!" he said and all his officers responded with

"*Vive la France!*" and drank their wine—as indeed did Longe and Houseman.

"*Vive l'Angleterre!*" proposed the colonel, inclining his glass graciously toward Longe, at his side, and to Houseman, who was sitting farther up the table. "*Vive l'Angleterre,*" came the response of many voices.

There had to be an end to this, thought Longe, if only a bomb through the roof. There was the scream of a plane diving and the chatter of machine guns. Still Huet was unperturbed. He raised his glass again: "*Vive l'Amérique,*" he declared. "*Vive l'Amérique,*" they all rejoined.

Huet looked coolly around the table. For a moment he sat even more stiffly upright in his chair. Longe felt that this must be the moment to which the colonel had been building up. "Stuff," he recorded, "was coming down all round." "*Messieurs,*" said Huet, "*je vous donne . . . la victoire!*" And the word "*victoire*" was not hurried—it was slow and proud and harsh and even determined. "*La victoire!*" they all echoed, some of them trying to repeat their colonel's rendering of the last word. It was all very Gaullian.

Because of the persistence of the attack, several people began to prepare for the possibility that the Germans might gain the high plateau very soon. Dr. Ganimède, only too conscious of what the fate might be of wounded men, sent his most serious patients to Tourtre, the hamlet two miles from St.-Martin where the OSS team was living. This was concealed in woods off the main road and might escape enemy attention. Vincent Beaume, for his part, made plans to transfer his concentration camp to Les Drevets in the woods above La Chapelle. He had a new inmate: one of the pilots of the attacking aircraft who had crashed in the Vercors foothills on his way back to Chabeuil. He had been brought up to the plateau by local Resistance men.

Beaume also gave orders that the engineers should move the

telephone exchange to Les Drevets. The lines had been severed in the attack on La Chapelle.

All day the air attacks continued. In the evening when Francis Cammaerts and Christine Granville, who had gone to Die, drove up toward the Col de Rousset they were worried by the glow they could see in the sky above the ring of mountains. They soon discovered what was causing it. The Germans had set fire to both Vassieux and La Chapelle with incendiary bombs.

Chavant and Huet drove separately to both towns, passing the ambulances and trucks that were taking the wounded to the hospital in St.-Martin. The Patron, to whom the people of the Vercors were so personal a cause, was utterly shocked. In La Chapelle he stood watching the flaming buildings, listening to his friend Benjamin Malossane's account of thefts from the shops. It was behavior he barely understood. When he saw Vincent Beaume in the street, he flung at him a stream of Dauphinois abuse because his men had not policed the town better—which was unfair, for Beaume and his staff had all been working desperately hard to help people save what they could from the fires. Then Chavant wrenched his jacket off and joined one of the groups of helpers.

At Vassieux, Yves Farge stood inside the burning church, filled with a sense of wonder that transcended his horror. "I've never seen anything so grand, so beautiful as the flames that enveloped the roof, that took possession of the great wooden beams beneath it, that devoured and illuminated the choir stalls in a last but magnificent rite. We leaped out of the church into the square that lay before it. At that moment the whole roof collapsed. Millions of red sparks whirled toward the sky. . . . The inhabitants of the town, together with their cattle, were waiting, scattered over the mountainside."

That evening the two American lieutenants, Vernon Hoppers and Chester Myers, dined with Huet in the officers'

mess in the Villa Bellon. During dinner, Myers suddenly became ill with intense nausea and an extreme pain in his side.
He was rushed to Dr. Ganimède, who diagnosed appendicitis. "I can't operate tonight," the doctor told the lieutenant
through his Canadian interpreter, "because I don't have
enough light. So I'm going to pack your side with ice and I'll
remove it first thing in the morning—I hope before the air attacks start." And he did. When the American regained con-
sciousness from the chloroform, the only anesthetic the doctor
possessed in the Vercors, Ganimède showed him his appendix
in a bottle. "If we hadn't packed you in ice," he said, "it would
have ruptured." Young Hoppers was to miss his comrade, for
many decisions lay ahead for him. Meanwhile, of course, Myers
was one of the wounded, the most vulnerable group within the
Vercors because it lacked mobility.

That night of July 14, it was a very bitter Bob Bennes who
sat in the radio shed tapping out a sarcastic signal to Constans in Algiers. "Received daytime parachute drop fourteenth.
About seventy-two planes. Very successful. Have been machine-
gunned on the ground ever since departure Allied aircraft.
Thanks."

At midnight, Chavant and Farge attended a crisis meeting
with Huet in the Villa Bellon. All the senior officers and regional commanders were present in the room, which was thick
with cigarette smoke.

"Tomorrow," said the colonel, "this will continue. After
that—" He broke off before adding, "The ground attack must
come soon. I've decided that the time has come to call up the
sédentaires." The *sédentaires* were the men who normally lived
and worked in the Vercors—the farmers, shopkeepers, foresters,
the drivers of buses and trucks, workers in the electricity station
and the telephone organization. All had continued with their

normal occupations since June 10, but now they would be assuming their posts as fighting men.

"We've had intelligence today," Huet went on, "that the Boche intend to arrest all men on the plateau for the STO [the German labor corps]. They intend to start by taking those in Villard. Patron, I think we should forestall them and bring all the men up here."

"All?" queried Chavant. He knew that many would be unwilling to leave Villard. It was time for the harvest and there was much work.

"All, Patron," insisted the colonel. "If necessary by force. Certainly it must appear that force is employed, in order to protect the wives from reprisals by the Boche."

Before dawn a convoy of trucks headed down the road alongside the Gorges de la Bourne and drove into Villard. In the leading vehicles were Chavant, Farge, and Jean Prévost. Prévost's men fired their guns into the air, banged on front doors, and ordered the male residents at gunpoint to dress and get into the trucks. They broke the windows of the hotel and captured two Gestapo men who were staying there. They made the curé of the church start tolling the bell as an alarm.

Jean Prévost and his men rode the trucks on the route back to the southern sector until the convoy reached the turning to Valchevrière. Then they jumped off and marched up the steep road toward the woods, singing "Auprès de ma blonde." Prévost was at the end of the column. He turned and waved to Yves Farge, who was a close friend, and saluted with a grin— then followed his men on up the track. It was the last time Farge would ever see him.

Huet's ploy was unsuccessful. When the Germans arrived in Villard two days later and discovered what had happened, they told the curé he had exactly twenty-four hours to get the men back again or they would burn the town. Huet, gambling that they would honor their undertaking, complied.

On that traumatic July 14, the remaining two men of Desmond Longe's Mission Eucalyptus arrived on the plateau. Lieutenant Conus, a large, ebullient, bearded character, who in civilian life was a big-game hunter in Chad, drove up the road from Die with his radio operator. They had been parachuted into the Ain mountains, where a car had been provided by the local Maquis. Conus was a man of great wit and, as he was soon to demonstrate, enormous courage.

The Germans meanwhile were learning from experience and taking great care with the convoys they were routing up the road from Aspres to Grenoble. In fact, Lieutenant Hoppers and his OSS team were far too busy fighting off air attacks to plan any more raids and Huet himself was too absorbed with the gigantic problem of how he was to hold the main assault when it came to think of small harassing operations. Nevertheless, the next convoy of size that went up the N 75 was halted before it reached Hoppers' "death trap" bend in the road near Lus-la-Croix-Haute and the women and children from the village were made to walk in front and beside the trucks to act as a screen.

Meanwhile, as aircraft from Chabeuil were bombing and machine-gunning the towns and roads of the plateau, General Pflaum and Colonel Schwehr in Grenoble held a final briefing conference of the officers who would take part in the assault. The main reconnaissance was over and the colonel had most of the information he needed. He had planned the operation in extremely thorough detail and was now proceeding to execute it with deliberate and unhurried care. Already he had reoccupied St.-Nizier in strength. During the next days, troops and tanks would be taking up position all around the plateau—in forward positions in the foothills and on every access road—as the first stage of a series of concerted attacks.

Standing beside his large wall map of the Vercors, he outlined the strategy of the attack to the officers who would be directing it. "The assault," he said, "will start at 0600 from four main points." He indicated them on the map as he described them. "In the north from St.-Nizier, troops will advance with the aim of taking possession of all towns in the northern sector as well as the Col de la Croix-Perrin, from which the terrorists could threaten our supply lines. They will then attack the southern plateau.

"In the south, an armored column will thrust from Valence along the Drôme River for the town of Die, striking north from there to the Col de Rousset.

"From the east, a strong force of Gebirgsjägers will break through the mule-track passes of the mountains. From the west we will attack from Pont-en-Royans under a covering barrage of heavy artillery.

"Four hours after the ground attack has started from these four directions, airborne troops will be dropped in the area of Vassieux, here in the heart of the plateau." Again he indicated the town on the map. "Their orders will be to dominate the air strip as fast as possible, take the town, and control all access roads to it from positions in these four hamlets here where buildings will provide them with cover. Once they have established firm possession of this part of the plateau, they will fight their way north and south—to the Gorges de la Bourne and the Col de Rousset—to help our forces attacking from the exterior by putting pressure on the terrorists from the rear.

"At every stage of the assault, our troops will be strongly supported by aircraft."

The colonel moved on to the second stage of his briefing: the operation that was to be put into effect after the plateau was in German hands. His orders were specific. All exits from the massif were to be blocked and anyone trying to escape was to be shot. The Vercors was to be systematically searched and all terrorists exterminated. Men aged seventeen to thirty who had not belonged to the Resistance or sustained it were to be arrested. Houses that had served as shelter or storage for terrorists were to be burned; farms were to be left with only the minimum number of cattle necessary to maintain the native population.

Schwehr's officers had acted against terrorists several times now and they knew what was expected of them, but they had never before attempted so formidable or sustained an operation. For the process of the combing of the forests was to continue for weeks, was to extend to the highest mountains, to the thickest parts of the forests.

Schwehr displayed another map of the Vercors. On this all the water sources had been outlined. "Hiding men can live on very little food for quite long periods," he said, "but they cannot survive without water. Like wild animals, they'll be forced sooner or later to make for the rivers, streams, and waterfalls that are shown here on the map. They will probably do this at night, since it will seem safer in darkness. Our troops must be waiting for them—with flares that can be fired to illuminate the banks when the terrorists approach to drink. They are, of course, to be killed as they do so."

Schwehr was confident that his operational plan would succeed. The strength he was deploying was overwhelming. The sole element that could prejudice the result was the air strip near Vassieux, which was why he had studied aerial photographs every day to discover the progress made by the labor teams. Work had been greatly curbed by air attack but the strip was almost completed, almost ready for planes to land. If the Allies were to fly in trained troops before the assault, then Schwehr's success prospects would be greatly reduced.

The runway was also the sole element that carried all Huet's hopes of relief from Algiers.

CHAPTER 15

On July 15, as the first elements of General Pflaum's troops were moving into position to attack the Vercors, General Jean de Lattre de Tassigny, commander of the French army that was to take part in the invasion of the South of France, arrived at the Algiers office of the U.S. general Caffey to discuss the operation.

July 15 was the official starting day, the first in the countdown of Operation Anvil (now renamed Dragoon). Early in the meeting, according to the minutes that are among the Allied headquarters papers, Caffey mentioned to De Tassigny that General Patch, the corps commander, was intending to drop French paratroopers into the Vercors as part of the assault plan.

De Tassigny vehemently opposed the idea. "It would be far more effective," he said, "for these troops to be employed in the Massif Central. From there they could strike south toward the advancing invasion troops."

Caffey, of course, was fully aware of De Gaulle's high-pressure campaign for his Operation C in the Massif Central and indeed of the Allied commanders' coolness toward the project. He limited his argument, however, to the fact that pure logistics made the Massif Central impractical for this purpose. "The planes," he explained, "will be coming from Italy. The Vercors is within range, but the Massif Central is not. If your proposal were to be adopted, General, it would mean that the aircraft would have to land for refueling on strips within France, and who knows how soon after the assault this would be possible?"

Caffey's argument appeared to make no impression on the French general. "It would be practical between D+7 and D+10," he insisted stubbornly, content to postpone the operation for seven to ten days after the opening of the attack, providing it was targeted into the Massif Central instead of the Vercors. Clearly, by that time, much of the effect of the operation on the rear of the enemy would be lost.

Even this, however, was not practical. Supreme Headquarters, Caffey explained patiently, was loaning the planes from England for the operation on the condition that they were back in Britain by D+10. The timing, therefore, would be far too narrow to plan a drop in the Massif Central.

De Tassigny fought on stubbornly, but he had lost the battle. The irony in the scene is remarkable. Despite the plight of the Vercors, which had been mobilized on the direct order of De Gaulle, his most senior field general was now doing his utmost to prevent a landing of paratroopers that was an inherent part of the Montagnards plan. Meanwhile, of course, the French *"paratouristes,"* so vitally needed in the Vercors, still remained inactive and impatient at Staouelli and Trapani and the planes originally scheduled for Operation Patrie had still flown no missions.

It is clear, too, that hardly any of the military staff seemed to realize the stature of the menace that faced the Vercors—certainly not General Patch, who appeared to assume that the situation there would be unchanged by the date of his assault, nor General Koenig, who seemed to believe that their success in holding the plateau in free French hands would encourage other Resistance enclaves.

On that very day when De Tassigny met Caffey, one of Constans' colleagues in SPOC, the U.S.-Anglo-French co-ordinating organization for Operation Anvil, issued a report about Maquis-controlled territory. "Perhaps," wrote Lieutenant Colonel Stewart McKenzie, "the most powerful area of all is in the Vercors plateau. . . . Its strength is altogether about 6,000 men. They are organized into military formations of light and heavy companies. . . ." This after all the desperate signals from Bob Bennes, from Zeller, from Cammaerts, from Desmond Longe. Not one hint of danger, of the fact that without immediate aid they could not possibly hold out.

One of the few men in Algiers who truly did seem to understand the situation was General Caffey, who believed that day that he had done something to help. In a note to General Cochet, he said that the previous night seventy-four planes had bombed Chabeuil. Again, however, he was misled. For no bombs had fallen on that airfield. Once more, it seems, another airfield in the Rhône Valley was attacked in error.

In the Vercors that day, July 15, the Germans blew up the tunnel at Engins, one of the two roads from Grenoble into the plateau, and also the bridge over the Isère below Royans in the west. It was the first indication to Huet in the Villa Bellon of what the enemy was planning to do. Two of the eight exit roads from the Vercors were now completely blocked. A third at St.-Nizier was occupied by a German force that was growing every day. Field guns were set up on the edge of the charred town, facing toward Villard.

During the next forty-eight hours, the news of the measured German build-up streamed into Huet's headquarters in St.-Martin—most of it routed through Vincent Beaume but some coming from other sources, such as Gaby and Jacqueline Groll, who got off their bicycles and picked flowers as they talked to German soldiers without exciting their suspicions.

Mountain troops of the 157th Reserve Division had been ordered from Chambéry to Grenoble. So, too, had units of the 9th Panzer tank division. Enemy engineers were setting up a direct telephone link between German headquarters in Grenoble and St.-Nazaire-en-Royans on the west side of the plateau—presumably so that communication for joint operations from both sides of the massif could be maintained.

Horse-drawn guns had been seen crossing the Drac River at various points on the eastern side of the plateau. At Seyssins, below St.-Nizier, there was a battery of enormous 105s. In the grounds of a château at La Paillasse, just south of Chabeuil, was a tank division, camouflaged in the trees. At the Salle de Fêtes in Valence, three hundred parachute harnesses had just been delivered.

For Huet, as the picture of ever-growing threat in the reports was reflected by his staff officers onto the wall map, it became clear that their only chance of survival was centered on the air strip and the easy route it would open up for reinforcement, for action from Algiers. According to his testimony in Paris, this was nearing completion and, although there are no signals on file from Tournissa to Algiers during this period, there can be little doubt, in view of its crucial importance, that he warned headquarters that it would be ready for its first aircraft by July 21—which is what he told his impatient commanding officer.

As for Huet's other vital need, the destruction of the enemy air base at Chabeuil, the situation that he faced, as reports flowed into the Villa Bellon at St.-Martin of the massing German forces all around the plateau, grew more unbelievable every day. Still, Allied headquarters was viewing this target, which to the people in the Vercors seemed so simple an objective for such major air forces, with incredible timidity. In Algiers, General Cochet had been vigorously promoting a plan for an attack on Chabeuil that would include the parachuting onto the airfield of an infantry "shock" battalion. But Allied Air Headquarters, Cochet signaled, were still challenging the facts reported so many times from the Vercors. "Aerial photos taken recently show only twenty-five Junkers 88s on the ground. Air command doubts the number of seventy [as Bennes had signaled recently] and hesitates to launch an operation of this importance and danger for poor results. Verify your intelligence carefully. Reply quickly." The question was almost academic. For people without anti-aircraft guns, twenty-five planes were quite enough.

Despite the growing crisis, the legal machinery of the Free Republic of the Vercors had been in motion as though there were no threat facing the plateau. In the morning of July 17 a court of which General Zeller was president and Geyer was a member condemned to death the *milicien* from Saulce-sur-Rhône—despite eloquent pleading by an attorney who had traveled all the way from Paris to defend him. His execution was scheduled for seven o'clock the next morning.

That night, as Huet worked late in his office in St.-Martin, a delegation of leading citizens from Die, including the prefect of the town, called to see him. "We've come, Colonel," explained the prefect, "to ask you to suspend sentence of the traitor. The Gestapo warned us today that, if he dies, six residents of our town will be shot. His life cannot be worth that price."

Huet sat back in his chair, his hands together, fingers straight, their tips touching. As always, to his visitors he seemed impassive, unmoved. Their request presented him with a difficult decision. Was the execution of one traitor an adequate reason for six loyal Frenchmen to die? On the face of it, there could be no argument. On the other hand, should not the law, following a formal trial, be carried out? And, indeed, since this man was the object of great hatred, would Huet's orders be obeyed if he did cancel the execution? Would the *milicien* be lynched?

"I'll give your request the most careful consideration," he told the delegation. "You have my sympathy, but it's not as easy as it seems. There are problems. I'll do my best."

Uncertainly, his visitors left his office, and for hours he worried about what he should do. It was not until three in the morning that he phoned Beaume. "The execution is to be deferred," he ordered, "and I'm holding you personally responsible for the prisoner's safety."

Beaume was aware of the danger. The firing squad might well take the prisoner by force. When he spoke to the guards on duty at the jail, they made it quite clear that they would certainly not jeopardize their own lives for a "cur like that" if there was a determined effort by outsiders to capture him. So the Second Bureau chief summoned Sergeant Bernstein of the Foreign Legion and his Discipline Section of egg-stealing teenagers and entrusted him with the task.

That morning, July 18, the almost leisurely preparations of the Germans for attack progressed one stage further. Barriers were thrown across all roads to the Vercors that had not been blocked by the blowing of tunnels or bridges. Parts of the approaches were mined. Machine guns were positioned at intervals along the ring road so that their arc of fire could cover anyone trying to escape.

The next day, in the southeast, the enemy pushed a column up into the pass of the Col de Grimone, which dominated the hills overlooking Lus-la-Croix-Haute. This was not one of the usual probes. They planned to stay. It was a starting battle position. The pass was not high, but it was well positioned for a thrust through the routes in the bigger mountains in the southeast ranges.

Desmond Longe kept an almost hour-by-hour record of these dramatic days. "Air attacks continued with first light . . . we are all very very tired. . . . In the morning Hervieux [Huet] gives me the latest reports on enemy movements. Looks like we're in for it. . . . The enemy appears definitely to be closing in on us from all sides of this road and river triangle. I have a curious feeling of being boxed in. . . .

"More and heavier air attacks. . . . The battle is warming up and I try to decide what is the best I can do to prepare for any eventuality. I warn my mission to prepare their kit and to keep themselves in the highest state of mobility in case of a quick dispersal. . . .

"We have withdrawn our posts from down in the valley but our patrols are in constant contact with the enemy. . . . John and I work almost to a standstill getting off frantic cables to London, the encoding takes such hours. . . .

"Hervieux has declared Martial Law throughout the Vercors. . . . Guards against parachutists have been posted. . . . At 4 A.M. this morning I was with Hervieux when the air attack increased. He begs me to have Chabeuil and St.-Nazaire bombed. I do my best with cables to Algiers and London but as usual neither answer. Cannot understand their attitude as it makes our position so stupid. We are here to present the facts to HQ and they just don't reply to our cables. . . . We try daily and nightly to explain to the French here that London and Algiers are trying but the weather is against the Allied Air Forces, but they reply by pointing to a sky-full of Huns. . . . I am tired and a little dispirited tonight as I know only too well that all our efforts are fruitless unless help comes quickly which I doubt. . . ."

All the radio operators were working enormously long hours, grabbing what sleep they could in the occasional lulls when they were not transmitting or receiving—for the labor of coding and decoding was immense. From Zeller, from Descour—who had, in fact, left the Vercors with Dom Guétet on a trip to a nearby range of mountains—from Cammaerts, from Longe, a stream of signals to Algiers was dispatched pleading for the bombing of the tank concentration at La Paillasse, for air attack on the three thousand Germans now camped at St.-Nizier, for some action against Chabeuil, for paratroopers and heavy weapons.

Even the Drôme Maquis, appalled at the constant gathering of German forces for the attack on the plateau, added their pleas to those within the Vercors, describing the burning of Vassieux and La Chapelle, and offering to support Cochet's "shock" paratroop operation on Chabeuil with an attack from the ground.

At last, on July 20, Longe sent a clear warning from Huet: "If we are to hold the imminent heavy attack, our requests for paratroopers and heavy weapons must be met. If the attack comes before they are met, then the Vercors cannot be held. Must remind you that if the Vercors troops are defeated, reprisals will be terrible. The meeting of our requests will need another daylight operation and fighters will have to cover the plateau so that the parachuted material can be collected."

Signals came in from Algiers. Constans, who was always obsessed with military structure, sent a message congratulating Huet on his reorganization of the military command of the plateau. At that moment, Huet had no need of congratulations. Another signal pointed out that six thousand Tricolor armbands had been parachuted into the plateau since June—but armbands were not much use against German batteries of 105 mm guns. On July 20 a message did arrive from Constans that, if there had not been so many similar wires before, would have given hope to the threatened men on the plateau: "We are doing what is necessary."

In Algiers the conflict between General Cochet and his superior commander in London about whose territory included the Vercors had developed to confrontation. On July 15 Jacques Soustelle had sent Cochet a sharp note reminding him that all orders regarding the Vercors must come from General Koenig only. The next day, when Cochet asked Constans to attend a meeting with one of his colleagues to discuss the situation on the plateau, both failed to appear. They were under instructions to accept no orders relating to the Vercors from General Cochet!

At Allied Air Headquarters in England, too, the attitude to requests for further supply drops into the Vercors met a very cool reception. According to testimony in Paris, aerial photographs had revealed that supplies dropped on July 14 still lay on the ground in the flat country around Vassieux. The Resistance men on the plateau did not seem to have taken the trouble to collect them. Presumably the aerial photographs did not reveal the German planes circling above the area, waiting to attack anyone who dared to approach the parachute canisters.

The morning of July 20 was brilliant and the early sun touched the Vercors peaks with purple. The summer heat, contained as it was between the rock walls of the plateau, was beginning to shimmer over the flat country. Had it not been for the planes that were always in the sky and the reports of German troops on the ring road, Huet might have found it hard to believe he was preparing for conflict. The beauty of the plateau, the butterflies, the birds, seemed far removed from death. The big brown and white cows grazing in the lush Vercors meadows looked fat and healthy. During those hours of waiting, the colonel must have thought often of his wife and his six children at Coublevie, so near to the north. Being so strong a Catholic, he must have prayed for strength, if not for intervention.

He knew that the attack must come very soon. During the night, fifteen guns, mounted on heavy tracked vehicles, had arrived at Grenoble station from Lyon. A long horse-drawn train of artillery had left the city, moving steadily along the ring road, although there were no reports yet to indicate where the Germans planned to deploy it. A battalion of mountain infantry had crossed the Drac River—presumably to attack from the east.

Then at three o'clock in the afternoon the desultory reports flowing into the office of Pierre Tanant suddenly increased in pace. A convoy of forty buses, crammed with infantry, had crossed the Isère from Grenoble and was heading along the ring road that skirted the north tip of the massif toward Romans. At every village it stopped to leave a contingent that varied in size depending on the importance that the position seemed to demand. For hours the phones in Tanant's office were ringing constantly as the lookouts around the plateau reported the arrival of the German units. From Sassenage, from Noyarey, from Veurey on the east of the Vercors tip—then from St.-Quentin, St.-Gervais, Cognin on the west side. At Cognin and St.-Just there were SS units. At St.-Nazaire, a battle was already in progress between the Germans and Resistance men.

Other German units had advanced in force from Valence in the southwest along the ring road that led to Die. They had attacked Vaunaveys, a village in the foothills not far from the main road where they knew there was a strong Maquis presence that would threaten their supply line, and then pushed on toward Crest, about seventeen miles west of Die.

From the southeast the picture drawn by the reports was the

same. More troops had joined the advance units in the pass of the Col de Grimone. Others had advanced to the Col de Menée. Both passes were on lanes that merged farther west at Châtillon into a single road that met the ring road to the east of Die. Already advance patrols had probed to Châtillon. But it meant that the Germans were thrusting at Die from both sides —and from Die the main road into the south wall of the Vercors snaked up steeply to the Col de Rousset.

Other troops had been stationed along the east side of the massif—at St.-Maurice-en-Trièves, at Clelles, at Lus-la-Croix-Haute, at Monestier-de-Clermont, at the entrance to every little lane that led up into the mountains. Tanks were on the move along the whole extent of the road on that side of the plateau, and it was soon clear to Huet as he studied the pattern of information that their role at this stage was not to attempt to strike up onto the plateau but to block the exits.

Meanwhile, the road to St.-Nizier from Grenoble was thick with troop columns and armored vehicles and guns and mobile kitchens and supply trucks.

In the late afternoon, as the total picture became clear, it began to rain heavily. With the help of Tanant's staff, who placed markers on the big wall map in the Villa Bellon, Huet analyzed the developing situation. They were surrounded by a force that was far larger than he had expected. The reports indicated that already there were some 15,000 troops in position to strike—with tanks and artillery and mortars and planes. And still intelligence messages indicated that other units were in motion toward the plateau from farther away.

When Huet held a meeting that evening with the Vercors leaders, everyone knew that the only thing that could save the plateau now was help from outside. Their main hope, of course, rested with the working parties on the runway. Captain Tournissa expected to complete it the next day. The timing was desperately narrow, but if they could hold the passes for just a few hours, Allied planes would then be able to land.

In the teeming rain, they all went to their posts. Beauregard was driven to St.-Julien by André Huillier in the green Renault with its bullet holes still ringed in red. The captain briefed the small staff in his command post, and bade good-by to Huillier, since he would not need a car until after the attack—and who knew what the situation would be then?

He drove down to the Pont de la Goule-Noire in a large truck and collected a company of Maquisards who had been ordered to wait there for him—the same veteran Maquisards that Huet had "inspected" at Plénouze the day he arrived on the plateau to assume command. The truck headed along the Villard road, then branched off north to Méaudre.

Beauregard's orders were to hold the Col de la Croix-Perrin, which dominated the Grenoble road in the north. The men traveled as far as they could by truck. Then they had to walk. Beauregard led the long file as they climbed through the woods up the side of the mountain toward the pass. The rain streamed down their faces, held their clothes clinging damp to their bodies, filled their shoes with water.

High above the Gorges de la Bourne, in dense, steep forest, Chabal's unit was stationed at the crucial position of Valchevrière. This was the place that, a week before, Vincent Beaume had warned Huet was inadequately guarded. Its main feature was a terrace that had been constructed for tourists—a belvedere as they called it—from which the view in daylight across the trees and the gorge toward Rencurel and the Col de Romeyère was one of the Vercors' many spectacular views. The belvedere dominated a lane—narrow but vital because it gave access to the south sector of the plateau—that led up through the forest from Villard.

The rain hammered on the leaves of the trees as the men

huddled in groups around the trunks to gain what little shelter they could. This helped a bit but not much, for the water still dripped on them as it seeped through the foliage.

Chabal, according to Richard Marillier, was in a pessimistic mood—and although this was not strange on the eve of a battle against enormously powerful forces, it was a little odd that this brave and experienced lieutenant should speak of it. His men relied on him completely, for this was the way he commanded them, and it cannot have strengthened their morale. "Listen," he said, "this is going to be tougher than we've experienced yet. . . . If things work out badly . . . if I'm killed, those of you who survive should make for the ridge of Le Coinchette." And he pointed south. "Then," wrote Marillier, "without waiting for comment, he strode off into the night. . . ."

Jean Prévost made a last tour of the posts in the line of passes he was responsible for holding, and gave orders for a few minor troop adjustments. Then he went to the field command post that he had set up to the south of his headquarters at Herbouilly, in a clearing formed by the angle of two tracks that led to different parts of his sector, to spend the hours that remained of darkness.

According to Yves Farge, he was writing a journal of his days in the Vercors in the same exercise book that he used for tear-out messages, and he must surely have recorded his emotions before the assault that would come at dawn. On that cold wet night, he can only have been consumed by a helpless sadness as he recalled the excitement that he and Pierre Dalloz had shared on that winter morning in the snow at Sassenage when they had suddenly conceived the potential of the Vercors as a mountain fortress.

At La Rivière, after the evening meal, Geyer had gone to see those men who were still billeted in the farm buildings to give them a few final words of encouragement. On the way back through the mud, he stopped at the barn where the horses were kept. Bouccaro, the white stallion he had ridden out of the 11th Cuirassiers barracks at Lyon, was among them. So, too, was the chestnut mare that Yves Beesau had stolen from Romans. They stood, as horses do, quietly but with endless minor movement—the swishing of a tail, the leaning of a neck, the occasional sudden bending of a hind leg. On the roof of the barn, the rain pounded monotonously.

The horses, Geyer was sure, would be tested very soon, as indeed would his whole concept of fighting on the plateau. The Vercors, he was still convinced, was guerrilla country and demanded guerrilla tactics—even though there were now some five thousand men under orders. Flexibility and consolidation, he believed, should provide the fundamental basis of their strategy, the deployment of large, highly mobile bodies of men who could exploit the rugged terrain—the passes, the gorges, the forests—to strike hard at the enemy and then withdraw to strike again from another direction. He was sure that, with imagination and boldness, they could offset the superiority of the enemy—and, to a degree, he was in due course to demonstrate his theories in practice.

The main reason why Geyer was convinced that Huet's policy was doomed was his decision to hold all the passes in the Vercors' vast perimeter, which inevitably meant that his forces were spread thinly over the line. Even more important, since it often took a long time in that terrain to move men from one pass to another, was the fact that this strategy would give the colonel little opportunity to adjust his tactics to any new situation that might emerge—as they always did in war. From the moment the Germans attacked, he would be stuck with his rigid battle lines.

Geyer completely discounted the orders that Huet believed he must carry out to hold the passes. He doubted if the para-

15. General Charles de Gaulle (*Photo A.F.P.*).

16. Fernand Grenier.

17. General Gabriel Cochet
(*Photo A.F.P.*).

18. Members of First Lieutenant Vernon Hoppers' American OSS team instructing Maquisards in weapons training.

19. Parade on Sunday, June 25, in St.-Martin's square. Captain Geyer, mounted, saluting the colors.

20. Captain Geyer with Chabal's unit.

21. Vassieux
from the air.

22. Le Grand Veymont, the Vercors' highest peak, which dominates the mountains of the southeast of the massif through which the German *Gebirgsjägers* attacked.

23. The Grotte de la Luire, site of Dr. Ganimède's hospital (*Editions Arthaud, Paris. Photo by A. Trincano*).

24. Wounded being tended in the Grotte de la Luire.

25. The ruins of La Chapelle after sustained bombing.

26. What remained of the Pont de la Goule-Noire, which spanned the Gorges de la Bourne, after it had been destroyed to check the German advance.

troopers would ever come and believed that they should adjust their strategy to the reality of their appalling situation.

He had not, of course, had the chance to express these views to his colonel. Even now, so Geyer insists, only hours before the German assault, Huet had still given him no orders. He had not summoned him to any meetings. Yet, despite the new instructions that section heads should report direct to the Villa Bellon, all the telephones from the command posts remained linked to Geyer's headquarters at La Rivière, and in practice the captain still controlled the southern plateau.

Certainly, however, the fact that the two men primarily responsible for the defense of the plateau were on such poor personal terms could only threaten the meager prospects of the people of the Vercors when the expected assault finally came at daylight.

Meanwhile, in the Villa Bellon on that wet night, Huet himself was considering whether anything more remained to be done. He had sat in the office with his staff analyzing the last of the reports of enemy activity. He had phoned Captain Ullman, the local commander at Rencurel, and ordered him to blow up the Pont de la Goule-Noire over the Gorges de la Bourne—an operation for which explosive had been fixed several days before. He had sent his adjutant Captain René Bousquet to l'Escoulin, in the Vercors foothills above Crest, for a final meeting with Colonel de Lassus, commander of the FFI forces in the Drôme Département that were responsible for the defense of the southern slopes of the massif.

He had summoned Major Desmond Longe and once again demanded the support of Allied planes. That, after all, was the purpose for which Longe had been parachuted into the Vercors—to inform headquarters so that they could take necessary action. Poor Longe. He was doing his best and was as frustrated as the colonel. "No sleep at all last night," he recorded in his journal. "John and I were either with Hervieux [Huet] and the General [Zeller] or working on codes. . . . Hervieux asks for fighter cover which I explain is impossible, but ask London just in case." London, the major wrote, did at least act on some of his requests, unlike Algiers who merely signaled that they were sending supplies that never arrived. "They always end their signals with Love to Pauline [Christine Granville]," Longe noted with irritation, adding, "We have no time for love here."

Huet's request to Longe was just one of the many last futile attempts to do something about his situation. He had exhausted his resources. As commander of the plateau, he had sent out a final order of the day to his men. He had written it with great care and much emotion and he knew it would now have reached the troops, if that was what they were, as they waited in the rain at their posts along the perimeter of this vast plateau. "Soldiers of the Vercors," he had declared, "the time has come for you to show your metal. It is the hour of battle. We will fight from our posts. We will engage the enemy wherever he is at all times and, above all, when he least expects it. We will harass him without ceasing. . . .

"The eyes of the whole country are fixed on us. We have faith in each other. We have right on our side. . . . The ideal that has motivated us and unites us will enable us to win."

As Huet studied the map in Tanant's office, he must have realized what little grounds he had for the confidence he had expressed in his order. A late signal came in from Constans and he reached for it eagerly with a spark of the illogical hope that never completely deserts desperate men, and read the message carefully:

"Having the following sent to you starting from the night of the 22/23: Two French teams of fifteen men each, fourteen officers and field sergeants; six bazookas with ammunition. . . . Ammunition for American mortars already dispatched. Fifteen heavy 50 mm machine guns; ninety light English mortars and shells. Medical material. Please indicate which is the most urgent and on what landing grounds they should be dropped. Courage."

The messages from Algiers still indicated a lack of comprehension of the real situation in the Vercors. The weapons would have been invaluable but they were too late. Huet knew that the resources at Constans' disposal were limited, that there were demands from other areas, but the staff colonel's signals indicated a basic misunderstanding, a kind of refusal to accept consciously the facts that the tired radio operators had been transmitting for weeks.

In his office, Huet stood alone with Tanant for a few minutes. Rain was lashing the window panes. Tanant, who had much respect for his colonel, was conscious of his anxiety although his commander never spoke of it—presumably, so the captain wrote later, because he did not want to damage the morale of the men who worked with him in the Villa Bellon. That night, however, Huet revealed more of himself than he ever had before. "You know, Laroche," he said, using Tanant's cover name, "I've never truly believed that more than one out of ten of us would survive. Still, we must do what we have to do." He gave a little shrug of his shoulders and, for once, his blue eyes softened.

Another message came in from Constans that was rushed up to the Villa Bellon by dispatch rider. "All our information indicates that the total enemy forces facing you are not more than three regiments. Total German forces deployed between the Rhône and the Isère, represented by the 157th Reserve Division, are ten thousand men at the maximum. I repeat: ten thousand men. . . . At present none of these units will be ready for battle in less than fifteen days. . . . Requesting for tomorrow sorties by fighters on enemy columns in south. . . .

All our information leads us to believe decline German morale. . . ."

Of all the messages from Algiers, this was the most ludicrous. Here they were, surrounded by thousands of enemy troops poised for assault within hours, supported by tanks, heavy artillery, and aircraft. Yet according to Algiers there were not as many Germans as they thought and even these would be unable to attack for fifteen days.

If Constans' information depicted the kind of futility at headquarters that outposts have often suffered from throughout history, it was dwarfed by another message. For it carried news that was so bad that it was barely believable. The signal is not in the official files, but the source is Huet himself at the Vercors inquiry in Paris and must be regarded as first class. The message stated that the runway—the runway that was to be ready within hours to receive Allied planes, the runway that truly provided their only hope of aid on an adequate scale—was *still* too small. Aircraft could not land on it, so Algiers asserted, because it was 60 meters (200 feet) too short and 10 meters (35 feet) too narrow.

Both Zeller and Huet are dead and cannot be consulted. There is evidence—from Desmond Longe in particular—that they met that night, but not of what they said to each other. It is impossible to believe, however, that Huet would not at least have telephoned his commanding general at Rang-des-Pourrets if he was not in the Villa Bellon. In his state of extreme frustration Huet must have said something to the effect: "The runway's long and flat, surely they can get some kind of aircraft down on it." And the general would have had to find an adequate answer, even though there can be no doubt that he shared the colonel's feelings. Certainly Zeller was familiar with danger. During his years in the Resistance he had faced it many times. Also, of course, he had suffered the terrible experience of knowing that his wife was being tortured by the Gestapo. They had both survived, though. So what could he have said to Huet? *"Courage, mon vieux?* While there is life there is hope?"* Doubtful. Cammaerts knew him well and insists that he was not a man to use clichés readily. Probably he just said, "Get some rest while you can."

One fact is known: the rain on the windows of the Villa Bellon. No doubt, at that moment, the noise seemed very loud.

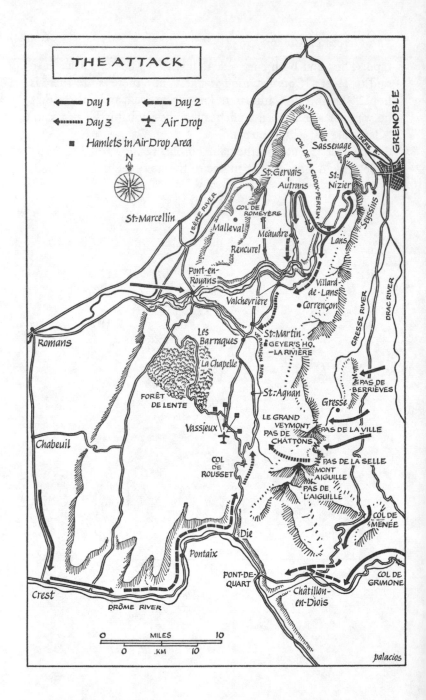

CHAPTER 16

For weeks, time for the Vercors had been running out. On that wet gray dawn of Friday, July 21, the final grains of sand were passing through the glass.

The first call to the Villa Bellon was made just after six o'clock. An enemy force of two thousand men was advancing from St.-Nizier, along the road toward Lans. Huet was awakened at once, although there was nothing he could do. The defense positions had been manned the night before. He drank coffee—the real coffee presented to him by the Americans—and waited.

Then news was phoned that the column was splitting at Lans. One part of it was driving on toward Villard, which of course was undefended, and the Gorges de la Bourne. The rest of the troops had turned north toward the Col de la Croix-Perrin, which Beauregard had been ordered to hold. The tactic was obvious. If the Germans succeeded in taking the pass they

would push on to Autrans, then turn south through Méaudre
to join up with the other column in a joint drive at the vital
gorge. As usual, it seemed, it would be Beauregard's men who
would bear the first impact of the attack.

By 9:30, three and a half hours after the first alert that the
enemy was on the move in the north, there had been no reports
from the other approaches to the plateau where Huet knew the
Germans were poised. It was then, as the minute hand of the
clock in the operations room moved to the half hour, that Bob
Bennes phoned Huet from his radio shed at La Britière.
"Planes approaching from the south, Colonel," he reported.
"They can't be from Algiers. We'd have been warned. They
must be German."

There was a strong temptation to hope they could be from
England. The two big daylight drops had come without previous signals, but Huet knew planes from England would not approach from the south. These aircraft were almost certainly
bringing German paratroopers, the one danger that he had
feared most of all—and indeed had made what plans he could
to combat. There were several units posted on the hills surrounding the open country at Vassieux whose prime purpose
was to attack troops dropping from the air.

From the balcony of the Villa Bellon, Huet watched the aircraft as they drew nearer, flying over the southern rim of mountains, not high above the peaks, in close formation.

Already Bennes was tapping out a signal to Algiers. "We are
under attack by paratroopers. We are defending ourselves." He
ended with the word "good-by"—not the usual "*au revoir*,"
which implies that there will be another meeting in the future,
but "*adieu*," which suggests that the parting is permanent.

On the runway near Vassieux, work had been in progress
since early light. In all, there were some four hundred people

spread out across the long, flat strip to the southwest of the town, digging, rolling, carting earth—making as much progress as they could before the Focke-Wulfs flew over the Forêt de Lente from Chabeuil. This morning the aircraft were later than usual.

Captain Haezebrouck, who was in charge of the defense of the strip under Geyer's command, was with Tournissa, the engineer, and a group of other people on the outskirts of the town when the first flight of planes roared noisily over the Col de Vassieux to the south. Because of the direction they came from, somebody shouted, "It's the Yanks! It's the Yanks!" But almost immediately the black crosses could be seen on the wings and someone also yelled, in panic, "It's the Boche!"

The assault progressed with the precision that had been planned. It consisted of waves of aircraft towing troop-filled gliders, supported by Focke-Wulfs and Dorniers that streaked ahead of the transports, over the open country around the town, bombing and machine-gunning. Then the gliders—fragile craft of light metal frames covered with thin fabric—were released. The biggest number came in to land near Vassieux and the runway. Others dropped near four hamlets—Jossaud, La Mure, Le Château, and Les Chaux—all of which were near the roads and lanes leading to the town and to the air strip. The strategy was brilliant, both in concept and in execution, for, by controlling the access roads in arcs of fire, these troops would be in a firm position to fight off any French counterattacks. The runway would then be in their control.

On the ground the impact of the sudden attack was overwhelming, for this was a vastly more devastating experience than the previous strafing, which had been traumatic enough. This was concentrated assault in strength. One of Haezebrouck's sergeants leaped for one of the machine guns that had been set up waiting on the edge of the air strip as part of the defense precautions and opened fire. Jacques Descour, the colonel's son, who was also under Haezebrouck's orders, rushed to another. Between them they shot down a towing aircraft, but the German attack, focused as it was on limited areas, was lethal. Both Haezebrouck and young Descour were killed. Tournissa and the sergeant were wounded. Great swaths were cut through the hundreds of workers on the air strip, running in panic, diving headlong on the ground as attack followed attack.

As the gliders came in to land, the troops within them flung out grenades. Then, as the flimsy aircraft bounced to a halt, SS men leaped out, blazing away both with machine guns and with flame throwers, running for their target buildings, shooting everyone they saw—men, women, and children. Within minutes, a hundred people lay dead on Tournissa's air strip. The engineer himself had been dragged to cover in a small underground grotto on the fringe of the town that had been fitted out previously as a first-aid post. In La Mure, the Maquis unit posted there was almost entirely annihilated.

The first stages of the attack were over very fast—just a few minutes—but throughout the day the supporting fighters were diving to attack all movement by Maquisard units against the Germans as they established their positions.

At La Rivière there was a brief disjointed warning phone message from Vassieux. One of Geyer's officers took the call. "Captain Hardy [Haezebrouck] is probably killed," he was told. "Captain Paquebot [Tournissa] is wounded. . . ." Then suddenly the line went dead.

At the time when the attack was launched, Chavant was sitting at his table in the café of the Hôtel Breyton in St.-Martin with Father Vincent and two others of the Committee of National Liberation. The Patron's first response on hearing of the approaching planes was that at last the Allies had honored the

promises they had given him in Algiers—which he had always
believed they would. When he was forced to accept that the
aircraft were German, the effect on this quiet, stolid man, who
rarely even raised his voice, was appalling. "He roared with
pain," Father Vincent recalls. "I had never seen him before in
an extreme emotional state and it was a terrible sight. He
pounded the café table with his fist, swearing that he'd been
betrayed."

In Huet's headquarters in St.-Martin, news of other attacks
began to flow in fast. In the southeast, enemy mountain troops
were attacking the French positions in the little mule track
passes of de Chattons and de la Selle between the high peaks
of Le Grand Veymont and Mont Aiguille. There were only ten
men defending each of the several passes in the range. They
were holding the enemy, but the heavy machine guns and mortars of Schwehr's Gebirgsjägers had permitted the enemy to get
well positioned.

In the south, the big German force from Valence, which included the 9th Panzer tank division, had advanced from Crest
along the ring road toward Die. They had been checked at a
barrage thrown across the road at Blacons, but Huet knew they
would be through that fast enough. His main hope was that
they could be held at Pontaix, where the road spanned the
Drôme by a bridge that offered good defense opportunities.

From the north, Huet learned that both German columns
were now attacking his positions—at the pass of the Col de la
Croix-Perrin and also at the approach from Villard to the
Gorges de la Bourne.

The SS troops at Vassieux, however, were clearly the biggest
danger. Huet called Geyer on the phone.

Vincent Beaume's telephone operators at the exchange,
which had been moved from La Chapelle to the wooded ham-

let of Les Drevets, made a practice of listening in to interesting conversations—which is why a verbatim report of Huet's frigid discussions with his prickly south-sector commander exists today. "Enemy troops have landed at Vassieux," the colonel told Geyer. "I want you to assemble what forces you need, surround the enemy, and attack."

"I'm aware of the situation, Colonel," answered the captain coldly. "I've already issued the necessary orders."

When Huet went on to discuss the attack strategy, Geyer said abruptly, "I repeat, Colonel, it's all in hand."

Huet, again displaying the strange reticence that marked his dealings with Geyer, apparently accepted this blunt refusal to discuss the details of a vitally important attack about which, as commander, he was surely entitled to be fully briefed. "Well, I have faith in you, Thivollet," he told the captain. "Keep me informed."

Geyer's big problem now was the lack of mobile communication. Because of the excellence of the telephone engineers on the plateau, all regular posts could be contacted, but as soon as units left these, Geyer immediately lost touch with them. Even before the colonel had phoned him, he had ordered counterattacks by the units he had posted on the hills overlooking Vassieux. At that stage, no one knew the exact number of Germans who had landed but it could not be very many—probably only two or three hundred. But the leaders of the French units soon discovered that the enemy troops were well armed and constantly protected by the planes hovering over the area, waiting to dive, guns blazing, on anyone moving to attack them. It became clear very fast that any effective attempt to recapture Vassieux and the hamlets would have to be mounted in darkness.

Given the situation he faced, Geyer did not disagree with Huet's orders to gather what forces he could and attack the German positions from all sides. He only wished he had more men available for the operation—which, as he knew, he would have had if the colonel had not been so rigid in his policy of trying to hold the whole vast Vercors rim as though the plateau was a small desert fort in the care of the Foreign Legion.

During that crisis morning, however, his main difficulty was to establish exactly where the Germans were installed so that he could frame his counterattack plan. He had troops pinned down on the hillsides, shooting at the enemy whenever they could from the cover of bushes and trees, despite the aircraft overhead, but he was not in direct contact with any of them. So he phoned Lieutenant Cathala, his commander at the Col de Rousset, the nearest permanent post to Vassieux, and ordered him to carry out a reconnaissance to discover the exact positions of the enemy.

Meanwhile, as the reconnaissance proceeded, Geyer grew anxious about the southeastern passes, which were not far from La Rivière. The news was not yet too bad. Lieutenant Calk, who was in charge of the handful of men spread through the entire range, reported that the Pas de Chattons and the Pas de la Selle, the two passes under attack, were holding well and enemy casualties were heavy. But Geyer knew that the forces in this area were quite inadequate for the size of the assault they were now facing. Even one man, so he was to write in his account of the battle, could stop large numbers of the enemy for a time in this kind of country if he was well positioned—as indeed the two Russians had demonstrated at the Pont Chabert in June—but he could not do so indefinitely.

The German Alpine troops would be reinforced all the time. There were reports that there were two thousand men behind them on the ring road. They were certain to attack other passes—for there were a sizable number of these tiny cuts in the mountains. In due course the enemy were certain to break a gap in the defenses. Since he was already scouring the plateau for men for his counterattack at Vassieux, Geyer was worried that he would have no reserves to plug this gap when it appeared.

Calk phoned again from the southeast. "There's a strange lull in the fighting," he said. "Do you think perhaps they're planning an airborne operation near La Grande Cabanne in the Plateau de Veymont?" This was a stretch of open country, rugged and irregular, that lay between the two lines of mountains running north–south which the Germans would have to break through to gain the plateau interior. The enemy Alpine troops had been attacking two passes in the first and far higher range until suddenly they had stopped shooting. This could well be an ominous sign, as the lieutenant suggested. Following the airborne operation at Vassieux, a landing in the Plateau de Veymont was an obvious danger. "It's possible," agreed Geyer; "keep me informed." Even if the enemy did drop troops by air onto this plateau, they would still have to penetrate the second range, but this was not so formidable an obstacle as the first line of mountains, which included Le Grand Veymont and Mont Aiguille.

"Enemy troops are approaching the Pas de la Ville," Calk went on. This was a third pass to the north of the other two, where the fighting had already been heavy. "I must have some more men and at least two more mortars. Also, I'm having enormous difficulty maintaining liaison between the passes. I've lost touch completely with Pré-Grandu." This last point was unnerving, for Pré-Grandu was in the second, inner mountain range which the Germans could not possibly have reached— unless they had done so by some cunning maneuver that had been undetected.

Geyer gave the young lieutenant what encouragement he could. "I'll try to get some more men to you," he said, and gave him formal orders that were recorded in his log: "Keep alert for paratroopers. Hold the passes at all costs. Even if you are forced to withdraw, stay in close contact with the enemy and counterattack as soon as you can."

Stirring words—but Geyer did try to meet his request. He phoned an order to the commander of the southwest region to send Calk what men he could spare. Soon afterward an officer and a dozen men set off toward the southeastern ranges, but, from the Forêt de Lente, it would take them many hours to get there.

Almost immediately, the phones in La Rivière brought news of attacks from the west. The enemy were approaching Izeron, reported the commander of the sector. From Izeron, not far from the ravaged Malleval, there was a small lane that reached to the Gorges de la Bourne. It could be important. Geyer tried to speak to the command post there but could not make contact—either because the Germans had captured it or because the slender Resistance force there was too busy fighting to answer the phone. Then came news from Royans, where the Bourne River flowed west into the Isère. Royans, St.-Nazaire, and the nearby villages were under attack and shelling by 105 mm guns.

Calk came through again on the phone from the southeast. The lull in the fighting was over. His men were under heavy attack. "I've just been to the Pas de la Ville," he reported. "The Boche are making an enormous effort there and bringing up a lot of artillery. We're still holding them in all passes but I'm in desperate need of those mortars. We don't have a hope of holding the Pas de la Selle without them."

Another call from farther south reported that other German forces had advanced from the two passes they had taken the day before—the Cols de Grimone and Menée—and were moving across the southeast tip of the Vercors toward the main ring road to the east of Die.

Geyer was in an impossible situation—which would, perhaps, have been marginally less impossible if his command post had been nearer the Villa Bellon in St.-Martin. For here he was trying to plan an assault at Vassieux, to keep control of a dozen passes, none of which had more than ten men to defend them, to give orders to troops on the far west of the plateau—all by remote control. He had no alternative to staying in his farmhouse, for the moment he left to examine any of these crisis areas in person he would be out of touch with the others.

At the Villa Bellon in St.-Martin, Huet's big staff was assessing the stream of information on the enemy attacks. They could only report a situation that all the time was growing more critical. Despite his desperate situation, Huet appeared cool and in command—to the extent that he *could* be in command. During one of the many meetings the colonel held that day, Lieutenant Conus, the bearded big-game hunter from Chad who had arrived in the Vercors to join Desmond Longe's mission on July 14, was in the Villa Bellon. Huet was searching in his mind for possible sources of help and his thinking was fixed on the Maquis in the surrounding mountains. The Drôme Maquis in the south were linked into the defense system of the plateau, but not far to the east there were large Resistance forces in the Oisans range. If they were to attack the Germans from the rear, it would create a diversion that would inevitably weaken the heavy pressure on the Vercors southeastern passes— which was so much stronger than Huet had expected.

Possibly the colonel could have contacted them by radio— though this link was fragile and might have involved routing the signal through Algiers—or by a liaison officer from Oisans who was actually in St.-Martin at that moment, waiting to return to his base. Presumably Huet believed that an officer of some stature was needed to give weight to his plea for help and he asked for volunteers.

"I'll go if you like," said Conus. He was only a lieutenant but, with his big frame and booming voice which made him seem like a character from one of Hemingway's African novels, he emanated authority. Huet accepted his offer gladly and sent him to Jean Prévost with a request that he provide him with a guide to lead him down the mountain to the ring road.

Conus traveled with Lieutenant Jail, the Oisans liaison officer, and Prévost did what he was asked. In the early hours of the morning the two men and their guide set off in the pouring rain up the steep mountainside, thick with forest, toward Corrençon, but they kept encountering German patrols and eventually, as dawn approached, they returned to Prévost's command post at Herbouilly, planning to attempt another route, farther to the south.

At last, toward evening, Geyer heard from Lieutenant Cathala, who had completed his reconnaissance of the situation at Vassieux. The Germans were firmly in control of their objectives, but the four hamlets were ranged in a semicircle to east, north, and west of the town. There was none to the south, where a strong unit of 11th Cuirassiers waited posted on a hill.

As he talked to Cathala on the phone, Geyer crystallized the plan for which all day troops had been moving into position on the hills surrounding Vassieux's open country, pending final instructions for the assault. A simultaneous attack would be launched on Vassieux from the south and on two of the hamlets—La Mure, the most northerly and the nearest to Les Barraques, where some of his best men were waiting, and Jossaud, the closest to the western hills where units from the Forêt de Lente were poised.

The operation was scheduled for nine o'clock that night. His force would consist of some four hundred men—probably quite a few more than the Germans yet had on the ground, although there is controversy about this. According to some accounts, twenty aircraft took part in the initial assault but reinforcements were flown in later. Ultimately, forty-five gliders were found lying in the area. Most, some forty-three of them, were small and capable of carrying only ten men, but there were two big craft large enough for twenty to thirty passengers.

The German units, however, consisted of well-trained troops, some of them foreign but supported and commanded by the SS. Even so, Geyer's force should in darkness have a good chance of overwhelming them.

That evening, as night enveloped the plateau and Geyer's troops moved toward their assault positions, the situation, as revealed by the flags showing the German positions on the big map in Huet's operations room, looked very grim. At Vassieux, the Germans now had a machine gun in the steeple of the ruined church that enabled them to fire on the approaches to the town on all sides. In the north, although the enemy had been held at the Gorges de la Bourne, they had made a detour to Corrençon—which gave them a good base to launch an attack at the top section of the eastern wall of Huet's citadel.

Jean Prévost's sector consisted, in effect, of the corner of this giant natural redoubt and the walls that formed it. His line stretched for some ten miles along the Gorges de la Bourne and the big mountain ridge—the Crête de l'Ange (Crest of the Angel)—that formed an angle with it. This was not a line in the usual sense of the word—at least, only on a map. It was a defense system constructed across wild forested mountain country, much of it impassable since it was sheer bare cliff. What Prévost had tried to do was to block every access, every cut, every slope that could be climbed—both with mines and with his four hundred men, who were far too few for the purpose. Eighty of these troops were concentrated under Chabal's command at Valchevrière, which dominated the only lane suitable for motor vehicles that reached through this tortuous eastern mountain complex to the interior of the plateau.

At Corrençon, the Germans were just outside Prévost's defense system, but only just. Already, by that first night, their advance units had been in contact with Chabal's outposts at Bois-Barbu, immediately below Valchevrière.

Meanwhile, communication had been completely lost with Beauregard. According to reports, the second German column that had struck north had swept through his defenses at the Col de la Croix-Perrin, advanced into Autrans, and, as expected, turned south to Méaudre, where they were now fighting stiff French opposition.

In the south, the enemy had advanced from the west along the ring road to Saillans, only twelve miles from Die—which, of course, was also being approached by a small force from the east.

By now, one or two people had escaped from Vassieux and the hamlets and their stories of SS brutality were appalling—of burning people alive in their homes, of the killing of civilians of all ages, of hangings by a special technique that made the death slow: two victims were suspended by the neck from opposite ends of the same rope that was thrown over a tree, so fixed that only one of them could just touch the ground with the tips of his toes. So they seesawed, death for each being postponed as he managed to get the tips of his toes onto the ground—until the other found the pressure on his neck unbearable and kicked, until ultimately they both became too exhausted to survive.

Almost everything now depended on the counterattack, and Huet was impatient for it to start. Shortly before nine he phoned Geyer to ask for news.

"The enemy is encircled," answered the captain, according to the transcript.

"How far are your men on the hills from Vassieux?"

"About fifty meters."

"Then your preparations are complete," said the colonel. "Order the assault."

"It needs to be simultaneous at all points, Colonel," Geyer explained a little over-patiently.

"Then fix a time."

"I need a heavy gun. I plan to give the attack signal by gun."

"I don't see the necessity," snapped Huet, presumably working on the assumption that if the attack started on one sector the others would hear it, "but if you must use a gun, take the one at Les Barraques—but do it quickly and keep me informed."

Geyer was exaggerating the situation a little. In fact, he did not know that all his troops were in position in the Vassieux hills. He had lost contact with the men from the Forêt de Lente assigned to attack Jossaud. The troops from Les Barraques had not yet moved forward to La Mure. Other units, who had been ordered from the Forêt des Coulmes near Rencurel in the northern sector, had not arrived. As always, Geyer was enormously hindered by his sheer inability to communicate or to be quickly informed. Had relations been better between the two men, he might have urged the colonel to allow him to delay the attack until the early hours of the morning, when he might have been able to establish closer control of it. As it was, his commander was demanding action and Geyer had to provide it. So he ordered the attack.

It was still pouring with rain, as it had been throughout this awful day, as young Lieutenant Vernon Hoppers and his OSS men waited on a hill to the south of Vassieux. He was the only officer with the unit now, since Chester Myers had been stricken by appendicitis. Near him were Lieutenant Cathala's men from the Col de Rousset. Not far away on his flank were the 11th Cuirassiers unit, which had been in action ever since the Germans had landed.

The young lieutenant was not very happy. The French who were to fight alongside him seemed to be very inadequate for the task—"most of them raw recruits having joined the Maquis just two days previously," as he reported later, although he was not being accurate. The town stood isolated in the open country—a mass of houses, dominated by the ruined church. For most of the day the stretch of open ground between Vassieux and the bushes and trees on the hill where they were now posted had been impassable. Everyone who had ventured forward onto it had immediately come under intense fire from the patrolling aircraft and the SS machine gunners in the buildings on the edge of the town.

After dark, Hoppers himself had moved forward toward their target on an exploratory reconnaissance, but he had not been able to get very close, for the enemy gunners were tautly alert, opening fire at any sound they thought they detected.

The tenor of Hoppers' report suggests little confidence, which is hardly surprising. The Americans were all conscious of the conflict between the French commanders, of the fact that, as the absent Lieutenant Chester Myers put it later, Geyer "seemed very jealous of his troops and area of responsibility." Their weapons—three mortars, two light machine guns, and some bazookas—were inadequate for an assault of this nature. They were going into battle alongside men whom the young South Carolinian officer could not even talk to except by interpreter.

No one had actually placed Hoppers in command of the attack, but the French seemed to accept that, as a serving American officer, he was their leader—though his uncertainty is clear in his report.

It would have been amazing if the assault, which clearly needed great determination, had succeeded under these conditions. The orders, however, were clear: they had to gain a foothold within Vassieux.

They advanced in the darkness, the rain on their faces. They came under heavy fire from the buildings on the fringe of the town and charged. Cathala's men had reached the first houses when, according to the French, Hoppers gave orders to retreat. The OSS lieutenant himself merely records that "we were driven off by automatic weapons." They dropped back some distance from the town, where they waited until it was light. Then enemy aircraft forced them to retreat to their former positions in the hills.

Geyer blamed Hoppers for this failure, but he had no success anywhere else. By the morning, the Germans were still in position in Vassieux and the four hamlets.

Meanwhile, that night, as Hoppers led the abortive attack on the town, Huet held a crisis conference in the Villa Bellon. It was attended by all the Vercors leaders—including General Zeller; Chavant; Father Vincent; Captain Bousquet, Huet's adjutant; Pierre Tanant, his chief of staff; as well as the SOE's Francis Cammaerts and Desmond Longe, together with Andre Paray, Longe's bilingual signals officer, whom he needed to interpret for him. Colonel Descour, of course, was still away—and still unaware of the death of his son. And naturally Narcisse Geyer was not present. At that moment he was far too occupied fighting the battle to attend, but it is doubtful if he would have been invited even if he had been able to spare the time.

They all sat around a large table in the Villa Bellon at which Huet, smoking as always, presided. Still the rain was beating on the windows. They could hear the thud of artillery, the sporadic hammering bursts of machine gun fire in the distance. Huet, haggard from lack of sleep, was taut but cool.

"Gentlemen," he said, "we must face the facts. Short of a miracle our lines will break—perhaps tomorrow, maybe the day after. . . . In my opinion, we have only one course: to disperse in small groups, to attempt to break out of the Vercors and continue the fight in our neighboring mountains." Always Huet had a sense of style that was marked by a Gaullian kind of grandeur. "We will be pursued by the enemy, of course," he said, "and we may die . . . but we will die with weapons in our hands. . . ."

It is a strange fact, known to all writers on momentous events, that the participants of crisis meetings often disagree in retrospect about what happened. According to one report, Bousquet, the adjutant, was utterly opposed to the colonel's proposal. Instead, he suggested they should fight their way out as an organized force—as General Koenig had done so brilliantly at Bir Hacheim. "The way is still open," he said, "the bridge at Quart to the east of Die. I was there myself this morning. I spoke to Alain. He has plenty of men and orders to hold the bridge open at all costs." Alain was the cover name for Pierre Reynaud, one of Francis Cammaerts' assistants, who had been given a large force of Drôme Maquisards specifically to protect this escape route across the river to the mountains in the south.

Huet did not believe that this idea was practical. How could the men, distributed over so huge an area, be assembled as a cohesive force? How could the enemy be checked while this part of the operation was in progress? Surely the plan could succeed only if it was executed swiftly, which would mean reliance on transport. But they did not have enough trucks for thousands of men.

Francis Cammaerts supported the colonel. "The one advantage we have over the Germans is local knowledge," he said. "There are plenty of men who know the mountains intimately to serve as guides. They could lead groups down the mountains without using the roads."

According to the writer Paul Dreyfus, who interviewed Chavant, Huet, and Zeller before they died, the Patron favored a breakout attempt, if not with all the troops on the plateau then with a substantial number, and urged that this should be by way of Villard. Cammaerts, however, always a keen admirer of

Chavant, insists that he never seriously suggested this. Certainly Villard, with Germans close to it in force, would not have seemed a good point at which to make the attempt.

A third alternative that they had all considered was to hold the plateau to the last man—and this indicates dramatically the genuine mood of martyrdom that existed on the doomed plateau on that wet and gloomy day. Cammaerts and Chavant had talked about it prior to the meeting before deciding, as the SOE agent recalls, that there was no point to it. "Already we knew we had tied down big German reserves for weeks while the assault was planned. Even if the original fortress concept of the Vercors remained unexploited, the mobilization of the plateau had served an important military purpose. But nothing further could be gained by prolonging the agony."

In fact, an attempt to fight their way out in force had great attractions for Huet. It offered scope for glory. It would mean that his name would be enshrined in the kind of epic legend that schoolchildren would learn about for centuries. It conformed entirely with the cool panache that he enjoyed, the panache that enabled him to drink toasts at lunch while under attack by German planes. The very concept of advancing down the mountains through enemy fire, with his head held high until he died, was extremely dramatic. And he had, after all, been raised in the cavalry, where audacity and dash were inherent in a long tradition.

However, he knew it was quite wrong, that it could only end in disaster. For even if they did succeed in breaking out through the enemy ring, they would be in flat open country—an easy target for German tanks.

Gradually, in that smoke-filled room, agreement was reached. It was not quite what Huet had originally suggested. An early escape attempt, even in small groups, it was argued, could well mean being "shot like rabbits" as they tried to cross the ring road. Surely it was better to wait hidden within the Vercors, the vast wilderness of which would provide ample refuge for them all until the Germans abandoned the plateau. They could then reform elsewhere.

"We're agreed then," said Huet finally. "We will continue fighting in all sectors for as long as we can. When this is no longer practical, I will give the order for simultaneous dispersal to fall-back positions, which all units will be allocated by my staff during the next few hours. From these we will continue the fight with guerrilla tactics." Which was, of course, what Geyer would long have argued if anyone had bothered to ask him.

The main decision had been taken but there were related matters—the prisoners, for example. What should they do with them? According to Desmond Longe, the suggestion by someone that they should all be shot was rejected curtly by the colonel. "When the dispersal order is given," ruled Huet, "they are to be released."

Then there was the question of Dr. Ganimède and his wounded. The accounts of the atrocities that the SS had already committed conjured up a horrible picture of what their future might be. "At least we should evacuate *them*," suggested Bousquet. In the Catholic hospital in Die, where nuns served as nurses, they would have a better chance. They might be spared the punitive treatment that clearly faced anyone captured in the Vercors.

Huet agreed. It was worth a try even though none of the options promised much. Then, with serious formality, he shook hands with everyone at the table, thanked them for everything they had done, apologized to Desmond Longe with a pained shrug of his shoulders and a wry reference to the handicaps he had faced—and wished them all good luck.

Chavant stayed at the table, his eyes grim, his shoulders hunched. All that day he had been a changed man. His faith in the staff officers at Algiers, which had survived for the six long weeks since the mobilization, had been shattered. Even worse, his visit to headquarters in May now seemed like a charade. All the eager questions from the colonels and generals, all the promises—and Chavant was convinced they *were* promises—now appeared to him to be veined with mockery.

Chavant was quiet and thoughtful, but he was also a man of action—as he had demonstrated often as a strike leader. Now, at the Villa Bellon after this traumatic desperate meeting, he called to Andre Paray, Longe's signals officer, and asked him to send a message to Algiers for him—to Colonel Constans. He had already drafted it on a piece of crumpled paper that he took from his pocket and handed to the American.

Of all the many signals that had been tapped out from the Vercors to Algiers over the past weeks—desperate pleas, reminders of responsibility, demands for action from such senior men as General Zeller and Colonel Descour—this outraged signal by a peasant patron was to have by far the most impact. It would in fact create a scandal involving De Gaulle himself and precipitate a Cabinet crisis.

Chavant was a veteran of in-fighting and he had considered the wording very carefully. He knew that, if his signal was to have any effect at all, if it was not to be processed like hundreds of others in the staff officers' filing trays, it would have to shock—and shock it surely did.

"Enemy troops parachuted onto Vassieux," the signal reported with a beginning that was deceptively mild. "We request immediate bombardment. We were promised that we would have to hold on for three weeks. Six weeks have passed since we set up our organization. We request supplies of men, food, and material. The morale of the population is excellent but will recoil quickly against you if you do not take immediate action and we will agree with them that those men who are in London and Algiers have understood nothing of our situation and will consider them criminals and cowards—repeat: criminals and cowards."

It was with a certain enthusiasm that Paray during the early hours of Saturday, July 22, tapped out that signal in his loft over the cattle shed at the farm above St.-Martin.

About the same time as Paray was transmitting Chavant's challenging message, the wounded were being carried out of Dr. Ganimède's hospital on the edge of the town. They were laid on stretchers in Huillier buses that had been stripped of their seats. In all, in the vehicles, there were a hundred and twenty people—including three doctors, seven nurses, a Jesuit priest who had traveled to the Vercors from Paris after the mobilization to offer his services, and thirty Maquisards to act as escort. The convoy set off toward Rousset, made a detour to the remote village of Tourtre to collect the more seriously wounded that Dr. Ganimède had cautiously transferred there a week before, and continued through the Rousset tunnel down the steep road to Die.

The streets of the ancient Drôme town were deserted as the column of buses headed for the Catholic hospital, but shooting could be heard not far away and a German plane was circling low overhead. When they reached the hospital, the mother superior welcomed them sadly but—according to Ganimède's son Jean—urged the doctor not to leave the wounded with her. "The Germans will be in the town within hours," she explained. "Our chief physician has already left. I've been given the task of burning the archives and doing what little I can to protect the wounded."

Ganimède held a hurried discussion with the other two doctors who had come down with him in the convoy. There *was* an alternative open to them. During the past weeks, as they had surveyed the plateau for possible hiding places for the wounded, they had considered a vast network of caves, hidden by thick trees in the mountainside near Rousset. The Grotte de la Luire was a huge cavern, with a roof height of twenty feet, that became a small passage as it reached back some four hundred yards within the mountain. From there it was linked to a complex system of narrow subterranean corridors that covered no less than seven thousand yards.

This giant warren in the hillside did not compare with a hospital as a place for wounded men. There were no washing or cooking facilities, of course, no piped running water, no heat— but they might well be safer there, as a refuge for "terrorists," than they would be when SS officers walked through the wards in Die in a very short time.

So yet another decision was taken. Three of the wounded elected to remain in Die and take their chances with the Germans. The rest opted with the doctors for the grotto, and the little convoy returned up the deserted mountain road. As they passed through the tunnel of the Col de Rousset a gray dawn was breaking. It was still raining.

The convoy headed along the St.-Martin road and then turned off into a lane that led toward the Forêt du Vercors, not far from the pass of Pré-Grandu in the inner line of mountains which a few hours earlier Lieutenant Calk had been so anxious about on the telephone to Geyer. The lane reached only to the fringe of the trees, and the last six hundred yards to the mouth of the grotto, up a steep mountain path, had to be covered on foot. Those wounded who could walk had to clamber up the slope through the woods as well as they could. The others had to be carried up laboriously on stretchers. In the huge cave they were laid out on slabs of rock or on the ground. The U.S. lieutenant Chester Myers, the appendix case, was one of those who were causing concern. At night a nurse was ordered to lie next to him.

Dr. Ganimède, who with Vincent Beaume had been a leader of one of the Resistance networks in Romans, was satisfied that the grotto provided their best hope. Because the mouth was almost completely covered by trees, it would not be seen even by German aircraft flying low. What was worrying him most during that early morning was that his medical supplies would have to be transported from St.-Martin. Would the German pilots note the traffic and particularly the passage of trucks up the lane below the grotto? The doctor hoped that they would be too busy supporting their fighting troops.

When sixteen-year-old Daniel Huillier, who had driven one of the hospital buses, returned to St.-Martin, his father told him that a general dispersal order would soon be given. He suggested he should take refuge in the grotto, but the boy refused. "No, Father," he said, "if I'm going to die, it's not going to happen in a hole."

CHAPTER 17

As the gray morning light came to the plateau, Huet studied his situation in the operations room of the Villa Bellon. Already his staff had moved the flags on the wall map to reflect the reports, received during the night, of the latest German positions.

On that morning of July 22, the second day of the attack, it was hard to find anything that could form the nucleus for any kind of hope. Even now, while they studied the map, they could hear the bombs as the planes from Chabeuil resumed the air assault that had now become so regular a pattern in their lives. But the tempo on this wet Saturday seemed to intensify. The pilots had become keener, as hounds do when they sense the fox is tiring. Nothing could move on the roads without enemy aircraft screaming down on it with guns hammering. La Chapelle was bombed yet again. The men waiting on the hillside around Vassieux were forced to lie flat as planes sprayed them with machine gun fire in repeated swoops.

In the southeastern passes the situation was clearly critical. The men holding them had been under fire for twenty-four hours and all the time the tempo of the assault was growing as, little by little, the Germans gained ground that enabled them to reposition their mortars and their guns, as enemy aircraft dived again and again, their bullets ricocheting off the rock faces.

The men in the passes were short of food, too, partly because it was sometimes hard to get it to them and partly because the whole plateau lacked adequate supplies of bread: the largest bakers in the southern sector, at La Chapelle, which had been under constant bombardment, had been destroyed.

In the northeast the situation was almost as ominous: all the signs below Valchevrière indicated that there would be a big attack that day.

In the south the Germans had made progress during the night, advancing on Die from both directions. They were now at Pontaix, only six miles west of the town, and at Châtillon in the east, close to the crucial bridge at Quart, which Pierre Reynaud had been assigned to hold open at all costs. Within hours tanks would be climbing the steep road to the Col de Rousset.

Early in the morning, Huet had phoned Geyer for another frigid discussion, demanding when Vassieux was going to be attacked again. "Colonel," answered Geyer, "it's been raining solidly for twenty-four hours. My men have been outside the whole of that time. They've had no sleep and little to eat. They're tired and hungry. They need rest and food if the assault is to be successful."

"Thivollet, I'm not satisfied," snapped Huet. "I'm ordering you to victual your men and finish this business as soon as possible."

The colonel knew that Geyer was right. The men were in no state to attack the SS men ensconced behind heavy machine guns in the town and the four hamlets, but there were times when weary men had to go into action. Something had to be done. The Germans could not be left unopposed in Vassieux. In their present positions they could be reinforced by more glider-borne troops. Soon they would stage a breakout, move onto the offensive, and, no doubt, attempt to advance toward the attack areas at the perimeter so that the defense positions in the main passes would be under assault from two directions at once.

Soon after eight o'clock, the Germans smashed the defenses in two of the southeastern passes—de Berrièves and de la Ville. Because the Pas de la Ville gave them access to Le Grand Veymont, the Vercors' highest peak, they were able to push Gebirgsjägers onto the other side of this mountain, so that they could fire down from above onto the defenders of the Pas de Chattons. Already they had badly wounded one man, and it was clear that this pass, too, would give unless reinforcements were sent in very fast indeed. But where were they to come from? Throughout that frenetic Saturday, Huet had to wrestle with this agonizing conflict. He could reinforce one sector only by reducing his defense force at another. As Pierre Tanant was to write, "It was like playing chess."

In fact, there *was* an additional source of manpower and Huet, knowing that somehow he had to find at least a hundred men to send up to those crucial passes, decided to tap it. There were sixty supply staff at the truck depot at St.-Agnan and the colonel ordered them into action with Lieutenant Calk, supported by one of the companies allocated to attack Vassieux and the hamlets. This was truly dredging the last of his resources, but anyone who could pull a trigger was better than no one.

Then Huet, feeling that Geyer was not displaying the necessary determination in his approach to the problem of Vassieux, took it out of his hands. He ordered Captain Maurice Bourgeois, one of Geyer's sector commanders, to make a daylight assault on La Mure, the most northerly of the four hamlets, at the same time as an attack was launched on Jossaud from the west. A staff officer from the Villa Bellon was given the task of co-ordinating the two operations.

They failed. In fact, they did not even start—for the same reason that all daylight attempts had proved abortive the previous day. The troops had barely begun to advance before they were pinned down by enemy aircraft, and reluctantly Huet was forced to postpone the action until darkness.

When Geyer heard about this at La Rivière, he smiled and shrugged his shoulders. When would his colonel ever learn?

It was during this crisis morning that news was phoned into the Villa Bellon that rendered the headquarters staff speechless, for the irony of it was intolerable. *German Junkers Ju 52s, big three-engined bombers, were landing on Tournissa's air strip at Vassieux!* They were bringing in supplies and evacuating the wounded. The runway that was too small for Allied planes—the runway on which planes could have brought in the mortars and artillery that they needed so desperately—was quite big enough for enemy bombers.

In Algiers, that Saturday morning of July 22, at roughly the same time as German planes were landing on the Vassieux air strip, Colonel Constans hurried to see Jacques Soustelle in his office in the old Arab palace below the Kasbah and requested an urgent interview. He handed him the explosive telegram from Chavant and at last, it seemed, Soustelle faced the fact that there was a crisis of unusual importance in the Vercors.

Earlier that day, Constans had again failed to attend a meeting summoned urgently by General Cochet to consider the critical situation in the Vercors—which, even though the message from Chavant had placed the staff colonel under pressure, was surprising. For even if others in Algiers had not yet realized the full facts of the assault on the plateau, Constans was fully conscious of them. Bob Bennes' dramatic *"adieu"* warning that they were under attack by German paratroopers had been processed by 11:15 the previous morning, some two hours after its dispatch from the Vercors.

Constans was caught up in a conflict between men who were senior to him, but, as an officer who could be in no doubt about the size of the German attack on the Vercors, he should surely have seen that the time had come to short-cut the administrative technicalities. Men were dying on the plateau and clearly the most urgent priority was to get aid to them, no matter which general commanded it.

This indeed was Cochet's view. He knew he had no jurisdiction over the defenders of the Vercors, he testified in Paris, but he was convinced he should use what power he had to help. He dispatched an emergency message to his liaison officer at Allied Air Headquarters in Italy, ordering him to request an urgent attack on the enemy troops and convoys taking part in the assault and, as usual, for the bombing of Chabeuil. Then he sent a bitter wire to Koenig in London. "Vercors your zone," he reminded his commander in chief, who had been so insistent that the massif was in the Northern Sector of France; "I can do nothing more."

Soustelle, now realizing the severity of the crisis, acted fast. Later, during the morning, Constans phoned Cochet and asked for the meeting he had boycotted to be reconvened. Soustelle himself called the general and asked him to give orders for a commando team to be sent immediately to the plateau. Suddenly it seemed that Cochet, whom everyone had been trying to ignore, whose summonses to conferences had been shrugged off, was persona grata—even in matters concerning the Vercors!

There were, as has been noted, French paratroopers at the Staouelli base near Algiers—the impatient *"paratouristes"*—six hundred of them. What is more, Soustelle was speaking with the full authority of the influential Committee of Action in France.

Even so, despite Soustelle's new sense of urgency, it was not easy to obtain immediate action from De Gaulle's complex network of power lines. Both the French Minister for War and also the Secretary of the National Defense Committee, which had so successfully stymied Fernand Grenier's Operation Patrie, insisted that the orders concerning the paratroopers did not permit them to be used for such operations as the Vercors. According to Cochet's testimony in Paris, they were formally reserved for De Gaulle's controversial Force C and the Massif Central.

Soustelle may have been to blame earlier for failing to supply the Vercors with the troops and weapons envisaged by Operation Montagnards, but no one could accuse him of inactivity now. Impatiently, he insisted that these interpretations of the orders were wrong, that he had the personal authority, at least, to send two hundred of the men at Staouelli. In fact, in the present situation, two hundred paratroopers could hardly affect the situation in the Vercors one way or the other, but at least Soustelle was trying at last.

Meanwhile, a strange pattern was developing in Desmond Longe's signals, which were now being routed through London since Andre Paray was having trouble maintaining direct radio contact with Algiers. Although a delayed message from him, received at 1:45 P.M., accurately reported the landing of airborne troops at Vassieux and the advance of tank-supported infantry to Saillans on the road to Die, a second signal created confusion in Algiers, which was already confused enough. "Need infantry . . . send onto Vassieux terrain that we hold. Our positions at the Col de Rousset have been turned by paratroopers. Strong air attack throughout the area. Bomb Chabeuil, St.-Nizier."

This was false, though how it came to be sent, whether or

not it was clever enemy activity or merely a mistake in transmission, remains a mystery. For certainly the French did not hold Vassieux, although another signal repeated this, nor had their positions been turned at the Col de Rousset. But it made Cochet warn his liaison officer at Air Headquarters to "be careful not to carry out any air operation against Vassieux, which seems to be held by the FFI. Request machine-gunning of convoys on the route Crest, Saillans, Die, and the southern slopes of the Col de Rousset. Reconnoiter by day to establish enemy positions."

At the end of that hectic day of July 22 Cochet signaled the Vercors, addressing his message to Zeller, Huet, and Cammaerts, assuring them that he was trying to arrange air attacks on the German columns and also to send paratroopers. "Conservation of men," he ordered, was "considered more important than conservation of terrain." The troops and munitions would be dropped on the "Pencil Sharpener" landing ground unless different instructions were signaled from the Vercors.

The prospect this suggested was horrifying. For "Pencil Sharpener" was near Vassieux and the French paratroopers would have been gunned down by the Germans before they hit the ground.

By now General de Gaulle had been informed of the Vercors crisis. He had only just returned from a highly successful visit to Washington, and his determination to push through his plans for Force C had been in no way blunted by the antipathy of the Allied chiefs. Only two days before, on July 20, as the Germans finally ringed the Vercors, he had attended a meeting with Sir Henry Wilson, the commander in chief of the Mediterranean Theater.

Wilson—as he reported to Eisenhower—refused to allow any of the invasion troops to be assigned to Force C, but he did agree somewhat reluctantly that French units who were not part of the assault army might be assembled for action after the landings.

Like Soustelle, De Gaulle acted fast as soon as he learned of the attack on the Vercors. He ordered General Béthouart, his chief of staff, to conduct an immediate investigation of the exact situation on the plateau and to report back to him.

Whether or not by this time De Gaulle had been informed about Chavant's dramatic signal from the Vercors is uncertain. What is sure, however, is that it was kept secret from General Cochet's liaison officer, who called at Colonel Constans' office every day.

Early that afternoon of July 22, the second day of the attack, the Germans launched their expected assault on Huet's northeastern perimeter. Most of the previous night, Chabal and his men had been kept awake by bursts of machine gun fire as the enemy ensured that its base for the attack, heavily wooded with firs, was clear of French units. Then, soon after dawn, the defenders heard the motors of the half-tracks as the German infantry was brought up in force.

All morning, Chabal and his men waited tensed in their positions ranged around the terraced belvedere of Valchevrière—overlooking the lane that wound up the steep mountainside through the thick forest of firs. This was one of the most crucial defense positions of the whole plateau, for it was an alternative route to the Vercors interior. The usual road to the southern sector from Villard, which bordered the Gorges de la Bourne, was virtually impassable. With its narrow approaches, dominated by huge boulders, and its tiny tunnels that often presented difficulties enough to tourist buses in peacetime, the road was relatively easy even for ill-equipped Maquisards to control. But the mountain lane that curled through the mountains high above the gorge offered more scope for assault. It was just wide enough for motorized transport—which included guns—and although it snaked in steep hairpin bends across no less than three mountain ridges and dipped into the valley below them, it did eventually emerge from a cut in the gaunt Roche Rousse near St.-Martin.

Chabal and his eighty-two men had done their utmost to block this obvious gap in the defenses, and Prévost saw it as so important that he had given the lieutenant almost a quarter of the force allocated to his entire sector. Felled trees barricaded the road and boxed in the belvedere and the other defense positions linked to it. All around them, the woods had been mined. The lieutenant had set up outposts on and near the road below him and also another in the trees above him. As always, the weapons of his men were unequal to those of the Germans—a few light machine guns, some bazookas, grenades, Sten guns, and rifles. Chabal himself, in a blue anorak, his regimental beret, and a pipe clenched between his teeth, held one of the bazookas.

Soon after two o'clock the Germans pushed forward a few advance troops to draw the fire of the outposts, so that they could establish where they were. Then they attacked, overwhelming three of Chabal's forward positions.

Jean Prévost sent up more men to support him. The lieutenant counterattacked and won back the outposts. When the Germans withdrew down the mountain, Jean Prévost sent a messenger to Huet at St.-Martin with a cheerful note worded: "Success at Valchevrière. Chabal has repulsed the enemy and inflicted heavy losses."

Huet was delighted—even though he knew there was little reason for optimism. Chabal was facing a German force that outnumbered him by more than ten to one; he could not possibly hold that narrow mountain road indefinitely. Good news had come in from the southeastern passes, too. Lieutenant Calk's men had regained the Pas de Chattons, but again this little victory could only be temporary. The enemy were through other passes, and for all practical purposes the defense of the first barrier of mountains in the southeast was cracking. As the situation had been ever since the mobilization in June, the only factor that could alter the inevitable progression to defeat was help from Algiers—or possibly, just possibly, an attack by the Oisans Maquis. This last could not be enough to hold the massive forces of the enemy, but it might buy a little time.

Lieutenant Conus, who had left the previous evening in the attempt to get through to Oisans, had not made much progress. After returning to Jean Prévost's headquarters at Herbouilly, he had set off again with Lieutenant Jail, the Oisans liaison officer, and two guides—taking their chance in daylight since time was so important. One of the guides had stepped on a mine that wounded him badly, concussed his comrade, and caused Conus himself severe bruising. Conus and Jail, however, decided to go on without guides. That night, after narrowly avoiding several German patrols, they slept for a few hours in a shepherd's hut near the Pas de la Balme, a few miles to the south of Valchevrière.

At La Rivière, as darkness came, Geyer was still trying to retain control of the units under his command, but he had lost touch completely with his forces in the west. The situation in the passes was confused by several false telephone calls made by French-speaking Germans. At one moment Huet phoned him with a report that there were two thousand enemy troops in the Forêt Domaniale du Vercors. If this was the case, it was all over, for the forest was barely three miles from Geyer's farmhouse and it meant that the Germans were through the second line of passes in force.

"I cannot believe this, Colonel," he told Huet, "but I'll investigate." It was always possible on that terrain to be taken by surprise.

Immediately, Geyer rang the Pas de Pré-Grandu, which the

enemy must have captured for the report to be true. This was
the pass that Huet's reinforcements had been sent up to support. Like Chabal's position farther north at Valchevrière, it
was a crucial point in the mountain defense. It was with some
relief that Geyer heard a familiar voice as the phone was answered. "So far everything's going well here," he was assured.
"There's been a light enemy infiltration but we're cleaning this
up now."

As it turned out, there was not much reason for his optimism. Colonel Schwehr's Gebirgsjägers were advancing through
several of the first line of passes in force. Desperately Geyer ordered reinforcements from the Col de Rousset and from the
Forêt de Lente in the west, but he was "playing chess," as
Tanant put it, for those men were almost certain to be badly
needed soon in their own sectors.

Then came news that the bridge over the Drôme River at
Quart that was to be held open at all costs as an escape route
was no longer defended. Pierre Reynaud, the man in command
of that sector of the southern slopes, phoned Geyer that they
had lost Châtillon and were withdrawing south. This opened
up Die completely from the east.

Huet's whole line was crumbling but still he went through
the motions of resistance. At Vassieux that night the Germans
fired flares so that any attack would be illuminated by their
stark white light. Despite this, the colonel insisted that the assault he had planned should still proceed, but Captain Bourgeois, like Geyer the night before, was terribly hindered by his
communication problems. There was the same lack of co-or-
dination, the same uncertainty. Also, the will of the tired men
who were ordered to attack was now badly sapped. Lieutenant
Hoppers and his OSS section advanced on Vassieux and "were
almost at the edge of the village before we realized that there
was no one with the section but six Maquis and again we had

to retreat into the woods." They stayed in cover and, as daylight came, shot at everything they could, claiming the destruction of three Junkers as they flew in to land on the air strip.

By dawn only one pass in the southeast was still causing the Germans trouble—the Pas de l'Aiguille—where the French were ensconced in a cave. So a squad of Gebirgsjägers climbed the mountain above it, let down a box of explosive on the end of a rope, and detonated it in the mouth of the cave. Every man within it was killed.

The end of the Free Republic of the Vercors was clearly near. Many of the liaison cars used by messengers could no longer be employed because of a lack of gasoline. But Huet had not given in yet. He was determined to attempt one more attack on Vassieux. He ordered Captain Bousquet, his adjutant, to take command and, since his weary men on the hills around Vassieux had now been at their posts for forty-eight hours, to employ a few units from the Forêt de Lente who had not yet been in action.

Early in the morning, Pierre Tanant rode up to the big forest by motorcycle to issue the orders but, as he was doing so, Huet discovered that already it was too late and had to send a dispatch rider after him with cancellation instructions. A message from Jean Prévost removed any lingering hopes he might have had. The moment he had been postponing since the big decision taken at the meeting two nights before had come at last.

The Germans had attacked Valchevrière again at dawn under the cover of a massive barrage of mortars. They had taken the outposts and had launched assault after assault on the belvedere. Chabal was calm, firing his bazooka, still with his pipe in his mouth. For hours the battle for the terrace continued. Chabal himself is reported to have killed twenty-seven of the enemy.

Meanwhile, the Germans were trying to turn the French position behind the high barricades of the belvedere, clambering up through the steep forest where the mines were not enough to stop them. Grimly the French fought off repeated attacks from three sides—the fourth side being formed by the mountain. Then finally the enemy gained some huge boulders that loomed out from the mountain high above the belvedere. Chabal had always known that his position was vulnerable from this point and he had indeed made some attempt to cover himself, but he did not have enough men to cope with every eventuality. Once the Germans were above him, it meant that his flanks were turned and the battle was almost over.

He ordered a counterattack but he knew that there was little chance of its succeeding. From their new position, the Germans could shoot down on the BCA men lying below them on the terrace, firing through the pillared balustrade constructed originally to prevent sightseers from falling down the mountainside. Chabal's men moved to avoid the lethal new danger, taking what cover they could, using trees and the barricade, but they were now between crossfire and their casualties increased fast. Men on both sides of Chabal were struck down.

During a lull in the fighting, he scribbled a quick note to Jean Prévost: "I am almost completely encircled. We are preparing to do a Sidi Brahim. *Vive la France!*" In 1845, at Sidi Brahim, some one hundred miles north of the Moroccan town of Marrakech, a French outpost was surrounded by desert tribesmen and three hundred and forty men were massacred. It had become a legendary event of French military history.

Chabal was shot very soon afterward, but he still went on firing, with blood staining his anorak. Then he remembered that he had a list of men in his pocket—men who might be regarded as "terrorists" by the Germans. He took it out, screwed the paper into a ball, and dropped it over the side of the belvedere. A moment later he was killed by a bullet in the head.

As soon as Huet heard that Valchevrière had fallen, he issued the disperse orders. Messengers hurried down from St.-Martin with instructions that contact with the enemy was to be broken off at 4:00 P.M. and all units were then to escape to the areas that had been allocated to them. Rear guards were under orders to hold various points on the roads to cover the retreat.

Andre Paray was summoned to the Villa Bellon. Huet wanted the American signals officer to remain with him as they withdrew so that, even at Revoulat, his fall-back position in the forested mountains to the south of Les Grands-Goulets, he would still be able to maintain radio contact with Allied Headquarters. This posed problems for Paray because the equipment was heavy and the latter stages of the journey to Revoulat would be on foot along steep forest trails.

Paray decided to abandon the transmitter that he used for contact with Algiers and to take only the machine he needed for radio communication with London—together with a battery and a charger that was operated, like a bicycle, by pedals.

Huet ordered Paray to meet him at Les Barraques, at the head of Les Grands-Goulets, at 4:30. Before the signals officer left St.-Martin, he transmitted one signal to London for the colonel. It was as bitter as Chavant's "criminals and cowards" accusation of the previous day, but more restrained:

"We have held on against three German divisions for fifty-six hours. Until now we have lost only a tiny piece of territory. The troops have fought courageously but desperately, for they are now physically exhausted and almost out of ammunition. Despite repeated requests, we are still fighting alone and have received neither support nor aid from the start of the battle. It was obvious that sooner or later the situation would become desperate and deteriorate into terrible misfortune on the Vercors plateau. We have done all that could be expected of us but are filled with sadness for the enormous responsibility of those who from far away deliberately engaged us in such a venture."

It is significant that this message is one of the signals that are not in the official French files, for there is no doubt that it was transmitted. It appears in full in the official report of Andre Paray, the man who sent it, in the OSS archives, currently held by the CIA in Washington. What *is* in the files is another message, sent from Revoulat a few hours later. This had a similar opening but none of the accusation, which probably explains why it is still available. In it Huet reported that he had ordered dispersion in small groups with a view to renewing the struggle if possible. Perhaps, as the evening drew on, he felt that the first, sent in the high emotion of defeat, had been a little tactless.

Early in the afternoon, the German troops who had broken through at Valchevrière appeared on the heights of the Roche Rousse overlooking St.-Martin. Soon after three o'clock the first shells were screaming across the valley to explode in the town.

When the news of Huet's dispersal order reached Rang-des-Pourrets, General Zeller departed by car with Francis Cammaerts, Christine Granville, and two SOE radio operators, each carrying their sets in black leather suitcases.

They drove to the tunnel of the Col de Rousset. There they left the vehicle and, led by a guide, scrambled on foot down the steep mountainside, which was covered by thick beech bushes. Way below them on the road they could see a big German column, led by three tanks, approaching from Die. Above, an enemy aircraft was flying in low sweeps over the mountainside, searching for signs of movement. Often, as the plane flew near them, they had to stay still, huddled under the bushes. Then, as they were halfway down the mountain, they heard the big explosion behind them as the Rousset tunnel was blown.

That night, in darkness, they crossed the ring road unseen by patrolling Germans and waded across the Drôme River. Cammaerts and his SOE team made contact with his network. Zeller was making for headquarters in North Africa to demand a meeting with De Gaulle.

When Geyer received the disperse order at La Rivière, he phoned those of his commanders whom he could contact and sent messengers to those he could not. All had been warned previously that they were to fall back into specified positions in the huge Forêt de Lente, which was, of course, familiar territory to them. The captain was determined that they should stay as a controlled force which, even if they had to remain hidden for a while, could after a short time be deployed for offensive operations.

His staff made hurried preparations to abandon the farm, burying documents and also some cans of film taken by a news cameraman who had been in the plateau with them. Both would be incriminating if found by the Germans, since they might identify "terrorists."

For two anxious hours, they could hear the explosions of the shells on St.-Martin as they got ready to leave. It was not until five o'clock that at last they set off with the horses and some motorized transport down the steep lane that led from La Rivière to the small road that lay parallel to the Vernaison River below. They headed for the ruins of La Chapelle and struck west by way of a small pass called the Col de Carri.

It was dark by the time they reached the forest and camped for the night, not far from the village of Lente. Immediately Geyer sent off horsemen to ensure that his commanders had successfully withdrawn and were in their allotted positions. Contact was established with five of them, but Geyer was certain that the remainder would reach their positions by morning. To the captain's pleased surprise, he found that Captain Tournissa, wounded on his air strip during the first attack on Vassieux, had been moved in darkness from the grotto first-aid post on the fringe of the town and was now with one of his units—badly hurt, but alive.

At Oscence, where the prison had been transferred a week before, Vincent Beaume received the order to free the prisoners. He did not agree with it, but it permitted him no options. Sourly he watched his detainees leave the camp, led by the night club singer from Grenoble. She was aiming for Royans, where she believed a German officer she knew would be waiting. Some of the Resistance men planned to mingle with the prisoners, hoping to escape from the plateau in this way, but when they reached Royans, the singer pointed them out. "Look out for the ones wearing American shoes," she advised the Germans, for these had of course been included in parachute drops.

Some of the tougher Maquisards, however, took the opportunity the breakup of the camp gave them to take the revenge that Beaume had prevented for six weeks. Several prisoners were shot on their way down the mountain.

Meanwhile, Lieutenant Conus, still trying to find his way out of the Vercors on his way to Oisans, had been captured by the Germans. They had interrogated him under torture and scheduled him for execution with a number of other French prisoners at the edge of a steep ravine near the village of St.-Guillaume.

He watched as his fellow captives were made to kneel in pairs before being shot in the back of the head by an officer, after which their lifeless bodies fell conveniently into the gorge. When it was his turn, Conus decided to make an escape attempt. As he knelt beside the ravine and the executing officer raised his revolver, the big-game hunter leaped backwards at him. The German fired—but missed. Conus jumped into the gorge, where fortunately his fall was broken by a tree. The Germans opened fire from above with submachine guns, but he managed to wade through the stream unhurt into some woods on the far bank. Luckily it was near evening. The darkness helped him to evade the rigorous search that followed and he succeeded in escaping. The next day he reached the Oisans with his sense of humor, at least, unscathed. He signaled London: "Arrested. Tortured. Shot. In good health."

Throughout the plateau, during that dramatic afternoon of July 23, men were making for cover to their assigned areas. In the north, Beauregard and his men had already fallen back into the wild mountain country near Plénouze where Huet had found them when he arrived to assume his command six weeks before. Jean Prévost moved south a few miles from his field command post with a group that included Lea Blaine, one of his liaison agents, and Jean Veyrat, Chavant's friend who had traveled with him to Algiers in May. They took refuge in the damp, dark Grotte aux Fées in the thick woods on the mountain above La Rivière.

Vincent Beaume and a party of some twelve people were heading for Revoulat, Huet's own designated fall-back area, but the Second Bureau chief planned to move on from there to the west side of La Montagne de l'Arp where a remote, heavily wooded plateau overlooked the foothills village of Ste.-Eulalie, where Beaume knew all the farmers in the district. He hoped they could be a source of food—a source that he knew he would need to use with care, for the Germans were certain to

watch the farms very closely and retribution on residents who
helped "terrorists" would be ruthless. Beaume's party had just
set off when he realized that they would have to go through the
western mine fields and sent one of his men back to headquarters in St.-Martin to get a Perspex sketch of the dangerous
areas. This could be laid over an ordinary map to show the
exact positions of the fields they must avoid.

Desmond Longe and John Houseman led the group that had
worked with them to the high woods near the Roche Rousse
opposite St.-Martin, where Huet had told the major to await
his instructions. Longe was anxious about Paray, with whom he
had lost touch.

Young Lieutenant Hoppers and his weary OSS team, who
had had barely any sleep for the past three days, were making
for the wild high country at Choranche, to the west of the plateau overlooking the Gorges de la Bourne. Exhausted as he
was, Hoppers was worrying about his comrade Chester Myers,
for since the hospital had been moved from St.-Martin he no
longer knew his whereabouts. Myers, of course, was already in
hiding with the rest of the sick and wounded in the Grotte de
la Luire.

There, all day, the nurses had worked very hard to transform
the huge cave, with water dripping from the ceiling, into the
nearest approach to a hospital that could be made of a grotto.
One of the doctors had operated on the urgent cases in the
Chaberts farmhouse, which lay in the valley near the road. By
dusk, his patients had been carried back up through the steep
woods to be laid down on the floor of the cave with the rest.
No one had told them that the disperse order had been given,
but the noise of battle that they had heard all day had di-
minished. By evening, too, the shelling of St.-Martin had
ceased and Dr. Ganimède assumed that the withdrawal had

started. This meant that German troops would soon be on the Rousset–St.-Martin road, that patrols might well drive up the approach lane to the woods that concealed the grotto.

In the flickering candlelight, shielded from the entrance, the old doctor surveyed his makeshift ward with its thirty-eight patients and seven nurses and wondered what the chances of their survival might be—the chances of thirty-four, that is, for four of them were wounded Wehrmacht prisoners. It was hard for Ganimède to be optimistic, but the presence of Father Yves de Montcheuil, the Jesuit priest from Paris, was some solace. That day he had held a mass in the cave. Ganimède hoped fervently that his prayers would be answered.

Huet's headquarters team of about twenty people assembled at Les Barraques. As Paray drove there from St.-Martin, he was forced to stop by shells dropping on the road ahead of him, and continued when the gunners eventually shifted their attention to another target area. Huet himself made a last visit to Rang-des-Pourrets and La Rivière to ensure that everyone had left, and then he joined the others—"haversack on his back, his rifle slung on his shoulder, his face contracted with emotion," as Pierre Tanant was to write.

Grimly he watched his final orders being carried out. The tunnel at the head of the route that reached down from Les Barraques beside Les Grands-Goulets was blocked with old vehicles. The road in front of it was blown up. The cars in which they had all driven to the assembly point were set on fire to prevent their being used by the Germans.

The food they had brought with them was distributed and they set off in two groups on foot from Les Barraques up the rocky forest paths on their way to Revoulat. Andre Paray's cumbersome radio equipment soon caused difficulties. Already he was overwhelmingly tired from sleepless nights. He stumbled under the weight of the transmitter and charger, several

times falling over as they clambered up the steep, uneven trail.
The others helped him as well as they could. After an hour
they reached Revoulat, which, like all the fall-back positions,
was in remote forested country. They made their camp within
the thick woods, which, so Tanant wrote, "would give us some
small protection against the dampness of the night."

Chavant was one of the last to leave St.-Martin before German troops entered the town. He was desolate with anger,
deeply concerned for the men and women of his plateau, especially for Mme Breyton, who had been such a bastion of their
lives while the Vercors had been an outlaw refuge. The Patron
was used to going underground and, for the next few days, he
moved constantly like a fox, always in darkness, using the country and the people that he knew so well.

In the high woods across the valley from St.-Martin, Desmond Longe and his group waited for the expected orders to
arrive from Huet—orders that, in fact, would never come, either because there was a mistake or because the unhappy colonel, with so many final things to cope with, had forgotten.
From their position in the woods they could hear shooting and
could see flames in the town. Fearing that German patrols
would already be scouring the country for fugitives, Longe ordered that there should be no talking and that certainly no fires
were to be lit.

For most of the day the weather had been fine but now, in
the darkness as the Vercors defenders made their way to their
hiding places or sat under the trees, chilled by the night air of
the mountains, once more it began to rain.

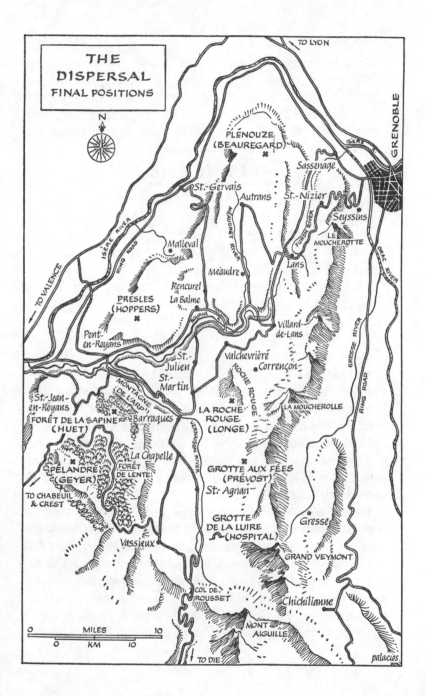

THE
DISPERSAL
FINAL POSITIONS

N

TO LYON

GRENOBLE

PLÉNOUZE
(BEAUREGARD)

Sassenage

St.-Gervais
Autrans   St.-Nizier

ISÈRE

Seyssins

LE
MOUCHEROTTE

MÉAUDRET RIVER

FURON RIVER

Malleval

Lans

TO VALENCE

RING ROAD

ISÈRE RIVER

Méaudre

DRAC RIVER

Rencurel
La Balme

PRESLES
(HOPPERS)

Villard-
de-Lans

BOURNE R.

Pont-
en-Royans

Valchevrièré
Corrençon

GRESSE RIVER

St.-
Julien

ROCHE ROUGE

St.-
Martin

RING ROAD

St.-Jean-
en-Royans

MONTAGNE
DE LAUP

LA ROCHE
ROUGE
(LONGE)

LA MOUCHEROLLE

FORÊT DE LA SAPINE
(HUET)

Barraques

VERNAISON RIVER

La Chapelle

GROTTE AUX FÉES
(PRÉVOST)

PÉLANDRE
(GEYER)

FORÊT
DE LENTE

St.-Agnan

TO CHABEUIL
& CREST

Gresse

GROTTE
DE LA LUIRE
(HOSPITAL)

Vassieux

GRAND VEYMONT

COL DE
ROUSSET

Chichilianne

MILES   10

MONT
AIGUILLE

KM   10

TO DIE

palacios

CHAPTER 18

For Geyer, the Forêt de Lente was home territory. He was suited by temperament to operating in heavily wooded country. During those spring months earlier that year, when the Lente forest had been his base, he and his commanders had come to know it intimately—the paths, the hills, the grottoes, the sawmills, the farms, the areas where the trees grew thickly, the parts that were so lightly timbered that a horseman could travel across them at a gallop.

There had, therefore, been a degree of satisfaction for this complex man as on the evening of the twenty-third, with his men and his regimental standard, he had ridden up into the tall fir forest that in the past had provided the timber for many of France's ships. Despite the anguish he felt over the appalling scenes that he knew would soon be enacted in the villages of the plateau as the German SS men directed punitive operations, he was pleased that soon he would be operating in an environment he completely understood. At last, after weeks when his actions had been curbed by Huet and his headquarters staff at St.-Martin, he would be able to take the initiative again. He would be able to deploy his units by exploiting the rough country he knew very well against an enemy who did not. The colonel, of course, was still his commanding officer, but the communication problem would make it far more difficult for him to issue binding orders.

After spending the night near Lente village, Geyer moved north with his men to Pélandré, a hamlet linked to a farm in one of the most rugged areas of the forest. Deliberately he avoided the houses and barns, for he knew that these were almost certain to be visited in due course by the Germans, and established his camp among close-growing trees at the head of the Vercors cliffs high above the village of Bouvante-le-Bas in the massif's western foothills.

As always, he had selected his site with great care. It was difficult country for anyone, unused to the forest, to move around in, and it had close natural boundaries that limited the approaches, thus making it less vulnerable to surprise attack. To the west were cliffs; to the north the pass of the Col de l'Echarasson; to the east the rocky mountain ridge of Taillebourse.

From his new command post, he sent out riders to order his commanders to move closer to him for easier control. Also, a lot of men who had lost touch with their units in the chaos of the withdrawal were wandering on their own about the forest. Some heard that he was at Pélandré and arrived at his headquarters seeking guidance. Others were picked up by his mounted patrols and brought in to the camp. These were directed to their units if they were among those in the forest. The remainder were formed into a new company.

On that initial day at Pélandré, one of the first men Geyer met was Captain Louis Bordeaux, a forestry expert who com-

manded the southwest sector of the Vercors and the man who
had established the first of the Maquis camps to be set up on
the plateau in 1943. To Geyer's horror, Bordeaux told him
that, instead of hiding in the forest, some of his men who came
from Royans had preferred to take the risk of returning to their
homes. "They must be stopped at once," ordered Geyer, "and
reformed ready for action as soon as possible." The disbanding
of Bordeaux' unit was one of the many misunderstandings of
Huet's disperse order. In fact, all that day, others who had
failed to appreciate the reason for remaining in the Vercors
were indeed being shot down "like rabbits," as predicted three
nights before during the crisis meeting in the Villa Bellon, as
they tried to break out of the German ring.

Escape, in fact, was not too difficult—as Francis Cammaerts
had demonstrated—because the ring road was so long that it
could not possibly be fully policed. But it required experience
in moving about hostile country, which was why, like Cammaerts, most of the veteran Maquisards survived.

Geyer's sharp order to reform his unit pleased Bordeaux, who
had been gloomy with the anguish of defeat. For he realized
that his commander saw the dispersal only as a tactical withdrawal. He hurried off to recall his men and soon reported to
Geyer that they were assembled and awaiting orders. Royans,
in fact, was the last place for anyone from the Vercors to think
of going, for the Germans set up a court-martial there and were
soon executing "terrorists."

Meanwhile, Geyer framed his new policy. As he had told
Bordeaux, he intended to attack, to show the enemy that the
French were not yet beaten in the Vercors. But he knew that
all his men were very tired after the long battle, that a period
of rest for the licking of wounds was vital before he swung
them onto the offensive again. Also, before then he wanted to
find out as much as he could about the German positions and
their patterns of activity—the routines and techniques of their

detachments as they scoured the plateau—so that he could devise a strategy that was tailored to the habits of the enemy.

So, maintaining close regular contact with his units, he ordered them to send out patrols, covering as wide an area as was possible without placing the men under too great a strain. As he had long predicted, his horses came into their own. They were on the move all the time, carrying messengers or men on patrol.

No one, Geyer insisted, was to attempt to attack the enemy. Information was the main requirement—information that could be vital to their survival during those first few days when it was hard to know what was happening, information that could be exploited later. It was a time, he believed, as it had been in April during the Milice campaign, for a low profile.

Despite this, there *was* some action on the first day after they had moved to Pélandré. One of the patrols, operating near the road to the Col de l'Echarasson that led down to the plain, encountered three civilians behaving suspiciously. They were released prisoners from Vincent Beaume's concentration camp. The officer in charge of the patrol interrogated them, became convinced that they had been sent back onto the plateau by the Germans to act as spies, and promptly had them shot. Geyer approved the action. Like the Croupe Vallier, he and his officers at La Rivière had long felt that Beaume was far too soft in his attitude to the known traitors in his care. "The responsibility of the Second Bureau was very great throughout this period," an entry in the 11th Cuirassiers log asserted after recording the executions, "and a rigorous inquiry should be made into a leniency that truly was exaggerated."

Without question, Beaume would have condemned these killings without trial, but for Geyer and his men this seemed no time to take chances. They had been driven like animals into the undergrowth. So far, although they knew little of what was happening in the villages of the plateau interior, they were in touch with the farms and rumors were circulating of terrible carnage in Vassieux and La Chapelle. Also, German units were already moving through the big forest, pillaging and burning the farms, often killing the people they found inside. Throughout the day, bursts of machine gun fire could be heard, echoing through the trees from the camp at Pélandré.

Within the Forêt de Lente, during that early period, the Germans seemed to be operating with great caution, taking care not to stray from the roads. Even so, Geyer ensured that all night guards at the camp should be posted in pairs, in case one fell asleep, and stay constantly alert. That first evening of the twenty-fourth, there were no alarms of patrolling Germans, but they did hear the noise that everyone in the Vercors had been yearning for since June 22—heavy explosions to the south and the sound of massed engines of a squadron of big Halifaxes. At last, after all those repeated pleas, the Allies had gotten around to bombing Chabeuil! At last they had found the correct airfield! The raid destroyed or damaged thirty German aircraft on the ground—some of the planes, no doubt, that had caused so much havoc among the troops on the plateau. Like so many of the events connected with the Vercors, it was useless because it came too late.

The next morning there were new arrivals at Pélandré. Lieutenant Moine, who had been with Geyer in the 11th Cuirassiers and also in his first group in the Grand-Serre, led his company of weary Senegalese into the camp, to be greeted by a warm welcome. The big African marksmen were totally exhausted, having marched south across the Gorges de la Bourne from the Forêt des Coulmes in the northern sector.

During the next few days, others, too, would come to the camp, and all the time the problems of how to feed everyone would grow—as it would for every group that was in refuge throughout the plateau. Most of them had taken a little food with them when they had withdrawn from the interior, but this was consumed very quickly. The farmers helped as much as they could, but in the face of the German policy of destroying those suspected of giving help to "terrorists" they were already in great danger.

While Geyer was setting up his headquarters at Pélandré, Huet moved on from Revoulat into country that was more remote and offered better cover. He, too, had been joined by men who had lost their units and, since his party now numbered about forty men, he divided it into three smaller groups that were easier to control. He led them, as Vincent Beaume had led his group, to Le Montagne de l'Arp, though he chose a different part of it—the Forêt de la Sapine, near the north side of the great chasm of Combe Laval.

"We had a terrible time," wrote Andre Paray of the journey, "never following the paths, stumbling at night on rocks, crawling on our knees. Hardly any food or water. Monday afternoon, the 24th, I collapsed. Even before leaving St.-Martin, I was overtired but the French refused to abandon me."

The new headquarters of the Vercors commander, still spread out in the three groups, was within reach of a farm, whose owners were very perturbed by the dangerous presence of the colonel and his men. However, as Tanant noted, they had a herd of cattle and, even more important, they possessed their own cistern, so that—unlike so many of the men in refuge in other parts of the plateau—they had a good supply of water.

Huet ordered that they should move the camp every day. Even so, Andre Paray succeeded in maintaining radio contact with London, although, as he noted in his report, "the Germans sometimes being too close, we would be compelled to stop transmitting and lie still." They possessed only one battery, which meant that the equipment could be used only for short periods at a time. Also, the "pedaltor," the strange bicycle-type machine with which they charged it, was noisy to use, so it could be operated only in darkness, when there was less danger of attracting the attention of enemy patrols. The pedaling was arduous work and several of the men would tackle it in turns.

The Forêt de la Sapine was not far as the crow flew from Pélandré, but because of the need to skirt Combe Laval anyone traveling between the two camps had a long journey. Despite this and all the other difficulties of communication, Huet and Geyer were soon engaged in conflict once more. Huet sent the captain orders by way of the Groupe Vallier to send patrols down to St.-Martin, Vassieux, and La Chapelle. Geyer believed that this would be madness at this early stage. His exhausted men were not yet fit enough for long missions that would be extremely dangerous and have dubious value. At present the Germans were everywhere, combing the plateau in rigorous searches for Resistance men. It was far better, he protested, to wait where they were until the main dynamic of the German operation had eased and the men had recovered their energies. That would be time for action. Under the new conditions in which they were all living, he was able to delay the execution of the order in a way that would have been more difficult before the German attack, but very soon Huet received more powerful support.

Colonel Descour returned to the Vercors on July 23, the night of the dispersal. With Dom Guétet, he was led by a guide through the German ring and the three of them made their way onto the plateau by way of steep mountain paths. Descour, of course, did not know of the courageous death of his son Jacques at Vassieux until at last he was informed by one of Geyer's patrols. According to Tanant, the colonel asked to be left alone. He remained in deep thought for a few minutes, racked with grief. Then, with a great effort, he gained control of himself and rejoined the others.

For Geyer, the arrival of the distraught regional commander created more problems. For Descour wanted even more aggressive action than Huet. He ordered Geyer to send two squadrons to the plateau interior—one to the Vassieux area and the other to Oscence, the last site of Beaume's prison camp. "The intention of Colonel Descour," the 11th Cuirassiers log records, "is to reoccupy the ground as soon as possible and to strike at the enemy columns on the main roads. . . ." Geyer protested that this was impractical, but the colonel did not waste time arguing. He bypassed him and gave his orders direct to two of Geyer's commanders—Captain Chastenay de Gery and Captain Jérôme Bagnaud. To Geyer's anxiety, for he doubted if he would see them again, the two squadrons left on their missions that night.

In Grenoble on July 25, as troops of the 157th Reserve Division were executing their anti-"terrorist" operation in the Vercors, General Karl Pflaum reported happily on the success of the attack to the commander in chief, German forces in the west, Field Marshal Von Rundstedt, in Paris, where the news of the operation was recorded in the command log as it came in during the next few days.

"Resistance of the enemy in the region to the southwest of Grenoble is broken. The terrorists have evacuated the camps and villages and are in flight, trying to slip away to the northwest. . . . Action against the terrorists in the region to the east of Valence proceeds. Contact made with airborne troops. Aircraft have successfully supported the operations of combat groups. . . . Vercors Operation: enemy resistance broken south and east. Camps and localities occupied until now by terrorists evacuated in haste with loss of arms, munitions, and food. Enemy, divided into small groups, is trying to escape across our lines of encirclement. . . ."

Meanwhile, Colonel Schwehr's orders to "find the gangs

of terrorists and exterminate them completely" were being ruthlessly executed. German patrols were systematically searching the plateau, section by section—exercising just a little care at this early stage in their probing of the deepest parts of the forests where "terrorist" ambushes were especially likely. The *ratissage* ("raking," or cleanup operation) bore the same signs of authorship as the attack, the same careful and methodical build-up. The German orders were to be thorough, which meant that the patrols had time. The more difficult areas could be left until later when, with the rest of the Vercors reduced to proper control, troops would go into the final pockets in sufficient strength to meet any remaining opposition no matter what scope there was for concealment or surprise attack.

In the villages, other units were conducting the characteristic operation of punishment, carrying the same warning to other Maquis areas, and the civilians that helped to sustain them, that the ravaging of St.-Donat had been intended to give to the Vercors. The Waffen SS, special troops often used for punitive purposes, and some of the much-feared Mongol prisoners had arrived on the massif. In Vassieux more than two hundred people were slaughtered, many of them old peasants. Some of the male bodies were found to be castrated. Others were killed slowly, such as one man and his son who were hanged together by the feet, their mouths just touching the ground, until they died of starvation after frantically eating earth. Several corpses were found with their eyes gouged out, breasts cut off, tongues removed. None of the dead were buried. They were left in the houses, in the streets, to decompose. One twelve-year-old girl, after the death of her parents, was trapped for days by fallen masonry in her destroyed home, begging passing SS men to give her some water. Each time they refused and laughed at her. She was found eventually and freed by Father Gagnol, the curé of Vassieux, who had confirmed her only three months earlier. Unhappily he was a little too late, for she died in the hospital.

In La Chapelle, among the twenty-five civilians who were killed, were sixteen people including the schoolmaster, taken, so the Germans announced, as "hostages," although they were not used as such. They were tortured all afternoon, their cries being heard throughout the town, and then shot in pairs that night in the square.

At L'Echarasson near Geyer's camp five Maquis, found in a farmhouse, were burned alive in the building. The girl who helped Desmond Longe's staff with their decoding was disemboweled and her intestines were wrapped around her neck.

According to Andre Paray, who returned to the Vercors after the German defeat, one fourteen-year-old girl from Corrençon was raped eleven times. Another woman was assaulted by seventeen soldiers while a German doctor held her pulse, telling the troops to wait at moments when she showed signs of fainting to allow her to recover.

The destruction was overwhelming. In Vassieux, 146 houses were destroyed—in La Chapelle, 160. Some of these were no doubt demolished in the bombings, but this would not have been the case in the tiny village of St.-Agnan near Rang-des-Pourrets, where 20 homes were burned, or St.-Julien, where 13 were razed to the ground.

Meanwhile, the arrest of the young men who were not technically terrorists, though the differentiation must have been arbitrary, was continuing, the church at St.-Martin being used as a detention center.

The roundup of livestock was approaching Texan standards: nearly three thousand head of cattle, thirteen hundred pigs, three hundred horses, and vast quantities of wheat, hay, and apples—much of which was transported out of the plateau by planes from Captain Tournissa's air strip. The price for living in a mountain fortress was heavy.

For the Maquisards and the men who had rallied to the plateau to fight in June, however, the main problem was to survive while the *ratissage* operation, the systematic combing of the plateau, was in progress. In those early hours after the dispersal, many of them were merely hungry and thirsty—but soon they would be facing starvation and the same desperate need for water that men have often known in the desert.

Late on July 25, huddled around Andre Paray's receiver in the Forêt de la Sapine, Huet and his officers heard great news. The stalemate in Normandy had ended. For six weeks, since D Day, the Allied armies had been contained on the Cherbourg peninsula. They had broadened the territory they controlled, but always the German line had held. That day, however, General Patton's tanks had at last broken a hole through the ring at St.-Lô, southeast of the big port, and were driving south in a big detour into the body of France before veering north. Close behind them, advancing through the gap the armor had made, were no less than three armies, fanning out for the drive to Paris. The position was good on other fronts. Russian troops, still advancing at the astonishing rate that was such an anxiety to Churchill, had reached the Vistula. In Italy, General Alexander's forward units were as far north as Pisa. As Pierre Tanant recorded, making the supposition that people in the Vercors had now been making for more than six weeks, "It all indicated that the invasion of Provence could not be long delayed."

On that day of July 25, events were emerging in Algiers that would splash the Vercors across the headlines, not as a story of heroism as it had been until then, but as a scandal. A provisional Consultative Assembly of all parties had been called to consider the issues raised by the liberation, and General de Gaulle opened proceedings with a major speech that, for both dramatic and external reasons, he regarded as extremely important.

His main theme was familiar to everyone with whom he had

been in contact since D Day. He still believed that, in the struggle for Europe, the role of the French, and the Resistance in particular, had not been given the credit that was due—as indeed it had not. Employing the rolling phrases that had inspired millions of French people during his radio broadcasts from London, he described the achievements of the FFI—the sabotage of German communications, the diversion of enemy troops from Normandy, the fact that there were parts of France into which the Germans could enter only at their peril, the pitched battles that had been fought in the mountains.

"Even at this moment," he declared, "the enemy is attacking the Vercors massif with forces of every service and major air support. According to unimpeachable reports, the Germans have already lost, in this incessant struggle [in France] since the beginning of June, at least eight thousand dead, more than two thousand prisoners, and a very large quantity of equipment. . . .

"It is certain that the number of troops that the Germans have been forced to use to fight against our men on metropolitan soil amounts to at least seven or eight divisions. Yet, in spite of the terrible repression that they have employed against our defenseless people, they have had no success in controlling the country. . . . Indeed, France knows from experience that this form of war costs human lives and ruined property. It is the government's duty to balance as far as possible the losses with the results. . . ."

This was either one of the most cynical speeches De Gaulle ever made or he had not yet been informed that in the Vercors, at least, the Germans had been completely successful, that the battle was certainly no longer in progress, that the losses bore no relation to the results. General Cochet, giving testimony in Paris with all documents before him, stated that Huet's final telegram, dispatched via London by Paray from their hiding place in Revoulat, was handed to General Béthouart at ten o'clock that morning. But this followed many signals over the past few days both from within the plateau and from the Maquis nearby that indicated that a tragedy was inevitable unless reinforcements in strength were dispatched without delay to the plateau.

Jacques Soustelle had done his utmost to arrange this. He had appealed to all French authorities who had control of any paratroops and also to the Allies, who were now engrossed in their program for the invasion of the South. General Cochet had flown to the Allied Air Force Headquarters in Italy to deploy what additional personal pressure he could. But Soustelle's effort had been started too late. Bad weather and the problems of assembling the men and weapons had presented obstacles that were too great to overcome in time. Even the few troops that Constans had mentioned in his last-minute signal to the Vercors, within hours of the assault, had to be dropped outside the plateau because, by the time of their take-off, Huet had already ordered the dispersal.

In view of the fact that De Gaulle had ordered Béthouart three days earlier to conduct a personal investigation into the Vercors situation, and that Jacques Soustelle, who was very close to him, was by then fully aware of the facts, it is impossible to believe that the General had not been informed of the truth by the time he mounted the rostrum to address the Consultative Assembly on July 25. The purpose of his speech, however, was to present a picture of French success, which would have been greatly marred by the spectacular defeat—due largely to his own errors and those of his senior staff, absorbed as they were in their grand concept of Operation C—that had just happened on the Vercors massif.

That day, however, there was one man in Algiers who believed he understood the facts of the Vercors tragedy very clearly: Fernand Grenier, the Air Minister, concerned with the abortive Operation Patrie. The previous evening, so Grenier has recorded, he received a visit from one of Soustelle's staff. Maybe this officer was, indeed, "sickened by the political maneuvers of the Gaullist politicians," as the communist Grenier wrote, or perhaps he had other reasons. Whatever his motive, he revealed to the Air Minister a story of which to this day Grenier insists he was until then totally ignorant. He had not been informed of the growing crisis revealed by the appeals for help from the Vercors as the Germans assembled their forces around the massif. Grenier's visitor did more than recount the facts. He handed the Air Minister a copy of the dramatic "criminals and cowards" message from Eugène Chavant, which had so far been kept secret.

For a communist engaged in a political battle with the right wing, this was ammunition indeed. It also provided protection, for Grenier claims that he feared a plot to blame him, as Air Minister, for the fact that adequate air support was never provided for the Vercors.

Already, before the arrival of Grenier's evening caller, a press conference had been arranged on July 27 for the Air Minister to bring newsmen up to date on the reorganization of French aviation services. It provided him with an ideal forum to exploit his new information without appearing to deploy the blunt method of a specially summoned press meeting.

During the conference, he spoke of the progress made by his ministry and paid tribute to the courage displayed by the men flying in French squadrons with Allied forces in the war theaters. "I would have liked," he added carefully, "to be able to tell you that we had not failed to give the Maquis the material and moral support of our airmen, [but] all my efforts have been in vain. I, at least, have a clear conscience, for I have done all I could to send our planes to aid those men of the Vercors and elsewhere.

"The French Air Force has deployed our resources to the maximum in [all] battle areas except the interior front, for, in spite of my efforts, I have been unable to overcome political opportunism—a true crime against our country."

This barely veiled accusation of De Gaulle—which the Algiers daily *Alger Républicain* published the next morning—was supported by a letter, phrased far more frankly, that Grenier dispatched that day to the General. Summarizing his attempts to gain his support for Operation Patrie, he charged De Gaulle with distorting the truth about the Allies' acceptance of the project. "The fact is," he wrote, "that during the development of these negotiations [regarding Patrie] the Vercors was attacked. For fifteen days the Maquis leaders have appealed in vain for the bombing of the airfield where German aircraft were massed. They have called in vain for heavy arms. Several times they have informed the French authorities and the Allied Command of formations of enemy tanks. The authorities and the headquarters have remained unmoved. Yesterday a large part of the FFI in the Vercors was crushed, and the final telegram of their leader contained this terrible accusation: 'You are criminals and cowards.' During the course of today, thousands of men have been massacred without the government making any effort, without the Allies going to their rescue.

"I do not intend, for my part, to be associated with a criminal policy that consists of assembling the resources for action and failing to employ them when our French brothers call for help. . . . The time has come to fix the responsibility where it should lie. . . ."

The day after Grenier's press conference, the Cabinet met in the Summer Palace. A furious De Gaulle stalked into the room with the Air Minister's letter in his hand. Before considering any matters on the agenda for the meeting, he read the letter aloud—then demanded Grenier's explanation. "When you have given this," he said, "I will present to you two alternatives. Either you will repudiate your letter and your words [at the press conference] or you will leave this room, no longer the Minister for Air."

Grenier defended himself strongly. "When the moment came for the national revolt," he declared, "it was the duty of all of us to support the FFI. . . . I found myself up against a brick wall. . . . When I learned of the crushing of the Vercors my anger exploded. . . ."

De Gaulle glared at him. "You know how to exploit the dead, Monsieur Grenier," he charged.

"I only know that, before my conscience and before the people of France," answered Grenier angrily, "I have done everything, absolutely everything, to help my comrades in the Resistance."

"You have stated," continued the General coldly, "that because of political opportunism, a crime has been committed against our country. You know very well that this is false. None of our planes [in the Patrie squadron] had the range to reach the Vercors—" He broke off, addressed the others. "Gentlemen, we will adjourn for half an hour. When we return, Monsieur Grenier, I will expect your retraction."

All the ministers withdrew from the room except for Grenier himself and François Billoux, the other communist member of De Gaulle's government. The two men decided that nothing could be gained by resignation, that it would be wise for Grenier to agree to issue a retraction of his charge—which was published the next day in the *Alger Républicain*. Grenier's statement was indeed groveling, even employing the same phraseology of his accusation of the previous day. It declared that the government had done everything possible to give material and moral aid to the Maquis and to the FFI, for "the government have always considered and continues to consider that at the moment when the supreme battle is being fought, political opportunism would be a crime against our country."

It was a total humiliation, accepted for the kind of hard tactical reasons that would have appealed to Lenin. For Grenier remained as Minister for Air. Later, however, he added a revealing postscript to the drama in his memoirs, entitled *C'était ainsi* . . . , by quoting a letter to him from Lieutenant Colonel Morlaix, the flying ace who was to have commanded Operation Patrie. "The Vercors," wrote Morlaix, "was the objective that we chose on which to base the Patrie plan. The distance from Calvi, the take-off airfield planned by General Bouscat, to Vassieux was exactly 360 kilometers [225 miles]. The aircraft to be used were: A-24, range 950 kilometers [590 miles]; Gleen, range 1,300 kilometers [810 miles]; Leo, range 1,500 kilometers [940 miles]."

Morlaix was an expert witness of unquestionable integrity. He was marked in no way by politics and was much respected by everyone. Jacques Soustelle himself paid admiring tribute to his reputation in his own memoirs, *Envers et contre tout*. So De Gaulle's charge that Grenier knew that the Vercors was outside the range of the Patrie aircraft was clearly ungrounded in the facts. Even the most limited of the planes available for the operation could have flown to the plateau—or to Chabeuil —with ample fuel for the return journey.

Perhaps the final comment on this aspect of the tragedy of the massif was made in *La Bataille du silence* by Jean Bruller, one of France's most celebrated writers, who ironically had used the pseudonym of "Vercors" since before the war. "The disastrous abandonment of the Vercors," he wrote, "illustrated the extent to which politics and rivalries had infiltrated the world of fighting France . . . feelings were no longer pure, everything began to become clouded like curdling milk. The resistance that Jean Moulin had so laboriously unified . . . split again into rival political factions, already preparing the ground for their future access to power. . . ."

CHAPTER 19

By July 27, the day of Grenier's outburst to the press in Algiers, the dynamic of the German manhunt in the Vercors had grown. The patrols, supported by dogs, were intensified. At night, the only time most of the hiding Maquisards dared move their positions, flares were constantly fired to reveal the sources of any sounds the waiting Germans believed they had heard. The noise of machine guns, loaded with tracer bullets, often broke the silence of the darkness. In many ways, the hours of quiet stillness between the bursts of gunfire were worse, for then the usual forest sounds—the cracking of a twig, the movement of a branch—carried menace. And all day aircraft flew low over the trees, the pilots searching for signs of campfires, of movement, of any human activity.

Two days after the dispersal, Lieutenant Hoppers and his OSS men, led by the Maquis guides who had been assigned to them, moved cautiously across the Gorges de la Bourne to the high country of Presles in the northern sector. From there they hoped to escape across the Isère and the ring road to the northwest—exactly, of course, what the Germans had anticipated. Fortunately they had met some local Maquisards who warned them that German troops were posted every hundred yards on that section of the road. Then, on the evening that they reached their new position, four hundred Germans arrived in Presles and the Americans had to retire deep into the woods. "For eleven days," Hoppers reported later, "the section lay in one spot, while German patrols scoured the woods and fired into the underbrush trying to scare the Maquis into the Isère valley, where many were shot trying to escape. For eleven days we ate nothing but raw potatoes and occasionally a little cheese. Not more than one man moved at a time—and then never more than fifty feet away from where we lay. The men were never allowed to speak above a whisper. The food which we did get was stolen at night from a farmer who lived close to the woods in which we were hiding."

In the Forêt de la Sapine, Huet was worrying about Hoppers' team. "Around July 27 or 28," reported Andre Paray, "we sent two men who knew the woods well to look for the commando group with the major [who he presumed was with the OSS men]. They failed to return."

The relentless German searching was causing Huet great anxiety, too. "Colonel Hervieux [Huet] sent a message to London," wrote Paray. "He did not know how much longer we could last as we were growing weaker and weaker. We had to contemplate abandoning all equipment. We could not walk for very long as we had not much strength left. . . .

"Toward evenings—not at night, as to find the way would have been impossible—we would in turn go to the farm with the object of getting a few supplies and some water. With German patrols I had some close calls. Once I was in a cherry tree as they went by. . . . We requested London to have containers of food and weapons ready to be dropped as soon as we gave the signal. . . .

"Twice . . . patrols [actually] came after us. We had been betrayed and were compelled to leave the vicinity of our farm rather in a hurry. We hid in the woods above. But we were saved by peasants who guided the patrols to other ruined farms. . . ."

Desmond Longe and his party were still in the woods of the Roche Rousse opposite St.-Martin waiting for Huet or Paray to contact them. "Food is very low and no water," Longe recorded in his journal; "we begin to squeeze moss for the moisture. . . ." To survive, they took it in turns to go out and search for food. One man delighted them by returning with part of a dead goat in his haversack and leading a live female who was in milk, having just borne a kid. Ravenously they drank the goat's milk and, since they dared not light a fire, ate strips of raw meat. But the she-goat was unhappy and began to cause them problems. "Three men have gone in search of water," recorded Longe. "We've had our ration of goat's milk but the goat is calling for her kid. We'll have to kill her or send her away before she exposes our position. My throat is terribly dry. Good old John [Houseman] has saved me by half a cup of moss water it has taken him nearly an hour to squeeze. This endless waiting in silence is dreadful. . . . Every time we drop off to sleep we each have the most vivid dreams of home and friends, food and flowing water. . . ."

The French who were with Longe's party began to risk returning to their homes. Each time any of them left, Longe insisted that the position of their camp should be changed just in case they fell into the hands of the Germans and talked or even, as he wondered in his more desperate moments, in case they were Milice spies.

"We are all getting weaker and are being hunted . . . once a [German] patrol was within touching distance of us, but fortunately neither they nor their dog discovered us. A wonder they did not hear my heart beating. . . . Water is nearly finished again and we squeeze moss and eat berries. . . ."

Finally Longe decided that they would cross the St.-Martin–Rousset road and go in search of Huet and Andre Paray. He knew that this was highly dangerous—and so it was. At one moment, he crept to the corner of a building and found himself face to face with three German soldiers who had also been creeping toward the corner along the adjoining wall. The troops were so surprised that Longe and Houseman were able to cover a good distance before they actually started shooting. Later, in the darkness, their movements were heard by machine gunners and, under the illumination of flares, they had to dive for cover into a wheat field under heavy fire from three different positions. They managed to slip away by morning, but they never found Huet.

During the morning of the twenty-seventh, a small Fieseler Storch reconnaissance plane flew over the trees that covered the Grotte de la Luire. It turned and flew back again over the area as though the attention of the pilot had been caught by something he wanted to verify. Even the second sweep failed to satisfy him, evidently, for once more he turned the plane so that he could study the mountainside, which was thick with timber.

Life in the grotto had settled down to a certain pattern. From the night they had arrived, Dr. Ganimède had insisted on a hospital routine. Meals, washing, dressing of wounds, even visits were scheduled for regular hours. Although they had other problems that were enormous, they had adequate food; but they distributed this frugally because the stock, once exhausted, would be difficult to replace. Local peasants had brought them a side of veal, which they stored in the cold of one of the deeper passages of the grotto, and they also possessed several sacks of oats that, by cooking in milk, they made into a kind of porridge.

The sterilizing unit, which was operated by gas from portable canisters, had to fulfill a second role as a cookstove. From the ceiling of the cave dripped ample supplies of water, which they disinfected with potassium permanganate.

The big danger was that, unlike the other refugees in the forests, they were immobile. They could not move if danger threatened—which was not remote since the grotto, like all the bigger caves, was marked on the maps of the Vercors.

It was because of this that Ganimède urged anyone who was well enough to leave. Four patients did so, taking refuge in a smaller grotto, about a mile distant.

This left thirty-six wounded—twenty-eight Maquisards, including one of the Senegalese; two civilian women casualties from the bombing at Vassieux; four prisoners, Poles who had been drafted into the Wehrmacht; Chester Myers, the OSS lieutenant; and Lilette Lesage, Descour's liaison agent, who had been shot in the thigh during the attack on Combovin in June. Lilette, of course, still carried the identity papers of a nurse. There were also seven genuine nurses, three doctors, Ganimède's wife and twenty-one-year-old son, Jean, and the Jesuit priest Father Yves de Montcheuil. Father Yves, who was renowned throughout France as a theologian, radiated a spiritual calm, and even those who were not of the faith took some comfort from the masses he held every day. Moreover, two Maquis patients had died since they had arrived in the grotto. Father Yves had been able to give them the last rites and supervise their burial.

The German plane whose pilot had shown such interest in the area that morning had caused Ganimède great anxiety—and the doctor's fears were soundly based. At four-thirty that afternoon in the cave everyone was lying down except Lilette

Lesage, who was sitting up on her mattress, her back against the wall. Suddenly she saw the gray-capped head of a German soldier appear above the ground outside the cave, his body still concealed by the mountainside. "They're here!" screamed someone. "*Terroristen!*" he shouted and immediately the grotto entrance was filled with some fifteen German troops, submachine guns aimed.

The four Polish prisoners realized the danger. "*Kameraden!*" one of them yelled in German. "Don't shoot! This is a military hospital!"

"Everyone! On your feet!" ordered a sergeant. "Hands in the air!"

Roughly, using their gun butts, the troops forced to their feet those patients capable of standing and made them line up against a wall with the doctors and nurses. A young SS officer entered the grotto. He was good-looking, polite, and fluent in both French and English.

Chester Myers was near the entrance and the German noticed the U.S. flash on his shoulder. "American, eh?" he said. "You have identification?" Myers showed his ID card. He examined it, looked up. "What are you doing here?" Myers told him. He nodded. "Well, Lieutenant," he said, "for you the war is over," and he ordered two men to escort Myers to a cottage near the main road that they had temporarily commandeered.

Then he noticed Father Yves. "You're a priest?" he asked in French.

"Yes."

"Why are you with these bandits?"

"It is my duty to be with the suffering."

Previously the nurses had carefully removed the uniforms that the Maquisards had so cherished during the days of Free Vercors and replaced them with peasant clothes, obtained from local farms. As an attempt to conceal the fact that they were Resistance men it failed. The officer examined their papers.

"These papers are false," he snapped. "You're terrorists!"—which, of course, under the German orders, was a death sentence.

The troops searched the grotto for arms, then ordered everyone who could walk to leave the cave under a strong escort of guards. Fourteen men remained as stretcher cases and when one of the nurses, Anita Winter, asked if she could stay with them, the officer shrugged his shoulders in uninterested agreement.

The others filed down the rocky pathway from the grotto toward the lane that led to the road. On the way the Senegalese slipped. "*Sale Boche!*" ("Filthy Boche") he exclaimed as he fell, and he was immediately beaten to death with gun butts. Then they were all made to walk to Rousset, where they were imprisoned for the night in an abandoned farmhouse.

After the main party had left the grotto, the Germans continued the rigorous search for arms that they had begun earlier. While this was in progress, Anita was permitted to give her patients some food and water. Then the Germans carried them on their stretchers down the hill and laid them side by side in a field below the cave. When Anita asked anxiously what they were doing, she was pushed roughly into a waiting truck. "*Au revoir!*" she called out to her wounded as she was dragged away. "Have faith!"

As the vehicle moved off down the road toward Rousset she heard the bursts of machine gun fire. By the time she joined the others in the farmhouse at Rousset, she was in hysterics.

One of the wounded had escaped when the Germans had arrived in the grotto. He had slipped away into the maze of subterranean passages beneath it and stayed there, shivering with cold, for three days, before daring to venture up to reconnoiter.

The next morning, in a field at Rousset, the Germans shot nine of the remaining wounded—including the uniformed lieutenant of the French Army who had broken his shoulder during the parachute drop with Captain Tournissa—and hanged one man. Of the patients, only Chester Myers, the American, was spared.

Together with the others from the grotto who had survived so far, he was taken to Grenoble by truck. When the vehicle drew up in front of the Caserne de Bonne barracks in the Boulevard Gambetta, Germans swarmed out of the building to take charge of the prisoners. Chester Myers was an object of fascination to them, for he was the first American officer any of them had seen.

Their interest in the OSS lieutenant gave Lilette Lesage a chance to escape. The driver of the truck, who had been friendly to her, made a movement with his head, indicating she should go while she could. So with the wife of Dr. Ganimède and his son, Jean, she walked off down the road without anyone appearing to notice.

It was almost the only bright moment in a story of continuing tragedy.

The seven nurses were deported to the infamous Ravensbrück concentration camp in Germany where one of them, Odette Malossane, was killed. Chester Myers ended up in a POW camp in Poland, from which he was liberated by the Russians. Dr. Ganimède succeeded in escaping from the Grenoble barracks during the confusion caused by an Allied air raid, but the other two doctors from the grotto and Father Yves were executed by a firing squad at the Polygon Artillery depot, not far from the Caserne de Bonne.

The priest had anticipated his death. For some reason he sensed that, of all of them, Lilette Lesage had the best chance of regaining her liberty. During the journey from the Vercors by truck he said to her, "If you survive, will you go to the Jesuit residence for me? Ask them to tell my father that I regret absolutely nothing."

On July 30, three days after the Germans discovered the Grotte de la Luire, Geyer's camp at Pélandré was also marked by tragedy. Colonel de Lassus, commander of the Maquis in the Drôme Département, whose responsibility included the southern slopes of the Vercors, arrived to talk to the captain about strategy. He also wanted to contact the Groupe Vallier, whom one of Geyer's patrols had seen the previous evening in a farmhouse near the Col de l'Echarasson. Yves Beesau, the 11th Cuirassiers lieutenant who had stolen the German commandant's mare from Romans, was present at the meeting with de Lassus and offered to go and get them. "It won't take long by horse," he said. He saddled the mare and set off at a canter through the trees toward the Echarasson pass to the north.

Geyer expected him to be back in some forty-five minutes. When after two hours he had not returned, Geyer began to grow anxious. Then one of the patrols who had been operating toward Echarasson that day reported that they had heard the sound of a galloping horse—*and* a burst of machine gun fire. Immediately Geyer himself led a search party to the area. He found Beesau—and the mare—lying dead together.

As Geyer rode back to Pélandré, with Beesau's body borne by his men behind him, he was desolate. The young lieutenant, with his daring and his easy laughter, had been one of his closest friends. Only a few days before, Geyer had met him as he was about to ride out of the camp unarmed. "Where are your weapons?" he asked him. "For the mission I have to carry out, Thivollet," he answered, "the speed of my horse is the best weapon." He had grinned and added, "Anyway, if I'm going to die, I'd be happy to die in the saddle."

Beesau had been very popular and the impact of his death induced a violent need for revenge at Pélandré. The next day Geyer and his men were given the opportunity.

Although the Germans had been raiding the farms on the plateau ever since the French had dispersed, they had not by

July 30 paid a visit to Pélandré. All the time they feared ambush by the Maquis and so far they had been very careful when
venturing into the Forêt de Lente, which provided so much
scope for it. Geyer, however, had always known that the time
would come when they would arrive at the Pélandré farm,
which was unoccupied, and he had planned what he described
as a "mousetrap" for them. Always he had men ranged around
the buildings, concealed in the woods in a large circle under orders to allow any visiting German raiding party to proceed
unchallenged up the approach lane. He would then close the
trap and block their exit.

Unhappily, when the Germans did come as predicted, the
plan did not quite work out as he had intended. The Senegalese, the first of the defending troops that they passed, were
taken by surprise and opened fire too soon. But in the battle
that followed, Geyer's men killed a lot of the enemy and forced
a retreat, which gave the captain a certain bitter satisfaction: at
least it showed them that the Maquis in the Vercors still possessed _some_ muscle. He knew, though, that the action was not
over. The Germans had only withdrawn to a safe distance
while they summoned reinforcements before moving in to the
attack again. This time, so Geyer planned, they would find no
one in the woods to defend the farm. The Maquis would have
disappeared—like skilled guerrillas, ready to strike again.

Disappearing was not easy, for the enemy was watching all
the escape routes. So, ingeniously, Geyer took his men down
the sheer side of the mountain—on ropes!—to new cover near
the village of Bouvante-le-Bas in the Vercors foothills below.
The method, clever though it was, did present certain problems. Horses possessed many advantages for wooded country,
but they could not climb down ropes. Nor, for that matter,
could wounded men.

Captain Tournissa and another officer who had been hurt at
Vassieux were left in a small hillside grotto that Geyer just

hoped would be unnoticed by the Germans when they scoured the area around the farm. The horses were tethered in a hiding place enclosed by trees and thick undergrowth. The obvious danger was that they might whinny.

The enemy returned as expected and burned the farm. And they scoured the area for the "terrorists" who had disappeared. The two men in charge of the horses had climbed to the high branches of a tree above the heads of their animals and watched a unit of enemy troops pass close by them. "The horses pricked their ears," they reported to Geyer later, "but they didn't move or make a sound. It was as if they sensed that if they were found they'd be deported to Germany." Fortunately Tournissa's grotto was not detected, either.

Geyer kept his men near Bouvante village for only a few hours. He was warned that the Germans planned an intensive search of that part of the valley. Guessing that they were unlikely to go back to Pélandré after destroying the farm, he ordered a return up the mountain—again by ropes. The ascent was much harder than the downward journey. Like all the French fugitives in the Vercors, Geyer's men had been greatly weakened by inadequate food. The exertion of pulling themselves up the cliffside was too much for many of them, but somehow, with help from others and additional ropes let down from above, they all managed to reach the top.

During the next few days, German operations in the west of the Vercors were intensified, both in the forest itself and in the villages in the foothills below. They were using larger units now, often amounting to five or six hundred men, sometimes supported with artillery, which enabled them to probe deeper into the forest from the roads. Under the new pressure, Geyer kept moving his camp, though he still continued to send out daily patrols. Sometimes there were confrontations with the enemy, even shooting, but Geyer's orders to his men were always to withdraw. He wanted battles only when he had made preparations.

All this time he had been growing increasingly anxious about his two squadrons that Descour had sent back into the Vercors interior. He had received no definite news from either of them, although the patrols kept hearing disturbing reports from the farms and villages they contacted. There was one report that Chastenay de Gery, a regular 11th Cuirassiers officer, had been in a tragic action near Lente that had ended with the death of more than a hundred of his men. But Geyer could get no confirmation of this despite repeated inquiries by his patrols.

Then at last one night an exhausted Captain Bagnaud, who commanded the second squadron, returned to the camp with sixty men. Chastenay de Gery, he confirmed, was indeed dead, like many of his squadron. All the evidence indicated that he had been tortured before he died. Geyer was filled with an immense anger when he heard—and an overwhelming desire to lead his men onto the offensive. In fact, he would not now have long to wait.

In the mountains on the other side of the plateau, Jean Prévost was finding his existence in hiding increasingly intolerable. Inactivity was not in his nature. To lie in the damp cold Grotte aux Fées—hungry, alarmed by every sound in the woods around them, unable even to take proper exercise—became impossible. At last, on July 31, after eight days in refuge, he could stand it no longer. He told his companions that he intended to attempt a breakout—to join Alain le Ray, who now commanded the Isère Maquis.

"That'd be madness," insisted Simon Nora, one of the group in the grotto.

Prévost, tense, gripped almost by claustrophobia, refused to listen. "I know what I have to do," he said. Faced with this determination, the others decided to go with him.

There were seven of them in all—six men and one young girl, Lea Blaine, his liaison agent. That night they set off north through the forest, skirting Corrençon, planning to leave the plateau by way of the Engins pass and Sassenage, the home of Pierre Dalloz and his wife, Henriette—although Pierre, with a price on his head, was no longer there.

Lea had trouble keeping up with the others—who were trying to cover as much ground as they could before daylight—and one of the men dropped back to stay with her. Soon after dawn, near a hamlet called Les Pouteils, the two of them were surprised by a German patrol and immediately gunned to death.

Prévost and the rest of the party arrived near Engins village later that morning. This was country that the writer knew very well indeed. Only a few months previously, before the plateau was mobilized, Prévost had taken an evening walk with Henriette Dalloz to the Pont Charvet, just above the village. Prévost had then been nearing his fortieth birthday and, so Henriette recalls, he remarked at one moment with a wry smile that "life begins at forty—or so they say." And because it was one of those age milestones on the road to death, Henriette had asked if he was afraid of dying.

"No," he had answered, "I don't think I fear death."

"When I die," she had commented, "I'd like to be buried near my mother in Sassenage church."

After a moment, watching the waters of the Furon tumbling over the rocks beneath the bridge, he had said, "I don't mind where I'm buried."

That morning Prévost and his four companions were tired from their sleepless night and the shortage of food in the grotto where they had lived for eight days. This could be one explanation why they did not stay in the woods until darkness before trying to cross what was one of the main roads into the Vercors —an obvious place for Germans to be stationed. They did, in fact, meet some peasants and asked them if the road was guarded. "We haven't seen any Germans at all today," they answered. Even so, trained as he was to life in the Vercors, it is surprising that Prévost did not carry out a very careful reconnaissance before taking action.

The peasants were wrong. There was a German post at the Pont Charvet—the exact spot where he had discussed dying with Henriette Dalloz. As Prévost and his comrades jumped down onto the road, they were seen. "*Achtung Terroristen!*" shouted one of the soldiers. Machine guns opened up. Prévost tried to clamber over the parapet but was shot down before he could do so. Three of the others died behind him. Only one, Simon Nora, who had not yet reached the road, escaped.

At the Côtes-de-Sassenage, below the bridge, in a house next to the Dalloz home where Prévost had helped Pierre conceive the idea of Operation Montagnards, Jacqueline and Gaby Groll, Huet's young couriers, heard the shooting. They knew the cause, for they often helped escaping Maquisards, but it was only later when Gaby, Henriette's sister, was shown photographs of the bodies that she realized who was among the victims.

CHAPTER 20

Three days later, on August 4, General Zeller landed by plane at Algiers' Aéroport de Maison-Blanche. After leaving the Vercors with Francis Cammaerts, he had toured the Maquis units in the mountains to the south of the Vercors, talking to their chiefs about their local situations, before being flown out of France via Corsica. On his arrival in North Africa, he had requested an interview with General de Gaulle, which was granted the following day.

The French leader was sympathetic to Zeller's angry complaints, but the Vercors was not a subject on which he wanted to dwell. He was concerned with the future. In ten days' time the Allied invasion, which of course included a French army, commanded by General de Lattre de Tassigny, would be launched onto the shores of Provence. De Gaulle handed Zeller a bulky file covered with blue cloth. "This is the operational plan," he said. "Sit down at that table there and study it. I'd like to know your views."

Quickly Zeller skimmed through the outline of the assault, which provided for landings on the vacation beaches of the Côte d'Azur on either side of St.-Raphaël, a drive to capture the ports of Toulon and Marseille, followed by a strike north up the valley of the Rhône. The plan was very detailed and the dates when the various military objectives were expected to be achieved were meticulously forecast. To Zeller's horror, he saw that the planners did not envisage the arrival of Allied troops in Genoble until D+90—three months after the assault! This would give the Germans ample time to continue their policy of attacking the Maquis centers one after the other with concentrated forces, to repeat what they had done in the Vercors— though with greater ease because nowhere else had the natural defenses of the massif. From his arrival on the plateau to set up his headquarters in June, Zeller had been warning Algiers that this would happen unless action was taken to prevent it. No one, of course, appeared to have taken any notice. Now, however, the assault plan meant that thousands more French Resistance men would die—quite needlessly—unless it was changed.

"General," he said when De Gaulle asked him what he thought, "this is far too cautious. If the Allies advance north through the mountains, in particular by the Route Napoléon, they will be virtually unchallenged. They'll be in Grenoble in days, not months."

De Gaulle, only too conscious of the Vercors debacle, which hardly suggested an easy passage to Grenoble, appeared astonished. Quickly Zeller summarized the situation in southeastern France. The German policy of concentrated force enabled them to attack individual targets with great success, to execute terrible reprisals on the Maquis and people who supported them. By contrast to the light weapons of the Resistance men, the enemy were amply equipped with guns, tanks, mortars—and trained troops. But this concentration inevitably meant that they no longer controlled large areas of the country —at least, only temporarily when their operations were focused on specific districts such as the Vercors. Everywhere else they were placed at great risk. No solitary German truck ever reached its destination. Small enemy units were extremely vulnerable. Even large convoys of transport, as Hoppers' joint OSS-Maquis attack at Lus-la-Croix-Haute had shown, were usually badly mauled in several actions before they completed their journeys.

In the mountains, which offered even greater scope for Maquis operations, the danger to the Germans was intensified. "Virtually the whole of the French Alps is in our hands for all practical purposes," Zeller insisted. "Once the assault troops have a firm bridgehead, it is vital that we lose no time in thrusting some armored columns north. With the support of the FFI they cannot fail to advance very fast. Large forces are not needed for this purpose—fifteen hundred, two thousand men will be enough. From Grenoble they'll be able to strike west across the Rhône Valley and cut off the enemy retreat from the coast."

"Are you sure?" asked the incredulous De Gaulle.

"Absolutely," Zeller insisted. Quickly, on a map, he showed his leader the position of the German garrison towns in the southeast—Digne, Sisteron, Gap, all surrounded by mountains. The Germans could not possibly hope to oppose Allied armor operating with the full support of the Maquis in Alpine country—with a complete information service of enemy positions and movements, with constant assault on the enemy rear, with every kind of obstructing tactic that the Resistance had already demonstrated it could execute to devastating effect. Zeller was convinced that the enemy would not dare attempt a challenge in the mountains.

"This is extremely important," said De Gaulle. "You must

leave immediately for Naples and explain what you have told me to General Patch, the corps commander."

The next morning Zeller left Algiers for Italy, flying low over the clear blue waters of the Bay of Naples, where many of the ships that would take part in the assault were already assembled under the protection of silver anti-aircraft balloons. Within an hour of landing, Zeller was in the office of General Patch. Standing before a large wall map of the operational area, he explained to the commander and his senior staff what he had told De Gaulle. The officers questioned him closely— about the German numbers, about the size of the Maquis, about the passes through which the armor would have to pass, about the precise support the FFI could give, about his capacity to control the Resistance men. "I'll give them their orders by radio," Zeller assured them, "and direct them to execute the operations you want." Patch and his staff were clearly impressed, for after Zeller left the office to fly back to Algiers, the U.S. general decided to act on his advice.

Nine days later, early in the morning of August 15, the event that the Resistance in the Southern Sector of France had been expecting ever since June 6 was finally set in motion. An invasion fleet of nearly twelve hundred ships approached the coast, with an assault force of three hundred thousand men. By that night a bridgehead on southern French soil was in Allied hands.

Two days later Patch signaled Zeller in Algiers: "Sixth Army corps is about to put into operation the Faisceau Plan," "Faisceau" being Zeller's cover name. "August 18 is probable date for the start of the operation which will consist at first of [an armored] regiment supported by tanks. If the operation progresses well, this will be reinforced with another division. Please send orders [to the FFI] to block enemy movements to the south of Lyon and to harass the enemy retreat on all routes during the night. Major air support will be given to the operation by day. Faisceau representatives must make contact as early as possible with the [Allied] columns and provide them with guides. . . ."

On the morning of the eighteenth, units of an armored brigade commanded by the U.S. general Frederic Butler advanced north up the mountain road along which, nearly a hundred and thirty years before, Napoleon had led his men on the march to Paris after his escape from Elba. That night American troops were at Sisteron. Two days later, forward U.S. units were only a few miles south of Grenoble.

In the Vercors, the German operation—the manhunt, the burning of the farms, the removal of the cattle, the killing of the "terrorists"—had been maintained with vigorous determination for two weeks. Then gradually the enemy troops began to leave the plateau. There were still Germans in the Vercors, reprisals were still savage, but from about August 10 the pressure on the hiding, half-starved Resistance men and women began to lessen. Movement about the plateau became much easier and the various groups began to make contact with each other.

Eugène Chavant, haggard and hollow-eyed, walked into Barraque-les-Feneys, a remote hamlet near Plénouze in the northern mountains that Beauregard and his men had been using as a refuge. Within hours, Pierre Tanant, acting on Huet's orders to survey his scattered forces prior to issuing them orders to reform, also arrived in the hamlet in search of the northern-sector commander.

Chavant, according to ex-Maquisard Gilbert Joseph in a waspish, critical book, was still devastated by the collapse of his dream for the Vercors, still extremely bitter about what he regarded as the treason of Algiers. In his haversack he carried with him Huet's final eve-of-battle order to his men, to his "soldiers of the Vercors," for the stirring phrases that the colonel had written in the deep emotion of those hours before the attack had greatly moved the Patron. During one of his evenings at Les Feneys, Chavant read it aloud to a group of Beauregard's Maquisards, speaking Huet's eloquent phrases—"The eyes of the whole country are fixed on us. . . . We have faith in each other. We have right on our side . . ."—with a proud but sad affection. "Eugène Chavant loved these words," Joseph commented acidly, "and his rough voice broke more than once during his reading. . . . Those of us who were listening did not have the heart to criticize this turgid prose. . . . It had the effect on us of an obituary notice"—which, of course, is what it was.

Gilbert Joseph was very young, still in his teens, and both he and his comrades had clearly become embittered, in a somewhat different way to Chavant, by the trauma of the past few weeks. It is doubtful, however, if the other Maquisards were quite as unmoved as Joseph was about Chavant's withered dream of the Vercors, quite as callous as he claimed to be about the ravaged but unbroken man who had been a central part of it, who had co-created the first Maquis camps, who had won the absolute faith of the villagers, who had forged the fragile alliance between the soldiers and the civilians, who had been betrayed by politicians and generals and issues that were bigger than the sufferings of a remote mountain plateau.

Others on the massif were on the move as the Germans slowly left the Vercors. Lieutenant Hoppers learned that the bridge over the Isère near St.-Marcellin was no longer guarded by the enemy. Cautiously he led his OSS men down the mountain and crossed the river. In a stolen truck they raced along the ring road, taking refuge eventually among the Maquis of the Belledonne range to the east of Grenoble.

Desmond Longe and John Houseman, who never succeeded in making any kind of contact with Huet or Paray, also left the

Vercors on the northwest side. They walked through the mountains to Switzerland. Later, Longe heard that Huet had received a report that his body had been reported swinging from a tree near Tourtre—not far from his first fall-back position.

On August 8, a week before the southern invasion, Beauregard had decided that the time had come for his men to go back onto the offensive. The captain set up a series of ambushes—by the Col de la Croix-Perrin, near St.-Nizier, and in the Gorges de la Bourne. According to Tanant's analysis, in a series of actions his men killed some twenty-seven Germans and wounded another fifty. But the new initiative was violently criticized by the local peasants, for the Germans responded by burning more farms before finally, on August 18, the last units left the ravaged plateau. Since Bastille Day, the Germans had killed eight hundred people.

By then the news of the Allied landings on the coast had rippled across the plateau. Huet ordered Tanant to set up a new headquarters in an abandoned convent near St.-Gervais, on the ring road to the northwest of the massif, and sent out a summons to his units to join him there to continue the fight.

He had left Geyer, with his squadrons, as an independent group, and had already given him orders to operate in the specific sector between Romans and St.-Marcellin that was allocated to him. The captain had moved very carefully from the forest. Too many of his officers and men had died—some of them horribly—during those awful weeks in the Forêt de Lente for him to take risks now. On August 13, after making sure that the Germans had left the villages below, he gave orders for a descent from the forest to La Baume-d'Hostun, a hamlet not far from the ring road—from which, as always, there was a fast easy escape route. His men camped on the grounds of a chateau. The 11th Cuirassiers standard, with its insignia of the Sun King and its fleurs-de-lis, was displayed in yet another headquarters. There were still Germans at Romans, Valence, and other nearby towns, so Geyer exercised great care. The Senegalese were entrusted with the duty twenty-four hours a day of guarding the camp against surprise attack, while Geyer's squadrons took station on the railroad track and on all the nearby roads under orders to attack German traffic.

Even then, Geyer limited the area of operations until he knew of the Allied landings in the South. Then he became bolder, clearly finding the scope for operations near the Vercors too small, and launched his units farther afield. They raided an enemy fuel train at St.-Marcel near Valence, killing twenty-five German troops. Repeatedly they attacked targets on the N 7, the main road from Lyon to the South, which, as the supply route to the German armies opposing the assault in the South, offered rich potential. At Tain one group destroyed eight trucks and killed several Germans; farther north, toward St.-Vallier, another team attacked a motor convoy with equally satisfying results in enemy casualties and crippled vehicles; yet a third made a strike at Ponsas. This knocked out only four trucks, but it garnered fifty enemy casualties. For four days, from August 17 to 21, Geyer's men took just a little revenge for what they and their comrades had suffered in the Vercors over the past weeks. They ranged up and down a twenty-mile stretch of that main arterial road, gaining success after success. Then Geyer called them back, for now, as his numbers were swelled by new recruits, he was under orders to attack a major target.

On the morning of August 22 Colonel Huet pedaled a bicycle furiously toward Le Pont-de-Claix, a little Drac River town under the Vercors' eastern cliffs, about five miles south of Grenoble. He was in a great hurry, his head held stiffly upright as always, his legs thrusting at the pedals with a muscled strength developed on the Vercors slopes.

During the previous night he had learned that the Germans were withdrawing from Grenoble. He had hastened to the city, whose people had awakened for the first time for four years to discover that they were free, to check that the report was true; then he had pushed on urgently toward Le Pont-de-Claix, where he had been informed that the advance units of the U. S. Army were waiting.

Huet rode into the little town, approached the first American tank he saw, and demanded to be taken to the commanding officer of the column. He was conducted to Lieutenant Colonel Philip Johnson and told him that the Germans had left Grenoble. "You can push on into the city," he urged the colonel through an interpreter. "We want to see American uniforms there today."

"But I've only got a tank squadron, an artillery battery, and a company of infantry," answered the colonel. "Most of my forces are still at Sisteron."

"*Foncez, foncez,*" repeated Huet.

"Okay," said the amiable American, and that afternoon U.S. tanks clattered slowly through the crowded streets of Grenoble to a delirious welcome. Thanks to Zeller, the objective that the planners had scheduled for D+90 had been reached on D+7!

At 0545 that same morning, Geyer's squadrons set off toward Romans, which had been menaced by U.S. guns until a Maquis messenger begged the American commander to postpone an attack that would inevitably destroy much of the town. The French, he said, would take it for him.

Geyer ranged his men on the approach roads to the town and at 0930, with the help of Romans Resistance men, launched his attack. The first objective was the station, where a munitions train had just arrived. The second was a big Citroën garage. The enemy defended both targets, then dropped back into their barracks.

The 11th Cuirassiers stormed the barracks, using machine guns and grenades, and set fire to the buildings. The Germans attempted a sudden breakout from the town at full speed in a convoy of trucks led by an armored car, but they were fought to a stop on the road. Geyer's men rounded up 109 prisoners and reported 35 enemy killed. It was hardly a great victory, but it was competent, and the collaborationist mayor of Romans was arrested. Certainly it was a heady experience for the survivors of the Vercors.

Again, though, Geyer, the once headstrong and impulsive Geyer whose clashes with the Patron had been so abrasive, was cautious. The Germans were not beaten yet. They were in force at Valence and in several towns on the main N 7. So he withdrew his troops, set up his headquarters outside the town, and ordered a constant state of alert. "Romans taken after a conflict of three hours," he reported to Huet. "The 11th Cuirassiers were equal to their task. . . . I have relatively small losses but I do not yet have figures. The Boche has suffered heavily. Big losses. At least a hundred prisoners. I have decided to keep the town in a state of siege. My troops will not stay in Romans. . . . Everything is going well. . . ."

His caution was justified. The German armies were withdrawing before the Allied advance from the South and Romans lay on a route to Lyon that provided a parallel alternative to the N 7. Nine days after Geyer's conquest, German tanks entered the town—and stayed there to hold it open for the retreating forces until a joint U.S.-Maquis force recaptured it. The second battle was fiercer than the first. To Geyer's sorrow, Captain Tournissa, who had survived Vassieux, who had endured the weeks in hiding in the forest, was killed. So, too, was Le Barbu, the bearded fighting priest, who had joined up with him again.

On July 23, the day after the liberation of Grenoble, Huet moved his headquarters to the city so that he could work closely with Lieutenant Colonel Johnson, whose tanks had "liberated" the town. Like Romans, Grenoble was still vulnerable because it lay on an escape route—in this case, to the northeast. Huet deployed his forces on the access roads, while other Maquis were alerted to the same need to stop an enemy in flight—but a dangerous enemy with a lot to lose and still armed with heavy guns.

Within hours a German column of twenty-five vehicles was reported approaching Grenoble from Lyon, obviously hoping to thrust its way past the city. On the road it was attacked by the Maquis at three different points before eventually being forced to turn back at St.-Jacques, near the tip of the Vercors arrow, by forces commanded by Captain Bousquet, Huet's adjutant.

There were, however, heavy concentrations of enemy troops to the east of Grenoble in the hills near Murianette. In an attempt to open the road, they opened fire on the city with 88 mm guns. Lieutenant Colonel Johnson ordered U.S. troops to attack in conjunction with French forces commanded by Huet. The American artillery was directed by a spotter aircraft that Huet, recalling how often German guns had been guided to their targets in the Vercors by planes from Chabeuil, must have noted with some satisfaction—especially since the enemy troops who were now flinching as the American shells exploded near them were men of General Pflaum's 157th Reserve Division, which had provided a large part of the force that had attacked the plateau.

He was soon to be gratified even more. The Germans at Murianette ceded victory. A Wehrmacht lieutenant bearing a white flag was brought to Colonel Johnson, who was standing with Huet. The officer asked if he could speak to the American colonel alone.

"Why?" asked Johnson.

The German officer hesitated, embarrassed, looking at Huet. "My orders," he said, "are to surrender my force only to an American officer."

Johnson laughed and put his arm around Huet's shoulders. "My comrade and I belong to the same army of liberation," he answered. "We will only accept your surrender together."

So it could be said that Huet won after all. The troops that had assaulted the Vercors, that had systematically combed it for hiding "terrorists" so that they would never fight again, were now prisoners of war. One of their officers had formally conceded the defeat of his regiment, which Huet had never done. It was a scene that, as he had lain in hiding in the Forêt de la Sapine, the French colonel would never have dared to imagine. It provided an ironic ending to the sad story of the Vercors.

AFTERWORD

It was not an ending, of course, for the Vercors became a legend and legends have no ending. Like the Charge of the Light Brigade, it became a subject of controversy, of accusation and counteraccusation, of political conflict, of military study. There have been books and articles written about it that placed the blame squarely in Algiers—as indeed does this one—and others that, in the cause of the politicians, have attacked the local commanders and even Chavant, claiming that he persisted with a dream that was unsupported by reality.

The epic of the Vercors remains the most famous of the Resistance dramas even though there were other actions against the Maquis that involved as many French and ended with even greater numbers dead. Perhaps, as the French historian Fernand Rude declared, this is because the whole concept of the plateau had panache, "this Free Vercors in the middle of a continent still under occupation, the big Tricolor flag floating above St.-Nizier in full view of Grenoble. It is certain that no other Maquis had the honor of being besieged by twenty thousand Germans. No other Maquis had the enemy mobilized against them—and immobilized so many of the enemy who at this moment were prevented from taking part in the battle for Normandy." It was, in other words, the romantic concept of the mountain fortress that ensured for the Vercors its role in history—a fortress under siege that, like Gordon at Khartoum, was not relieved in time.

Certainly most of the men who played the leading roles have been honored. A square in Grenoble today bears the name of Eugène Chavant, who is buried in the cemetery of St.-Nizier. Huet, Descour, and Costa de Beauregard all ended up as generals. Narcisse Geyer, too, was honored, as was his regiment. In formal ceremony, General de Lattre de Tassigny, who had pleaded so persistently with General Caffey against the parachuting of troops into the Vercors, pinned the Croix de Guerre to the 11th Cuirassiers standard. De Gaulle conferred on the captain the title of "Chevalier de la Légion d'Honneur" and permitted him officially to assume his cover name. He became Colonel Geyer-la-Thivollet—only a colonel, perhaps, among so many generals, because his style and independence may not have appealed to those authorities concerned with appointment to the higher ranks.

De Gaulle's uneasy alliance with Fernand Grenier, following the Air Minister's retracting of his charges against the General, did not last very long. In September of 1944, barely two months after Grenier's dramatic challenge, De Gaulle dismissed him from the Cabinet. Three years later, Grenier resumed the attack with his "Dossier on the Vercors" in *Les Lettres Françaises* and fought out a bitter conflict in print with Jacques Soustelle, whom he charged by implication with the French President with guilt for the tragedy.

One source that would have been invaluable for this book

has not been available. The journal that Jean Prévost told Yves Farge that he kept during his time in the Vercors was never found, although the Baudelaire manuscript on which he worked at the Herbouilly farmhouse survived and was duly published. Prévost's son Alain, who was with him on the plateau, wrote a novel about his father in the Vercors but, although the great Jean Bruller ("Vercors") declared in a letter published in the book that the leading character closely resembled Prévost, the novel provided little detailed information that could be used in *Tears of Glory*.

The Vercors itself is marked with monuments to the dead, not only in the cemeteries, but also in the passes, on pathways in the woods, on the roads, in the fields—on the exact spots where they died. Apart from this, much of the massif is unchanged. The soaring pillared towers of rock still dominate the plain, the fat cattle still graze in those rich meadows, tourist buses still edge their way through the rock tunnels beside the Gorges de la Bourne, the trees still grow thickly around the belvedere where Chabal died at Valchevrière. And customers still sit at the tables of the Hôtel Breyton—now named L'Hôtel du Vercors—from which Chavant directed and inspired his people and dreamed of greatness for his plateau.

Sources

The number of people who have co-operated in the preparation of this book, in many cases giving many hours of their time over a long period, is formidable and my debt to them is great. Most, of course, were participants in the events concerning the Vercors, but not all of them. In particular, I am grateful for the enormous help I have received from Paul Dreyfus, author of the fine *Vercors: Citadelle de la Liberté*, who has been most generous in his guidance and assistance and has kindly read this manuscript before publication.

Also, I have much appreciated the warm co-operation of Joseph La Picirella, one of Geyer's men, who, while not perhaps aspiring to the professional literary level of Dreyfus, has written an excellent and deeply researched day-by-day record of those dramatic months in his *Témoignages sur le Vercors*. Both La Picirella and his wife, Jacqueline, have devoted a lot of hours to providing me with extremely useful material. He is director of the impressive Musée de la Résistance in Vassieux, which records much of the Vercors story and of the massacre in particular. It is visited by many thousands of people every year.

Vincent Beaume has been an invaluable source both as an important participant as Huet's Second Bureau chief and also as the Drôme Département correspondent of Le Comité d'Histoire de la Deuxième Guerre Mondiale. He has provided me with an enormous amount of eye-witness correspondence—far too voluminous to list—as well as his own personal record and many hours of interview.

Pierre Dalloz, too, has been very helpful—as indeed has his wife, Henriette. He has furnished me with correspondence that he has conducted with many of the leading characters in the Vercors controversies, and has permitted me to read his own lengthy memoirs. I am a little sad that his important role in the Vercors story is not as fully reflected in this book as it merits, but this is an unhappy result of my focus on the events from January to August 1944 when Dalloz was elsewhere.

I must express my gratitude, too, to Aimé Requet, a famous figure in the Grenoble Resistance who, although he did not take a direct part in the Vercors conflict, has given me much documentation, guidance, and contact with important sources. Also to Michael R. D. Foot, author of the prestigious *SOE in France*, who has provided considerable assistance and offered valuable avenues of research.

Others who have given me so much time that special mention must be made include Francis Cammaerts, Generals Marcel Descour and Costa de Beauregard, Desmond Longe, Richard Marillier, Lilette Lesage, and Colonel Geyer-la-Thivollet. I have appreciated, too, the opportunity of interviewing Jacques Soustelle, Fernand Grenier, Madame Eugène Chavant, Father Johannes Vincent, Gabrielle and Jacqueline Groll, Léon Vincent-Martin, Marin Dentella, David Astor, Terence Kilmartin, and Yves Samuel, and of corresponding with General Jean Constans, Chester Myers, and M. H. Thackwaite.

I am especially grateful to Henri Michel, who not only discussed the issues of the Vercors with me but also made available to me the resources of the library of Le Comité d'Histoire de la Deuxième Guerre Mondiale where the librarians M. Rosier, M. Perret-Gentil, and Mme Mercier were invaluable. The transcripts of the Commission d'Études du Vercors conducted

by the Comité, at which several of the leading characters in the
Vercors story (in London, in Algiers, and within the plateau)
gave their version of events, has been one of the prime research
sources of this book.

My thanks are also due to the Central Intelligence Agency in
Washington for providing me with the OSS records relating to
the Vercors; to the veterans of the OSS in New York; to the
BBC Archives Department in Reading, England, for the messages transmitted to the Resistance; to the Public Record
Office, London, for access to the Allied headquarters files, to
Colonel E. G. Boxhall of the British Foreign and Common-
wealth Office for his great assistance concerning SOE records;
to the Bibliothèque Nationale in Paris, to the British Museum
in London, and to Jean Bailey of the London Library, who, as
always, has been tireless in her efforts to uncover sources for
me.

Some mention should be made about the Allied headquarters files since, although many records have now been
declassified, a number of the documents relating to the French
Resistance held in the Public Record Office in London are still
secret—mainly, I understand, because of war codes still in use.
However, in my search for any trace of Opération Montagnards
or the famous signal "Le chamois des alpes bondit," the
classified files have been investigated for me by officials permitted to view them. They have been unable to find any reference
to the operation or to the signal. As stated in the text, the latter does not appear on the BBC's list of coded messages transmitted on the night of June 4–5. So, although the operation
was approved by top French circles including General de
Gaulle himself, it does not seem to have been discussed at an
official level—at least not at a level official enough to be recorded—with the Allied service chiefs.

A number of people have permitted me to read personal documents, written in most cases soon after the events with which

this book is concerned occurred in the Vercors, and for this facility I am indeed grateful. They are described in detail in the bibliography.

Finally, I would like to thank those who have given me invaluable help in producing the book: Elly Oosterbos, Michelette Marimootoo, and Elaine Arari who have provided enormous assistance with the research, Janet Brunning who without complaint has typed and retyped the manuscript in its many drafts, and my wife, family, and friend who have shared the book with me for so long without any signs of wearying of the subject.

Bibliography

UNPUBLISHED

BBC ARCHIVES, Caversham, Reading, England Lists of coded messages transmitted to the Resistance on BBC French Service and plain language broadcasts.

BEAUME, VINCENT Two manuscripts of personal experiences in and near the Vercors: (1) Prior to the mobilization in June 1944; (2) After the mobilization.

BUNDESARCHIV-MILITÄRARCHIV, Freiburg, Germany War diary, commander in chief, West.

CHAVANT, EUGÈNE Address given during a conference on the Vercors in Grenoble, February 1945.

DALLOZ, PIERRE A long and highly detailed personal account of experiences relating to the Vercors—on the plateau, and in Paris, London, and Algiers.

GEYER-LA-THIVOLLET, COLONEL NARCISSE A long personal account of his experiences with the 11th Cuirassiers, most of which relates to the Vercors period.

HOPPERS, LIEUTENANT VERNON Operational Report of Operation Justine (the OSS mission to the Vercors).

JOURNAL DE MARCHE DU 11ME RÉGIMENT DE CUIRASSIERS (Période du Vercors) The day-to-day log of the regiment.

LONGE, MAJOR DESMOND A long manuscript of personal experiences in the Vercors, much of it in the form of a daily journal.

MALOSSANE, BENJAMIN Address at a conference (undated) by the civil administrator, Southern Sector.

MARILLIER, RICHARD A manuscript, written in third-person book form, of his experiences with Chabal's unit.

PARAY, LIEUTENANT ANDRE Very long, highly detailed Activity Report of Mission Eucalyptus (Longe) and Paray's personal experiences after the dispersal with Huet.

PUBLIC RECORD OFFICE, London Headquarters files including War Room daily situation reports, SPOC files, correspondence between Supreme Allied Headquarters and Allied Forces Headquarters Mediterranean, documents relating to Allied support of the French Resistance, French Resistance support of Operation Anvil (Dragoon). File Nos: DEF/2/76; 495; 496; 1151. WO/204/1964: 1947; 5754.

LE VERCORS LIBRE Four issues edited by Vincent Beaume.

PUBLISHED

ARON, ROBERT *De Gaulle before Paris* (1962).

BEAUREGARD, GENERAL COSTA DE "Le Vercors Juin 1944–Projets et realités," *La Revue Historique de l'Armée*, No. 4 (1972).

BEGUIN, ALBERT *Le Livre noir du Vercors* (1944).

BRISAC, PAUL *Le Historique de la zone Nord du Vercors* (photocopy—date unknown).

—— *Combats de St.-Nizier: Le Pionnier du Vercors* (photocopy—date unknown).

COOKRIDGE, E. H. *They Came from the Sky* (1965).

DACIER, JEAN *Ceux du Maquis. Coups de main et combats. L'Épopée d'une compagnie FFI du Vercors* (1945).

DE GAULLE, GENERAL CHARLES *War Memoirs* (1956).

DESCOUR, GENERAL MARCEL "La Tragédie du Vercors: Nous fumes prisonniers de la mission rescue," *Le Monde*, August 29, 1974.

DEVAL, JEANNE *L'Année terrible* (1946).

DOUILLET, JEAN *Valchevrière, le chemin de croix du Vercors* (1950).

DREYFUS, PAUL *Vercors: Citadelle de la Liberté* (1969).

—— *Histoire de la résistance en Vercors* (1975).

EHRLICH, BLAKE *Resistance: France 1940–1945* (1965).

EISENHOWER, GENERAL DWIGHT D. *Crusade in Europe* (1947).

FARGE, YVES *Rebelles, soldats et citoyens* (1946).

FOOT, MICHAEL R. D.   *SOE in France* (1966).

GRENIER, FERNAND   *C'était ainsi . . .* (1970).

—— "Nous ouvrons le dossier du Vercors": *Les Lettres Françaises* (October 23, 1947).

JOSEPH, GILBERT   *Combattant du Vercors* (1972).

LA PICIRELLA, JOSEPH   *Témoignages sur le Vercors* (undated).

MICHEL, HENRI   *Histoire de la Résistance en France* (1965).

NAL, COMMANDANT LOUIS, and AIMÉ REQUET   *Le Bataille de Grenoble* (1964).

PONS, PAUL   *De la résistance et la libération* (undated).

PRÉVOST, ALAIN   *Le peuple impopulaire* (1956).

RUDE, FERNAND   "Le dialogue Vercors-Alger. Télégrammes échangés pendant la bataille," *Revue d'histoire de la Deuxième Guerre Mondiale*, No. 49 (January 1963).

SOUSTELLE, JACQUES   *Envers et contre tout* (1950).

TANANT, PIERRE   *Vercors: Haut-lieu de France* (1947).

TROUSSIER, ASPIRANT FRANCISQUE   *Le combat des Ecouges: Le Pionnier du Vercors* (photocopy—date unknown).

VERCORS (JEAN BRULLER)   *La Bataille du silence* (1966).

Index

DATE DUE

Sep 29 '79			
Oct 12 '79			
Oct 26 '79			
Nov 10 '79			
Dec 24 '79			
AP 19 '80			
MY 16 '80			
OC 20 '86			
DE 15 '89			
AP 15 '91			
SE '91			
NO 6 '91			
NO 26 '91			
JE 24 '94			

DEMCO 38-297